A HISTORY OF ALCOHOLISM

A History of Alcoholism

JEAN-CHARLES SOURNIA

WITH AN INTRODUCTION BY ROY PORTER

TRANSLATED BY NICK HINDLEY AND
GARETH STANTON

Basil Blackwell

Copyright © Jean-Charles Sournia 1990
Copyright © Introduction, Roy Porter 1990
First published in French as *Histoire de l'alcoolisme*
© Éditions Flammarion, Paris, 1986
English translation first published 1990

Basil Blackwell Ltd
108 Cowley Road, Oxford OX4 1JF, UK

Basil Blackwell Inc.
3 Cambridge Center
Cambridge, Massachusetts 02142, USA

British Library Cataloguing in Publication Data
A CIP catalogue record for this book is available
from the British Library.

Library of Congress Cataloging in Publication Data
Sournia, Jean Charles.
[Histoire de l'alcoolisme. English]
A history of alcoholism/Jean-Charles Sournia : with an
introduction by Roy Porter : translated by Nicholas Hindley and Gareth Stanton.
p.   cm.
Translation of Histoire de l'alcoolisme.
Includes index.
ISBN 0–631–16026–4
1. Alcoholism–History.   2. Drinking of alcoholic beverages–History.
I. Title
HV5020.S6813 1990   89–15138
394.1′3′09–dc20   CIP

Typeset in 10½ on 12½pt Sabon
by Footnote Graphics, Warminster, Wiltshire
Printed in Great Britain by
T. J. Press Ltd, Padstow, Cornwall

CONTENTS

vi   *Contents*

Contents   vii

ACKNOWLEDGEMENTS

THE publisher and author are grateful to the following for permission to use and for their help in supplying photographs: Courtesy of the Trustees of The British Museum, London (Plate 1); Hulton Picture Library, London (Plates 3, 7, 11, 12, 15 and 17); Hulton Picture Library/© The Bettman Archive (Plate 18); Kunsthistorisches Museum, Vienna (Plate 4); The Mansell Collection, London (Plates 8, 9, 13, 14 and 16); Martin von Wagner Museum, University of Wuerzburg (Plate 2: photo K. Oehrlein); The Museum of London (Plate 10); Courtesy of the Trustees, The National Gallery, London (Plate 5); Wellcome Institute Library, London (Plate 6).

INTRODUCTION

IT is a long time since historians ceased to be the chroniclers of kings and battles, and concentrated instead on the grand forces that determine social existence: the succession of modes of production, the history of class and class conflict, the evolution of ideologies and mentalities. It is only rather recently, however, that they have come to recognize the significance of subjects nearer home and apparently more humble – the history of the home itself, of sex and the family, of gender, of domestic existence and material culture.

Not least in importance amongst these, as any anthropologist might have pointed out, are the histories of food and drink, for they link together so many facets of existence: the biological and medical dimensions of diet, the economic issues of subsistence and agriculture, and the social symbolism of communal eating and drinking (ritually enshrined in the Christian Eucharist itself). It is no accident that historians and archaeologists of material culture find that the most telling indices of changing patterns and levels of consumption are the implements used for eating and drinking – cutlery, crockery, silverware and so forth.

It is rather peculiar, then, that the cultural histories of eating and drinking have been so little studied. Food and nutrition have begun to receive their share of historical attention, partly because of the interest shown by *Annales*-school historians and historical demographers in the elementary struggle for survival down the ages, the perennial Malthusian ecological battles between man and a hostile environment. But what people have drunk, and the cultural language of their drinking habits, remain almost wholly neglected by scholars. Prima facie, this appears quite extraordinary, given the degree to which contemporary Western society relies upon drinking as a social signifier, or, indeed, the degree to which academics are themselves noted for their fondness for a good vintage. One must only presume that drinking still seems to lack the seriousness that qualifies a topic for historical research, or perhaps one should conclude that for academics, rather as for society at large, drinking is an activity more readily indulged in than overtly acknowledged.

For all these reasons, Professor Sournia's history of alcoholism is particularly welcome. It constitutes the first fully-documented, cross-cultural, chronological account, published in English, of one major facet of the history of drinking – the story of alcohol abuse – and it examines that topic with all the skill one has come to expect from a leading French historian of medicine. Its particular virtue, however, lies in grappling with a far wider problem, by setting the history of the condition of alcoholism in the context of those emergent European socio-cultural values that, by the nineteenth century, were beginning to identify persistent excessive drinking as a pathological state, whose treatment ought to lie within the province of the medical profession. In other words, this book is not simply a history of drinking, or even of drunkenness, but an analysis of the formation in public opinion at large of those attitudes that eventually – though only after a very long gestation – generated the belief that addiction to drink was a disease and that the habitual drunkard was a sick person. Professor Sournia is as aware of the contingency of this formulation as he is concerned subsequently to demonstrate the profound ambiguities that the notions of alcoholism and of the alcoholic have conveyed in twentieth-century society.

It may be helpful, in the present introduction, to unpick these strands, or distinct conceptual levels, and examine them in rather greater detail. Historically speaking, it is no surprise that Mediterranean and Northern European civilization began, from early times, to produce alcoholic substances through fermentation, brewing and distillation. After all, transforming surplus and perishable agricultural produce – grapes, grain, potatoes or whatever – into alcoholic liquor is an efficient way of preventing waste through spoilage, and of providing beverages to drink, where non-alcoholic ones such as water may be scarce, unpalatable or subject to deterioration and thus a health menace. Classical Antiquity transformed wine-drinking into a social event, both profane and sacred, and Christianity specifically licensed the consumption of alcohol through the sacrament of the Eucharist, in which wine literally becomes (in the Roman Catholic formulary), or symbolized (in the Calvinist construal), the blood of the Saviour.

Thus Latinate culture endorsed what the logic of the emergent economy of medieval and early modern Europe urged – the use of alcohol, not only as a beverage and as a source of stored nourishment, but, in addition, as a social lubricant. Wherever and whenever people gathered – as friends, as strangers, as masters and men, or even as rivals – for the sake of festivities, fellowship, or hard-headed business, drinking accompanied the proceedings, to establish fellowship, seal a deal, reconcile a quarrel, toast one's loyalty or drink others' health. One might almost say that the consumption of alcohol was the index that constituted a social gathering, just as the inn or tavern became synonymous with the urban location where people met for formal or informal convivial gatherings. In early modern England, a rural celebration was commonly known as an 'ale'.

Social drinking often, indeed all too often, spilled over into drunkenness. From Noah through Falstaff and beyond, the drunk, indeed the sot, has been an endless source of amusement for caricaturists, artists and writers, and the target of the wrath of moralists, preachers and magistrates. In a tough world of grinding work, when the few oppressed the many, under a harsh sky scarcely mitigated by the comforts of civilization, and when sickness was hardly relieved by effective medicines or pain-killers, drinking oneself into oblivion provided for many the only escape from the penal servitude of daily existence. For the labouring classes, perennially pinched by penury, habituated to hunger and cold, the occasional largesse of a barrel of beer provided by the lord or master, at harvest home, Yuletide, or perhaps at a wake, might offer the only opportunity for debauch from one year's end to the next.

The resulting bouts of drunkenness were condemned by magistrates and priests alike. As with every other case of appetite slipping the reins of reason, the Church regarded it as sinful, for it spelt the reduction of man to the level of the beasts (like the dog unto his vomit). Yet traditional society did not regard excessive drinking as amongst the most heinous of transgressions. One reason for this was that it was a weakness of all classes, not a vice exclusive to the poor. As is shown so well in Richard Gough's *History of Myddle*, an account of life in a Shropshire village written around the turn of the eighteenth century, many of the more substantial inhabitants simply drank their fortunes away. Everyone is familiar with the notorious three-bottle men of Georgian England, including leading politicians such as Pitt the Younger and Richard Sheridan. The man who did not get blind drunk once in a while was often regarded with more suspicion than he who did.

Under the old regime, the worst fate likely to befall the drunk was to spend the night in a lock-up. Even the law looked upon drunkenness with some leniency: the Scottish plea of diminished responsibility in the case of homicide evolved from the eighteenth century, in order to accommodate the high percentage of felonies committed while in a state of inebriation.

When and why, then, did the traditional attitudes towards chronic drunkenness – expressing mild, ineffective and generalized disapproval – begin to harden, leading to the widespread temperance, abstinence and teetotal movements, which became so prominent a feature on the nine-teenth-century 'moral reformist' map, to the campaigns for prohibition, which came to fruition above all in the USA, and to the crystallization of the very idea of alcoholism? It is certainly arguable, as Professor Sournia documents, that the problem of drunkenness objectively became far worse from the eighteenth century onwards. Industrialization created vast new floating urban populations of proletarianized males, mainly without family restraints, who readily poured out their wages on liquor. From the London 'gin craze' of the 1730–50 era onwards, consumption of cheap spirits, in particular whisky, schnapps, absinthe and vodka, also created acute and chronic health problems, leading in turn to unemployment and destitution.

One result was that drunkenness became associated with all those vertiginous public-order problems that followed in the wake of the first half-century of industrialization in many European nations – or at least it became associated with them in the minds of the propertied classes, terrified lest proletarian disorderliness should galvanize itself into rev-olutionary spirit. It was, in other words, during the nineteenth century that drunkenness was transformed, within the mental outlooks of official society, into a deeply disturbing social problem.

Focusing concern upon drunkenness served many purposes for social activists. On the one hand, it acted as a useful social indicator. As the bourgeois and genteel classes progressively rendered their own life-styles more respectable – indeed, more 'sober', in all senses of the word – it became easier for them to stigmatize the labouring or dangerous classes as the drunken classes. The drunk thus became a class apart, almost another race. In such circumstances, it became very easy to blame drink – or at least those who failed to resist the urge to drink – for all the social evils of the day. In the eyes of the sterner reformers, the squalor all around was the product not of capitalism, exploitation, starvation wages or urban neglect, but of the habit of squandering earnings upon drink.

Nevertheless, this new preoccupation with drunkenness, character-ized as the malaise of malaises, also contained a message of hope. The drunk (so argued reformers, religious and secular alike) could be redeemed. Hence the appeal of temperance as a call from the respectable classes to the 'great unwashed' to rescue themselves from the demon drink: a crusade which attracted an authentic following amongst the more 'improving' sections of the working class themselves.

Herein lay the potential attractiveness of a new formulation, regard-ing habitual drunkenness neither as a symptom of social dislocation, nor even as a personal moral dereliction, but rather as a state of sickness. It is not hard, as Professor Sournia argues, to find medical authors from the eighteenth century onwards discussing persistent excessive indulgence in alcohol both as the *cause* of illness, mental and physical, and also as itself a sickness, or even a disease. Before the close of the eighteenth century, Benjamin Rush in the USA and Thomas Trotter in Britain had both contended that habitual drunkenness was the enduring symptom of some mental craving or obsession, itself perhaps excited in the first place by excessive consumption of alcohol: drunkenness could thus come to be viewed as a disorder of the mind. Then, during the first half of the nineteenth century, a succession of eminent medical investigators throughout Europe incorporated what finally became officially termed 'alcoholism' within their taxonomy of diseases.

From Trotter onwards, doctors looked upon this 'medicalization' of hard drinking as a triumph of progress, both scientific and social. On the one hand, it constituted a truer understanding of a condition so long improperly and ineffectually denounced by preachers as a sin and by moralists as a vice; rather, argued the doctors, alcoholism was more akin to epilepsy or psycho-nervous conditions, properly the business not of do-gooders, but of doctors. For that reason, such medicalization promised social benefit, because, it was contended, now that it was properly understood at last, it could actually be treated. Here it is useful to remember, as Michel Foucault and other historians have insisted, that the nineteenth century saw numerous departments of life, including the understanding of sexuality and criminal proclivities, reconstituted as objects of discourse within the field of medicine, within the same 'progressive' ideology.

The tendency of radical historians nowadays is to regard this process of the medicalization of abnormality – including abnormally heavy drinking – as a measure simultaneously indicative of medical empire-building and also socially scapegoating in respect of its objects or 'victims'. This may well be so, but it is also important not to risk anachronism. For during the last hundred and fifty years, the deployment of the 'disease concept' of alcoholism has commonly served as the intellectual rationale for active campaigns for the positive reclamation of habitual drunkards by medico-social means. 'Medicalization' can be a liberal strategy for relieving the individual of the stigma of guilt (by treating his drunkenness not as a culpable vice, but as a biological disposition, rather in the manner, say, of diabetes), while also drawing upon medicine's perennial optimism about cure. Once drunkenness is seen as a disease, the drunk ceases to be regarded simply as a 'bad lot' and can be more readily thought of as a suitable case for treatment.

In these ways, Professor Sournia shows how currents independently generated in nineteenth-century medicine flowed parallel with, and merged into, the growing social panic over the problem of proletarian drunkenness in a modernizing society. Thus among the general public an ideological consciousness evolved that was simultaneously more agitated about drunkenness, yet, through the invention of the idea of the alcoholic, more optimistic about the possibilities of treatment, reform and cure. It must be emphasized, for instance, how eager organizations such as Alcoholics Anonymous, and their individual clients, have been to utilize the notion of alcohol dependence as a sickness. A just parallel is perhaps afforded by the transformation of attitudes towards the insane. Early Victorian public opinion grew more perturbed about the threat the insane allegedly posed to social progress. None the less, swayed by influential medical views, it also believed that insanity was a treatable disorder, and that the new insane asylums would prove to be instruments for transforming the mentally disordered into the mentally healthy.

This powerful formulation of the 'disease' concept of alcoholism, however, far from resolving the problem of habitual drunkenness and alcohol dependence, involved further complexities in theory, while, in the event, it contributed disappointingly little in progress. As Professor Sournia's masterly discussion of the chequered developments of the last hundred years shows so well, what promised to be the final clarification has instead created greater confusion.

For one thing, the view that alcoholism is a disease could perfectly readily be incorporated into one of the most pessimistic strands of late-nineteenth-century medico-scientific thinking: degenerationism – the idea (the dark side of evolutionism) that acquired disorders of body and mind would be inherited in progressively more severe forms in subsequent generations. Many medical and social analysts contended that the children of drunkards would be born with defects, perhaps a liability to promiscuity or mental disability, precipitating a slippery slope towards imbecilism and ultimately racial suicide. As eminent recent historians of the eugenics movement have pointed out, drunkenness was widely taken as a prime symptom of a dysgenic disposition.

Thus medical science seemed itself to be looking both ways as to the likely prognoses, individual and social, of alcohol dependence. Furthermore, during the last century, the medical profession has proved remarkably uncertain as to the optimal methods for treating the condition it appropriated to itself as a disease. On the one hand, drug therapies and, on the other, psycho-therapeutic methods have been attempted, and mixtures of both as well. No certain and long-term solutions have been discovered, however, and after 'cures', recidivism rates remain high. Moreover, today's doctors seem no nearer a consensus as to how to cure alcohol dependence than when, precisely two centuries ago, certain physicians, such as John Coakley Lettsom, advocated weaning drunkards off liquor step by step, whereas others, such as Thomas Trotter, believed 'all or nothing' was the only way. Alcoholism treatment has remained a happy hunting ground for the quack. Perhaps more than Professor Sournia's text indicates, the drift nowadays in the medical profession, at least in the English-speaking world, is to express considerable misgivings as to the advantages of treating alcohol dependence primarily as a medical, rather than as a personal-cum-social, problem.

As Professor Sournia shrewdly notes, setting chronic alcoholism in the hands of the medical profession has proved a mixed blessing. It has been all too easy, as a consequence, for society thereby to wash its hands of responsibility for the problem altogether, leaving it to doctors, as if it were akin to chickenpox or Parkinson's disease. And in turn, the medical profession, profoundly oriented towards clinical and curative, rather than preventive, medicine, has never directed its energies into crusading against all those aspects of modern consumer-capitalist culture that encourage the alcoholic's progress. The net outcome is that today's European and North American societies are ones in which individuals, manufacturers and governments alike, for their various reasons, are all happy to conspire in turning a blind eye to alcohol abuse. As with tobacco smoking, alcohol abuse is growing more severe amongst certain sections of the population (above all, the young and women), although it is possibly alleviating amongst traditional groups (proletarian males). What is more, there is every prospect that alcoholism will grow ever more acute as a problem in third-world countries open to capitalist multinationals. As long as alcohol dependence is largely seen as a problem for doctors to treat, there is little prospect that its wider social challenge will be met.

This book combines two great virtues. On the one hand, it provides the reader with abundant detailed information in many fields – about medical developments; about the actual consumption levels of alcohol and the recorded incidence of alcoholism in many nations; about movements, led by reformers, sufferers and ex-sufferers alike, to counter and combat the problem. Much of this information, particularly about reformist movements in continental countries, has hitherto been hardly accessible to the English-speaking reader, and it provides an excellent comparative foil to the more familiar story of the temperance movement in nineteenth-century England and to prohibitionism in twentieth-century America.

On the other hand, it rightly insists that alcoholism is not simply a 'given', a positive fact of life, of society and of biology. People have always got drunk, but they have not always been called alcoholics, nor have they always called themselves by that label. And the moral, personal and social connotations of such categories have never been rigidly fixed, but have always been the subject of negotiation, depending upon circumstance, class, gender and so forth. Professor Sournia's book expertly charts the interweaving of the history of drinking, with the history of social reform, and the history of medicine, to show the particular way in which the 'problem of alcoholism' is a specifically modern formulation, though one showing few signs of resolving itself into a thing of the past.

ROY PORTER
Wellcome Institute

PREFACE

THE solid components of man's diet have been the subject of numerous historical studies, but, with the notable exception of wine, the liquids he drinks have long been neglected. This book sets out to show how attitudes to the *excessive consumption of alcoholic drink* have changed through time. Such an undertaking poses problems, not least those of terminology. *Consumption* refers to the quantity of liquid absorbed by the individual when he drinks; experts prefer to talk of *alcoholic intake*, thereby expressing a purely quantitative idea without moral overtones or reference to alcohol-related diseases.

To define exactly where *excess* begins is rather more difficult. Do we see it in the man whose drinking upsets his family and professional life, and who is deemed by others to be an *excessive drinker*, or do we confine it to the cirrhotic who consumes more alcohol than his body can take? The effects of alcohol vary so greatly from individual to individual, and depend so much on the manner of drinking that any definition of excess will seem inadequate. Acceptable thresholds of alcohol intake are defined by others and not by the drinker. They vary within societies according to social group and occupation and they change with time – each generation has its own way of drinking.

The language of drink is nuanced, embracing different aspects of the phenomenon to a far greater degree than might be expected from simple variations on the word *drunk* in English or *ivre* in French. Such niceties of language are not gratuitous. In relation to alcohol they reflect society's ambivalence towards a pattern of behaviour which in some situations is greeted with approval and in others condemned out of hand.

In the nineteen centuries considered in part I, *ivrognerie* and *intempérance* were the only words available in common French usage to describe the effects of excessive alcohol consumption. With the emergence of *alcoolisme* in 1849 the heavy drinker entered a new domain of observation and scrutiny, namely that of medicine. The term had a learned ring to it which suited doctors. However, it did not remain exclusive to them, but soon became fashionable with the general public, thereby acquiring the moral nuances and stigmata attached to its predecessors.

Like everybody else, doctors remain products of society, they speak its language and are raised on its ideas, even if, by recourse to dubious statistics, they purport to provide a rational explanation for its myths. Even when they do expose the harmful effects of alcohol intake, they come up against so many vested interests and are often so impassioned in their 'struggle' that the public tires of anti-alcoholism and its message.

With the advance of medical science the term 'alcoholism' has acquired several new meanings. Its inventor used it to describe the mental and physical effects of alcohol observed in the individual. Statisticians soon began to use it in reference to populations suffering the effects of alcohol, and as a result we have come to speak of alcoholism existing within countries or professions. The term was principally used in these two ways until the middle of this century and it is this period of a hundred years, during which alcoholism played such an important part in society and when much was written about it, that will be considered in part II.

Since the 1950s alcoholism has come under psycho-social and psycho-pathological scrutiny, as has the particular kind of dependency it induces. No longer is the alcoholic the object merely of moral condemnation; instead the reasons for his dependence are studied in the hope of freeing him from it. Part III will examine the contemporary period.

The alcohols are a large family of chemical compounds that are by no means all fit for human consumption; indeed some are poisonous. When the word 'alcohol' is used, it is generally *ethyl alcohol* or *ethanol* which is meant. Doctors speak of *ethanolic* breath when they are speaking amongst themselves in the presence of a patient whom they do not want to condemn by using the word 'alcoholic'. Such a term does not escape the moral overtones implicit in its predecessors. With the advent of the new approach to alcoholic disease, the French now speak of *alcoologie*, a scientific discipline which, protected by the neutrality of science (as was *alcoolisme* one hundred years before), attempts to inspire social or medical prevention of what today is still referred to as *alcoholism*.

Man's worthy desire to overcome the vices that assail him gives rise to the language of war, studded with struggles and fights leading to victories or defeats. Temperance battles with intemperance, virtue with vice, and hygiene with infection; the anti-alcohol movement has had its triumphs and reverses.

The history of alcoholism – one which goes back several thousand years and which will probably never end as long as man lives – has never been chronicled. This work tries to do this using studies already in existence and which in the main deal with contemporary times. If nothing else, it will show man's insatiable thirst for a pleasant poison and the ways in which his cravings for it have been satisfied or resisted through the ages. It has only been possible to consider the Western world in this book, but it should be remembered that the Near and Far East have long been familiar with fermented liquor.

Finally, I would like to thank the numerous institutions that have assisted me in the course of my research, in particular the *Haut Comité d'études et d'informations sur l'alcoolisme*, the *Comité nationale de défense contre l'alcoolisme* and the *Institute d'alcoologie* in Paris; the Wellcome Institute for the History of Medicine and Alcohol Concern in London; and the Alcohol and Drugs Addiction Research Foundation in Toronto.

PART I

THE HISTORY OF ALCOHOLISM

1

Drinkers in Antiquity

DRUNKENNESS AND SOCIETY

FERMENTED drinks date back thousands of years. Although the exact nature of their original discovery remains open to speculation, it seems likely that they predate agriculture. Alcohol has become widespread and although there are examples of peoples who achieve effects similar to those of alcohol by different means, these are rare. The different states induced by alcohol range from simple elation, enabling the individual to relax and lose his inhibitions, to deepest coma and death. So much mystery surrounds the effects of alcohol that many peoples see them as divine in origin. Self-transcendence brings man closer to the gods and the happiness he discovers in the process generates an irrepressible desire to repeat the experience again and again.[1]

Mankind's consumption of alcohol has always been associated with festivity. The euphoria of the drinker is such that he abandons his inhibitions, and while he shows off to others, he discovers in them similar new-found vigour and insight. Through drink the individual no longer faces the human condition alone; the group discovers new solidarity and is strengthened. There are very few occasions that are not marked by the consumption of alcohol. The pretexts for festivity are innumerable: a successful hunt, victory over the enemy, various important social events such as birth, initiation, marriage, death and migration. There is, however, another side to such celebrations, which is often forgotten: they give the group the opportunity to survey the behaviour of each of its members. Like all aspects of daily life, drinking obeys a pre-established ritual, which varies from group to group. The rules of the game state that we should drink just enough for everyone to share in the fun without transgressing into aggression or stupor. Excessive drinking can lead to violence, which would threaten the group. If festivities are to take place in a general climate of goodwill, participants have to recognize their own capacities and drink enough to join in without over-indulging. It is a game for society and the individual: a dangerous and therefore attractive game.

Each group has its own drinking rites and each member ensures their proper execution. He who does not drink according to the rules, especially if he drinks too much, commits a crime. Such crimes are multiplied, as the drunk not only upsets social hierarchies by his behaviour, but also defies sexual taboos and the familial constraints, which form the basis of the society. From then on he is guilty and must be punished. This notion of the violation of social ritual appears at every stage in the history of drunkenness.

THE FIRST DRINKERS

The ancient populations of the Far and Middle East had a number of substances at their disposal capable of producing fermented drink. It seems that honey furnished the first drinkable ethanol: all the nations of the West and the Old World came to be familiar with mead. In the prehistoric period, the western Mediterranean had at its disposal dates, cereals, grapes and many other fruits. Egyptian papyri provide evidence of several alcoholic drinks, and the frescos in the tombs show drunken people. Inscriptions from Ugarit and Sumer also carry allusions to intemperance.

The law code of the Babylonian king Hammurabi, dating from 1700 BC, mentions the sale of wine. Commercial activity played such a role in the consumption of alcohol that the passages of the code are worthy of attention.[2]

If a female seller of date-wine with seasame has not accepted corn as the price of drink, but silver by the full weight has been accepted, and has made the price of drink less than the price of corn, then the wine-seller shall be prosecuted and thrown into the water. (paragraph 108)

If rebels meet in the house of a wine-seller and she does not seize them and take them to the palace, that wine-seller shall be slain. (paragraph 109)

If a priestess who has not remained in the convent shall open a wine-shop, or enter a wine-shop for drink, that woman shall be burned. (paragraph 110)

These fragments speak for themselves. The commerce in wine was already something that needed to be controlled. Alcohol loosened tongues and plotters gave themselves away. The trade in wine was run by women and it was their job to report any potential trouble; these women were of low station, since wine-selling was degrading work. (In Western society too, the profession has never been well regarded, even though governments are eager for the revenue it generates. To be a tavern keeper in France was not considered respectable until after the Revolution.)

The Bible contains nearly two hundred references to vineyards and wine, and there are also references to drunkenness. The oldest of these concerns Noah who, according to the account in Genesis, was unaware of the intoxicating properties of wine, drank too much and fell asleep.[3] The important point of the story is not the drunkenness of the patriarch, but the behaviour of his sons, who laughed at his naked body until finally one of them reclothed him. The scandal was not that he was drunk, but that he was naked. Sex and alcohol have always been linked.

Both the Old Testament and the Talmud make ample reference to the virtues of strong drink:[4] it gives courage and enables the poor and unhappy to forget their trials.[5] The vine is a recurrent symbol of wealth and peace. Excesses are also described: the extreme drunkenness of a woman is criticized in the Book of Samuel,[6] and in Proverbs we find a description of an inveterate drunkard with his short temper, bloodshot eyes, strange visions and hallucinations.[7] It was because of wine that Lot was able to commit incest with his daughters. Only through drink was he able to forget the gravity of his transgression and guarantee the family's succession.[8] Nevertheless, the dangers of wine called for some limitations. Drunks were forbidden entry to the temple and priests could not drink inside. Both judges and the performers of ritual sacrifices were forbidden from drinking while discharging their duties.

Ancient Judaism speaks of groups voluntarily practising abstinence. One such reference concerns the Nazarenes, an early Jewish–Christian sect. For a certain period they had to avoid all products of the vine and refrain from cutting their hair. At the end of this time the Nazarene was required to cleanse himself. By deliberately depriving himself of one of God's bounties he had offended Him, and in order to rejoin society a sacrifice was required.

Abstinence was also practised by the Rechabites, descendants of Jonabab, the son of Rechab, who live in the Yemen and the United States to this day. This sect renounced the sedentary life, agriculture and its products, grains and the vine, to return to its former nomadic ways in the desert.[9] Examples of this kind only reappear in the nineteenth century: indeed one Protestant temperance society was to use the abstinence of the Rechabites as a model for its own behaviour.

DIONYSUS–BACCHUS

The Ancient Greek world was a society where wine played a considerable role. The Greeks drank mead from the earliest times and probably developed the cultivation of Caucasian vines around 1000 BC. Legend would have it that it was Dionysus who taught them how to make wine. His story is well known: considered by some to be the son of Zeus and a Theban princess, and by others to be of Thracian origin, he is said to have fled to Egypt to escape the fury of the jealous Hera. It was there that he learnt to make wine. The cult of Dionysus was also called the cult of Bacchus. The public ceremonies that it inspired were often linked to 'phallopheries', rustic fertility rites featuring choirs, dances and parades, out of which were born poetry, comedy and drama. Initially, the Greeks resisted these foreign rites, which pushed men and women to the worst excesses, but they rapidly became part of daily life. There was, however, a certain opposition among the cultivated classes, whose allegiance remained with Apollo. This opposition between Dionysus and Apollo, between spontaneity, fantasy and joy as symbols of mystical intoxication and carnival, and the more rigorous qualities of self-control and individual reason, persists today.

Although there are no quantitative data available, the epics and the tragic and comic theatre provide innumerable examples of alcoholic excess. They range from Elpenor, the foolish and cowardly companion of Ulysses, who, having drunk too much, fell from a roof and broke his neck,[10] to the unfortunate Polyxenos, a habitual drunkard, who slipped on a wet road after drinking and died.[11] The virtues of wine have been sung by many, among them Homer, Anacreon and Euripides.[12] The Greeks wrote the first poems dedicated to wine, but these give no clue to contemporary drinking habits. Legendary drinkers existed, but excessive drinking was frowned upon. The Greeks despised the Thracians because they drank too much, and the Macedonians met with similar disapproval. It is a social tendency throughout the world to mistrust the foreigner as other, with his different styles and drinking habits. To drink moderately was acceptable. Alcibiades recalled that no one had ever seen Socrates drunk.[13] During the banquets or 'symposia' (literally meaning a drinking party), wine awoke the spirits, enlivened the company and increased one's appreciation of the dancers, but moderation was recommended. It ill behove a gentleman to drink heavily.

In the fifth century BC, Plato outlined what he considered to be correct behaviour in relation to alcohol.[14] He forbade wine to those under 18 years old, authorized its use on condition that it was in moderation to those under 30, and placed no limits on those older than 40. (The Aztecs had a similar attitude, punishing drunkenness among the young, but authorizing it in the old.[15]) Water alone was to be consumed by soldiers and certain other professional groups, such as ship's helmsmen, judges and magistrates, for the reason that alcohol might dull their faculties.

His advice was not always followed. All armies at war drink to give themselves courage and there is no lack of examples, even in Ancient Greece, where unforeseen defeats or victories can be attributed simply to drunkenness in the ranks. For obvious reasons, slaves were also required to abstain: the slave who dared to match his master's drinking was acting above his station, since alcohol led to arrogance and violence, and was thus a threat to social order. Colonizers all over the world have instituted similar restrictions: the whites with their black slaves; the American pioneers with the red Indians; the Canadians with the Eskimos. (The Spartans had different ideas: the helots were made to drink so that the young citizens might witness the evils of alcohol.) Plato also addressed the recurrent association of sex with alcohol, and maintained that couples wishing to have children should abstain from drinking during the night.

Plato was not a legislator. He only expressed his personal vision of an ideal state and wrote for the educated class, to which he himself belonged. Eyewitness accounts suggest that Greek towns had their quota of heavy drinkers, women amongst them, and it is known that in Athens the policing of taverns was strict and that public drunkenness was punished. There is further evidence to suggest that habitual drunkenness was commonplace, whether in public places or in the home.

An accurate assessment of the scale of the phenomenon in Greek society is impossible, since doctors made no record of what today we would call chronic alcoholism. (Hippocrates describes one of his patients who fell ill after overindulging in love and wine. The man complained of stiffness, vomiting, insomnia, palpitations, delirium and incoherent speech – symptoms more suggestive of acute alcoholic poisoning than chronic intoxication.) Furthermore, it is difficult for us to interpret with any certainty the causes of symptoms observed at the time; thus when Hippocrates describes a patient with what today would be considered classic symptoms of the *delirium tremens* – delirium with fitful plucking movements and fumbling with the sheets – we cannot assume that the man was an inveterate drunkard.[16] (In medical terminology, 'acute' is used to describe a disease when it comes sharply to a crisis, whereas 'chronic' is used when the disease lingers for possibly months or years.)

How is it that the astute clinicians who wrote the Hippocratic tracts between the sixth and second centuries BC failed to observe the damage caused by excessive drinking, when drunks undoubtedly existed? One difficulty lies in the area of mental disturbances. Failing intellect and mental incoherence attributable to alcohol can develop in relatively young individuals still in their twenties, but this is often masked by other forms of mental illness, which even today doctors have difficulty in classifying. Doctors have not yet established the relationship of cause and effect between certain psychiatric disturbances and the repeated abuse of alcohol. Identification of physical lesions due to alcohol may have been complicated by the fact that the average life expectancy at that time was about 40 years: cirrhosis of the liver, damage to the pancreas and the cancers caused by ethanol require several decades of abuse before manifesting themselves. Even if some individuals did succumb at an early age, the number of clinical cases was probably too small to have attracted the attention of doctors. Another reason for physicians' failure to recognize the problem was that wine was an important agent in the medicinal pharmacopoeia:[17] although they counselled against abuse, they freely prescribed wine for fevers and to fortify the milk of wet-nurses – a practice that had spread to the point of absurdity by the nineteenth century.

Few deaths in Antiquity have excited as much interest as that of Alexander the Great, who died in Babylon in 323 BC. His demise is described in the contemporary accounts of Eumenes of Cardia and Diodorus of Sicily and the much later works of Plutarch and Arrian from the first and second centuries AD.

As Littré demonstrated more than a hundred years ago, Alexander died on the eleventh day of an acute attack of malaria.[18] The part played by alcohol in his behaviour, however, is interesting. All too often modern biographers of Alexander have proved to be mere hagiographers, vaunting the inspired insights of their hero, his political sense and his creative, enduring reforms. He was, however, subject to the passions of ordinary men and his taste for wine could not escape medical attention. His case illustrates further the difficulties of retrospective diagnosis.

Alexander was born into a milieu where drunkenness was common. His father, Philip the Second of Macedonia, conqueror, authoritarian and womanizer, took part in numerous orgies at his court and often made decisions while he was drunk. His mother, Olympias, in spite of her husband's opposition, became a fervent follower of Bacchus. (Little is known of the nature of the libations the cult of Dionysus required of its members. It must not be forgotten, however, that what information we do have on this subject is furnished by the Greeks, who regarded the Macedonians as drunkards. Alexander's bouts of drunkenness, however, are well documented.[19]) Each of his many victories provided a pretext for drinking with his companions, and his billeted troops also drank between campaigns. Certain excesses committed during his drinking sessions are well known. In 330, the burning of Persepolis occurred. It is possible that the king played no personal role in this, but he was drunk on the day. During another orgy, in 328, he slew his best friend Cleitus, who dared to contradict him. When his dear friend Hephaestion died (he too had been drinking), Alexander retired to his tent for three days and then had the doctor responsible for Hephaestion's care hanged, together with several of his countrymen. On the basis of such excesses we can suppose that there were others.

It is apparent, then, that Alexander did not follow the counsel of moderation given to him by his teacher Aristotle and his behaviour bears witness to his excessive drinking. During the last seven years of his life, he had no more than strained relations with his friends. He no longer tolerated their criticisms, justified as they were, given the nature of his wayward enterprises. He lost his temper with them, drank and was then struck by remorse. Apparently happy and charming in the company of drinkers like himself, he was apt to become aggressive and violent without warning.

As a figure of such renown, Alexander has aroused the interest of modern psychiatrists. Psychoanalysts cite his stormy relationship with his father and, in contrast, the passionate feelings he had for his mother to justify the constant anguish, which sought relief in ever-renewed conquests. Others consider him to have been a manic depressive of the cyclothymic type: a condition characterized by cyclical alternation from exhilaration to depression. His mood-changes and crazed actions – sometimes found in young drinkers – might usefully be interpreted as personality disorders due to alcohol.

It is not possible to attribute the death of the great Macedonian king to an acute episode of drunkenness, since no mention of alcohol is made during the last days of his life. However, attempts have been made to interpret the sudden death of a man who was still young in years as the result of the sudden withdrawal from alcohol, which was occasioned by his fever. Stopping drinking in itself is not enough to have been the cause of death, but it may well have played a role – it is now known that deaths that occur during attempts to break some form of dependency are almost always attributable to external causes. In Alexander's case, malaria attacked an already weakened constitution.[20]

This short review of alcoholism in Ancient Greece would not be complete without mention of the influence of Greek civilization on our own attitudes to wine and alcohol. Many authors have drawn attention to this.[21] Since the Greeks, the drinking of wine, both alone and in company, has been equated with happiness, life, blood, well-being, warmth and virility. Wine and, latterly, other forms of alcohol have been the inspiration of writers and poets across the centuries, throughout the world. The symbolism that surrounds alcohol, despite the received wisdom, is not strictly Judaeo-Christian in origin. Rather, it predates both Judaism and Christianity, and its roots lie in man's desire to escape the treadmill of his daily existence. The cultures of the western Mediterranean, however, played an important part in the diffusion of this symbolism – the mythology of wine – which persists as an irrational force driving men to drink.

THE SPREAD OF THE VINE AND CHRISTIANITY UNDER THE ROMANS

Vines existed in Italy for several centuries before the period of Greek colonization, but wine itself was a rare commodity and it seems that the inhabitants of the Greek colonies in ancient Italy knew of no other form of fermented drink. After the second century BC, vine cultivation increased. This was the result of a drop in the value of grains, coupled with a dietary shift from the consumption of gruels to bread, which made it necessary to drink while eating.[22] Prior to this time, the Romans drank water and the peasants grape juice (wine was so scarce that women were forbidden to drink it), but now all social classes began to drink wine. Wine became more easily obtainable and the Bacchanalia developed into major public celebrations, becoming so unruly that they required regulation. Men were supposedly forbidden to participate in the ceremonies of the female followers. Cato the Elder (234–149 BC) recommended that wine be drunk in moderation and defended its medicinal value; the flowers of juniper, myrtle, hellebore and pomegranate soaked in wine were useful against snake bites, constipation, gout, indigestion, diarrhoea and other illnesses.

During the first century BC, wine production in Italy increased enormously and export became highly lucrative. Local consumption also grew apace and there are a considerable number of allusions to drink and drunkenness in the literature of the period. Numerous illustrious heavy drinkers lived at this time: the general Sulla; Mark Antony, who wrote a book about his drinking habits; Marcus Tullius Cicero, son of the famous orator; Lucius Piso, who stopped drinking the day he took public office; and Cossus, the prefect of Rome, who arrived drunk at the Senate one day and promptly fell asleep.

Roman poetry between 200 BC and 200 AD celebrates the glory of wine. Poems were destined to be sung or read during banquets. Their subject matter is drawn from the behaviour of those present. Petronius' *Satyricon* presents us, in Trimalcion's banquet, with the scene of a freedmen's orgy. Seneca speaks of those who drink without getting drunk and of others who succumb with the greatest of ease, and Pliny describes men who drink incessantly, even in the baths. Here are clinical cases of chronic intoxication indeed – alcohol dependence as we know it today. The true extent of the pathological phenomenon remains uncertain, since these writers belonged to the educated classes and the picture they paint pertains only to Rome, not to other imperial cities or social milieux. For this reason, it can only be conjecture to state, as Gibbon did, that generalized drunkenness was one of the causes of the collapse of the Roman Empire.[23] Hypotheses, such as those propounded in the nineteenth century by writers who adhered to a moralizing view of history, can stimulate our explorations of historical pathology, but only become plausible when substantiated by the necessary documentary evidence.[24]

The Byzantine Empire survived a further millennium and its history is studded with great drinkers.[25] Antioch, at one time the true commercial capital, was considered to be a seat of debauchery, and Julian the Apostate who, despite his sobriety, enjoyed Lutician wines, had numerous problems with the town's wine-sellers.[26] St John Chrysostome spoke out against the citizens' drunken habits. Emperor Michael III (842–67) was justifiably nicknamed the drunkard; when speaking in public, he stammered to such an extent that the people would cry out, 'You've had too much to drink again'.[27]

More interesting from the medical point of view is the remark made by Simeon Seth, a doctor practising in Constantinople in the eleventh century AD. He wrote that drinking wine to excess caused inflammation of the liver, a condition he treated with pomegranate syrup. Although we cannot say what he meant by 'inflammation', his awareness of an association between hepatic damage and heavy drinking is worthy of note.

During the same era Muhammad Rhazes, an Arabic-speaking Persian doctor, seems to have been more interested in nervous disorders brought about by drinking. One of his aphorisms (no. 162) declares: 'Great damage is done by wine when it is abused and used regularly to get drunk. Delirium, hemiplegia, paralysis of the voice, croup, sudden death, acute illness, pains in the ligaments, as well as other illnesses that would take too long to list attack the heavy drinker.'

To the west of the Byzantine Empire, Italian wine was drunk in increasing quantities and vineyards were planted in areas where they had previously been unknown. According to Strabo, the Ligurians drank only beer made from barley. The Celts who invaded the peninsula in the sixth century gorged themselves on wine, and Rome was taken amidst scenes of great drunkenness. The Gauls, fond of their ale, were forever considered drunkards by the Latins.

The Roman vine was first grown in what is now eastern France and its cultivation spread along the great routes of communication – the Naurouze line and the Rhone valley – subsequently taking a hold in the Narbonne area.[28] The inhabitants of these regions were great wine lovers and seem to have valued it both religiously and commercially. Roman merchants grew very prosperous supplying Gaul, and it is to be supposed that Caesar was encouraged in his conquests by traders in search of new openings: mercantile interests have always inspired colonial enterprises.

Defying Domitian (81–96), Gallo-Roman cultivators began to plant vines and in the space of two centuries cultivation spread throughout Gaul, extending to the Meuse and Moselle, and then across the Channel. Trade from Italy rapidly declined after the first century and, in turn, traders, north and south of the Loire alike, developed commercial links with the North Sea coast and Germany.

The Germanic peoples, the Francs, Saxons and Scandinavians traditionally drank mead and, subsequently, barley beer. The use of hops did not become widespread until after the ninth century. If Roman visitors are to be believed, these people drank in great quantities. Viking folklore abounds with accounts of prodigious drinking. The sagas deal with drinking matches and the trials faced by their heroes. Such drinking sessions were probably episodic and took place to celebrate victories, alliances and initiations. They are testimony to the vitality of these peoples and not, as the Romans considered, their general barbarity. The bishop poet Fortunat attacked Count Dagaulf in typical fashion: 'Would that sad ale and the impurities it contains kill him off, may dropsy take him.' Could it be that the popular consciousness had already registered that dropsy occurred in heavy drinkers before doctors became aware of the fact? The Chronicle of the Merovingian court suggests that the Francs did not alter their drinking habits on accession to their modest thrones. The numerous cases of drunkenness are exemplified by the death of Clovis in 657. The son of a drunkard and a drinker himself, he seems to have suffered from several lapses into alcoholic delirium before dying at the age of 21.[29]

The spread of the vine coincided with the spread of Christianity in Europe. The Church, drawing upon a familiar xenophobic theme, viewed intemperance as a pagan vice and concluded that drinking was barbaric. In the fifth century, Saint Jerome reproached a drunken Christian woman for behaving like a pagan. A century later, Salvien, a priest at Marseilles, accused some Christians of drinking like unbelievers. Such condemnation was selective. When the evangelization of the Germans began, the Church forbade the use of beer, but wine-drinking was hailed as a sign of conversion. Charlemagne issued a capitulary forbidding the funeral feasts that were traditional among the Germans. He reasoned that too much drinking occurred, especially when the dead man had been a clan chief. (The Church had already forbidden other practices such as that of eating the deceased's horse in order to appropriate his virtues.) Charlemagne himself drank very little and recommended sobriety for the laity, monks, priests and nuns. For the army he outlawed not wine, but its abuse. He did not forbid what he could not prevent. None the less he had drunks whipped for their first offence and pilloried repeated offenders. The Germans took no notice of such measures; the funeral feasts continued and the Church was forced to 'christianize' numerous pagan ceremonies.

Drinking was prevalent amongst priests and laity alike. In the sixth century, Gregory of Tours observed that wine had replaced ale as the popular drink of the Parisian taverns and he speaks of the repeated drunkenness of the clergy. He cites the cases of five vicars who were habitual drinkers and describes cases of alcoholic delirium. Childebert the First (511–58) proclaimed that drunkenness was an offence in the eyes of God; his slaves were given one hundred strokes of the rod, if they were found drunk. During the period from the end of the sixth century to the ninth, several synods spoke out against the abuse of wine, claiming that it provoked serious illness, undermined the intelligence and led to evil deeds.

2
Wine and Eaux-de-vie

In Western Europe, the following centuries were marked by a complex evolution in viticulture, which was to have a profound effect on wine consumption. Bad years for the growers were rare (one example was the period following the Great Plague, from 1358 to 1360, when labour shortages pushed up wages and agricultural produce was expensive). Cross-breeding led to new strains of vine, and vineyards that failed to keep pace with increasing yields or that faced difficulties getting wine to market were abandoned. Wine-growing was regarded as highly prestigious and this was a factor responsible for its extensive spread in the period up to the fifteenth century; princes and the bourgeoisie alike possessed their few acres of vines, and even town-dwellers aspired to ownership of a smallholding close to the suburbs. The monasteries and clergy also played a role;[1] the extent of their cultivation was far in excess of their requirement for communion-wine. A considerable part of their vast domains was given over to viticulture. This interest was the result of two considerations: vines were relatively easy to cultivate, and the revenue from wine sales was more stable than that possible on the grain market. For the Church, the vine was not just a sign of wealth; it was also a rich source of income.

Wine-drinking became more common between the sixth and sixteenth centuries and as its popularity increased, a new sense of discrimination developed. The best barrels were enjoyed by kings and princes or exported to northern countries, where they were greatly appreciated. Wines not favoured in this way were to be found on the tables of the middle classes. In rural areas, growers drank what they had been unable to sell and, in the days before the French Revolution, landless peasants drank water. As the towns grew in size, the number of consumers increased. From the twelfth century onwards, artisans, workers and servants began to drink wine, albeit of a poorer quality than that consumed by their superiors. In 1664, an Italian traveller observed that the 300,000 inhabitants of Lyons drank more than the combined population of twelve Italian towns.[2] It seems likely that the numbers of heavy drinkers grew in line with total consumption, but little attention was given to this subject in the Middle Ages. Members of the aristocracy drank heavily themselves and saw no harm in such conduct; indeed Dante, who was quick to describe the torments reserved for sinners of all kinds, makes no mention of drinkers in the *Inferno*.

The fables of the Middle Ages tell of drunks who are fooled into marriage or ruined in business. Rabelais took his character Pantagruel from a mystery play in which the eponymous devil stuffs the mouths of the damned with salt because no penance is worse than an unquenchable thirst. In his short work, *The Orgy*, Laurent de Médicis mocks one of his companions who goes searching for his lost thirst.[3] Being drunk is humorous, but the damaging effects of prolonged drinking are ignored. Poems and songs dedicated to drinking are also found in the literature of the Renaissance, and odes to wine, in a style reminiscent of Anacreon, continued to flourish until the beginning of the twentieth century.

Doctors themselves contributed to the increased consumption of alcohol among their patients; following teachings that can be traced back to Antiquity, they prescribed wine to aid bowel function and digestion and to fortify the blood. Medical thought in the Middle Ages argued the superiority of wine over water, and doctors took sides in rivalries between the growers: there was fierce competition between Burgundy and Champagne and the Ile-de-France and Auxerre districts. One of the treatises on good health that were so popular during the Middle Ages, Cuba's *Hortus sanitatis* (Garden of Health), maintains that 'wine helps both digestion which takes place in the stomach and the second digestion in the liver; because it is such a natural product no meat or drink promotes the body's warmth as it can ... It purifies clouded blood and opens all inlets, channels and veins of the body.'[4]

Warnings were voiced, but these went unheeded. In 1596, Barthélemy de Laffumas, an adviser to Henri IV, denounced drinking that 'all too often ruins homes and families'.[5] The Greek monk Agapios, in a work published in 1647, stated that excessive drinking was harmful to the brain and nerves, and was at the root of numerous maladies such as paralysis, apoplexy, convulsions and trembling.[6] A medical thesis submitted by Berger in 1667 asked the question: 'Does wine shorten our lives and harm our health?' Although the author begins by listing the points in favour of wine, he answers the question in the affirmative and describes the damage done by excessive drinking: shaking hands, loss of memory, ulcerated eyes, thirst, disturbed sleep, jerky gait, sluggishness, gaping expression.[7] This work contains a number of valid clinical observations justly attributed to their cause, but such perception was not widespread.

Outside France, condemnations of drinking were also rare. For many years England had served as a privileged market for the quality wines of Aquitaine, which were a great favourite with the rich, although the poorer classes remained beer-drinkers. One visitor to London noted as early as the thirteenth century that: 'The town has only two curses, fire and drunken idiots.' A poem by John Skelton, written in the sixteenth century, portrays a female beer-seller in the vicinity of one of Henry VIII's castles. The poet described the way her clients paid in kind, but he is most interested in her appearance: she was paralysed in various places, her joints were gout-ridden, her head and hands trembled, she was fat, her breath was bitter and she smelt of beer.[8] In the east of Germany beer was popular, but the preference in the west was for wine. There is a manuscript describing 'the horrible vice of drunkenness', dating from around 1531, but the work of V. Obsopoeus is more considered. His Latin poem, *The Art of Drinking*, published in 1582, describes the joys of wine. He goes on, however, to deplore the contemporary manner of always drinking to get drunk, which he considers to be the behaviour of fools, who have no respect for real companionship.[9] The Russians were particularly fond of beer and Saint Basil preached against drunkenness. In China, where rice was one of many cereals used to make alcoholic drinks, there was a common saying: 'First the man takes a glass, then the glass takes a glass, finally the glass takes the man'.[10]

Further changes were necessary before the West became fully aware of the dangers of drink. In France, the demand in expanding urban areas increased and vineyards developed that were capable of producing cheap wine in plenty; those producing poor wines or situated far from urban centres were abandoned. In the west of France (with the exception of the Loire valley), these factors resulted in an increase in cider consumption, but that was to remain a country drink. In the course of one year, just before the Revolution, 250,000 *muids* of wine were drunk in Paris compared with only 2,000 of cider.[11] (The Parisian *muid* was equivalent to 268 litres/58.5 gallons.)

THE STILL

New, more dangerous alternatives to traditional fermented drinks were to emerge. Arnaud de Villeneuve is attributed with the discovery of alcohol in the thirteenth century, but it is likely that this volatile and highly flammable liquid had already been isolated by other alchemists. Its physical properties resulted in the Latin name *spiritus*. In Arabic, it was referred to by a generic term for all products of combustion: *kohl* is the name of the black powder still used as eye make-up. An apparatus called an *alambic* (an Arabic deformation of a Greek word) was used to heat a fermented drink and the resultant alcohol vapours condensed as they cooled. The system was very simple, requiring only a source of heat, a cauldron (traditionally called the curbite), with a tube, often coiled, running off it.

In the encyclopaedic work of Raymond Lulle, a doctor and philosopher of the same era, alcohol is described as *aqua vitae*, water of life, because of its invigorating properties. Here again, it is not certain that he coined the term, but this was its first appearance in print. Initially, spirit of wine was only used for medicinal purposes, but this state of affairs did not last. In some countries the original pharmaceutical label was retained and it became known as *aquavit*; elsewhere it was called *branntwein* (burnt wine, whence brandy), after its mode of production, or *aguardiente*, the water that burns.

The Dutch were probably the earliest to distil drinks other than wine, when they made the first gins from juniper. The first mention of a still in Sweden, where the first grain alcohol was made from beer, dates from 1469. From 1498 onwards, alcohol was sold as a remedy by apothecaries, but demand grew and a century later the *cabaretiers* took over the trade. From the end of the sixteenth century, distilled drinks were to be found throughout the West. People's lives could now be made sweeter with products containing 50 per cent ethanol; these were cheaper and faster-acting than wine, but increased the chances of addiction.

The appearance of the new drinks was lamented by certain moralists. The French accused the Italians of introducing distilling techniques, the Germans said the same of the French, and the English claimed that their soldiers had been introduced to gin-drinking in Holland during the wars of the sixteenth century. There was a rapid change in drinking habits which soon became widespread, and even the upper classes took to eaux-de-vie, once they became more refined and varied.

Dutch merchants played a considerable role in the development of French eaux-de-vie. In the sixteenth century they became regular clients at the Atlantic ports, where they purchased wine of all types in large quantities. The quality of the wine was of no interest to them; it was not destined for the home market, but for re-export and once in Holland it was 'tainted', according to a contemporary expression, using processes that were kept secret from their suppliers.[12] With the exception of the English, who were long-time connoisseurs, they provided their buyers – Frisians, Germans and Scandinavians – with the first fortified wines, drinks to which sugar, spices and alcohol were added.

In some areas of France, the Dutch lack of regard for quality had the effect of encouraging the production of mediocre wines that would have found no other buyers at the time. In the form of eaux-de-vie, these wines were shipped at Bordeaux, La Rochelle and Nantes. Growers in the regions of Gascony, Aunis and Saintonge were the most sensitive to this demand and produced good cognacs and armagnacs from poor-quality wines.[13] These regions then, as now, were the best known, but Anjou and the Lower Languedoc followed their example. By the end of the eighteenth century, wine from the Orléan district was of such poor quality that the region was known only for its eaux-de-vie and vinegar.

Connoisseurs and farmers who were aware of the problem deplored this decline in the wine industry. In 1868, Guyot was moved to condemn 'this current, this torrent ... which covers everything with vines which make excellent eaux-de-vie, but never produce anything other than dreadful wines'.[14] However, there was nothing to hinder this preference for eaux-de-vie and *marcs*, and stills spread throughout the French provinces. In western districts, ciders were distilled; elsewhere, the juices of fruits such as cherries, pears and plums were used. In this fashion, numerous regions produced white alcohols (*alcools blancs*). Some of these had a distinctive flavour, but others, because of rudimentary production and storage methods, tasted awful and had as their sole virtue a high alcohol content.

Strong liquor was being drunk everywhere. Using the same basic techniques and custom-built stills, each country soon fashioned its own preferences. The Scots made *whisky*, which soon became known as *Scotch*; Swedish peasants had their *aquavits*; the Germans produced *branntwein* and *schnapps*; the Russians made *vodka*; and in the Balkans, people drank a plum brandy called *slibovitza*. The western Mediterranean succumbed to *arak* and *raki*, made with rice from the Far East. The extensive cultivation of sugar in the West Indies gave rise to the slave trade. Boats abandoned their human cargo in the Caribbean and loaded up with alcohol: *rum* destined for North America and France, and *punch* for the English.

Old French legislation confined access to *cabarets* to travellers, wagoners and coachmen. The local inhabitants could only buy *vin à pot*; they went to the shop with their own receptacle, chose from the wines on tap and returned home. In 1587, an edict passed by Henri III abolished this restriction and the *cabaret* henceforth catered for both local and passing trade. This change was to alter the nature of the institution. For the local inhabitants, it became a meeting place: some-where to chat and exchange news. Doubtless the repeal of the law made it easier to buy alcohol, but whether, as Dion suggested, this led to the rise of alcoholism in France remains open to conjecture.[15] We will never know whether wine consumption increased dramatically among the common townsfolk at the time or whether they simply switched their drinking from home to the *cabaret*. The relation between alcoholism and access to alcohol posited by Dion remains a vexed question today.

As the number of customers increased, wine-selling became more profitable and in consequence the number of *cabarets* grew. At the end of the sixteenth century, de Laffumas spoke out against this increase and the rapid fortunes being amassed by owners of such establishments.[16] In Lyon, in 1664, an Italian visitor noted 'that every house is a *cabaret* and, curiously, none of them lack customers'.

Since every aspect of the trade in wine and spirits represents a source of revenue to governments, it comes as no shock that they supervise it closely. In France, taxes on wine dated from the time of Charlemagne and were collected and increased regularly. Whenever a king was short of funds, he would consult his aides and order an increase in taxes; they were raised to pay the ransoms of both Jean Le Bon, imprisoned in London during the fourteenth century, and François I, the prisoner of Charles V of Spain in Madrid during the sixteenth century. Given the availability of eaux-de-vie, it is surprising that fiscal agents waited until the reign of Louis XIV (1638–1715) to tax them at the same level as wine. In the days before uniform taxation, tariffs varied so much that disputes, frauds and smuggling were common. The fact that governments derive an income from alcohol sales is seen in some quarters to legitimate its consumption, and bars and taverns have become a focus of attention for the activities of both temperance movements and tax inspectors.

3

From the Enlightenment to
Magnus Huss, 1700–1850

B Y the beginning of the eighteenth century certain Western societies, or at least a few enlightened individuals, were beginning to express concern at the increasing level of drunkenness. Such a phenomenon did not occur simultaneously in every country, nor did it always manifest itself in the same way.

Those concerned by the general lack of temperance were few and far between, at best forming small groups. Their concern, rather surprisingly, was based on social rather than medical grounds: drunkenness was upsetting social order in that the lower classes, thought to be the sole indulgers in alcoholic excess, were becoming unruly. It was only some hundred years later that the medical argument became more coherent. Not until the mid-nineteenth century did governments become sufficiently worried to take action; until this time politicians left the subject well alone.

ENGLAND: BEER STREET AND GIN LANE

Gin conquered England in the sixteenth century. In *Pierce Pennilesse, his supplication to the Devill*, published in 1592, Thomas Nashe dedicates a whole chapter to the subject.[1] He deplores the consumption of gin imported from the Netherlands and criticizes, in particular, the new habit of drinking to get drunk, which led to vulgar, violent behaviour. He elaborates seven types of drunkenness, ranging from monkey-like to lion-like.

The British government introduced tax benefits in the seventeenth century to encourage distillation of local grain at the expense of the Dutch, and there was accordingly a steep rise in consumption – 11 million gallons in 1750 as opposed to 527,000 gallons in 1685.

In England there was greater social variation in drinking habits than in France, where the main difference was one of quality of wine drunk. The English aristocracy and wealthy classes consumed French or Portuguese wines, French brandy or West Indian rum punch flavoured with local fruit, whereas the poor drank beer and, increasingly, gin. The excesses of many a nobleman, politician or intellectual were well known, but it was those of the poor that were harmful to the nation.[2] It is hardly surprising that attitudes differed on either side of the Channel: where drunkenness was a cause for English concern, the French disregarded it.

English demographers and statisticians – the European leaders in these disciplines – lent weight to the notion of generalized excesses amongst the people. Despite regular increases in the English population at the end of the seventeenth century and the beginning of the eighteenth century, and in spite of considerable movement from the countryside to London, the number of people living in the city actually fell. Infant mortality was enormous: between 1730 and 1749, only a quarter of the children baptized reached the age of five.[3] At this time, in London taverns and even shops one could get drunk for a penny, and for twopence one could drink oneself into a stupor in the knowledge that a bed for the night would be provided. Although contemporary writers blamed gin-drinking for high infant mortality and increasing crime, it is likely that gross overcrowding and unemployment had much to do with these problems. Whatever the case, this era engendered two notions that were to become widespread in the following two hundred years – namely that only the poor were drunkards and that drunkenness gave rise to crime.

The problem was not just confined to London, although there it was at its most serious; it was also to be found throughout the country. Hogarth's satirical writings and engravings depict scenes from rural election campaigns where votes are bought with measures of beer and gin.

Between 1720 and 1736, attempts were made to restrict the sales of gin and prices were raised; riots were only narrowly avoided and few attempts were made to implement these unpopular measures. Towards the middle of the eighteenth century the authorities began to show concern. Petitions were lodged and a commission of inquiry revealed, for example, that in the St Giles area of London as many as one in five houses had set up as a gin shop.

The writer Henry Fielding, who was also a criminal magistrate in London, published one report and several accounts that dealt with poverty and vice in the less salubrious areas of the capital. He came to the conclusion that alcohol played a considerable role in the crime-ridden lives of many citizens.[4] The popular press was full of terrifying accounts of the woes of prostitution and infanticide, and of stories of women convicted scores of times for being drunk in the streets.[5] (Female drunkenness has always been seen as more serious and degrading than the equivalent male excess, in spite of the fact that historically male dissipation has led to far greater domestic hardships.)

Hogarth also showed concern. Two moralizing engravings printed in a cheap, poor-quality edition were sold in their thousands. 'Beer St' shows a flourishing London scene with prosperous houses, clean streets and a well-kept tavern; an impoverished pawnbroker tries to conduct his business, while a tidily dressed woman suckles her baby. In 'Gin Lane', the same scene has become a living hell: the houses are run down, drunkards quarrel in the streets, the pawnbroker is doing a flourishing trade and the woman, now unkempt and dirty, beats her child. These didactic engravings were not preaching abstinence, they deplored only the drinking of gin; they imply that had English people not given themselves up to this diabolic potion and stuck to good, traditional English beer, all would have been well. Drinking as such was not criticized; gin alone was seen as the root of all evil.

This line of thought led to the introduction of effective regulatory measures in 1751. Gin consumption fell from 11 million gallons in 1750 to 2 million in 1758. Unfortunately this did nothing to resolve the English drinking problem. Today we know how easily drinking habits can change and, although the increase in the popularity of tea and coffee at this time is well documented, no records were kept of the quantities of beer and rum consumed in place of gin.[6] A further difficulty is encountered in that an assessment of the quantity of alcohol consumed cannot be based on the number of alarmist tracts written against it. (It is for this reason that, in spite of the vast amount of English writing on the subject, it is impossible to say who drank the most, the English, the French, or the Germans.)

The newly-formed Methodist Church founded by John Wesley (1703–91) was one of several movements that broke away from the formalism of the Anglican Church during this period. Wesley wanted to fight against the dechristianization of the people and to restore a way of life closely based on the teachings of the Gospels. In 1769, he recommended that Methodists should abstain from distilled liquor, he forbade all preachers to indulge in alcohol of this kind and he demanded that all distillation should be outlawed. Once again, we encounter the notion that fermented drink such as wine and beer is harmless ('hygienic' even, as it was dubbed a century later) and that distilled liquor – whether rum, brandy, punch or gin – is harmful. (The truth, of course, is that the toxicity of any alcoholic drink depends solely on the concentration of alcohol it contains.)

With the onset of industrialization, urban populations grew in the newly-created suburbs and in hospitals doctors became increasingly aware of the effects of heavy alcohol consumption on the human body. Medical reports on the subject, however, were rare and were confined to the specialist journals. Greater publicity was achieved by the writings of Thomas Trotter (1761–1832), himself a doctor, who at the turn of the nineteenth century was one of the first to relate alcoholism to the increasing numbers of patients in the new, specialized mental hospitals.[7] Crime, illness and 'pauperism' (a term created in England in the 1830s) were also on the increase. Doctors working in the asylums were quick to take up the cause, and in 1850 Forbes Wilson mentioned that four inmates in five were there through overindulgence in distilled liquor; Holloran, however, put the figure at one in five.[8]

Trotter considered the heavy drinker to be ill: 'Drunkenness is an illness of unknown cause which upsets the healthy equilibrium of the body.' He also implicated alcohol as a cause of dropsy, gout, apoplexy and epilepsy. In treating the ailment Trotter relied more on trust and determination in his patients than he did on sermons and moralizations.

Medical attention was also drawn to certain liver abnormalities by Black in Dublin (1817) and Baillie in London (1873). The former described the appearance of the organ in two drinkers examined at autopsy: the tissue was shrunken to a third of its normal size, hard, and covered with nodules. The condition was later termed 'cirrhosis' by Laennec.[9] Black was cautious in summarizing his findings: 'this condition is often found in heavy drinkers although as yet a specific link between their lifestyle and this disorder has not been established'. Laennec, as we shall see, also failed to make a link between cause and effect in cirrhosis and when Thomson, in 1841, described 'gin-drinker's liver' he went unnoticed.

The phrase 'delirium tremens', coined by Sutton, also dates from this era, although this condition, characterized by bouts of extreme agitation, had been recognized previously. (In 1696, Grubel described a mania 'provoked by excessive drinking of gin'.) Guillaume-Fabrice de Hilden (1560–1634) recommended blood-letting as a treatment, whereas Stoll de Leyde in 1788 proposed the use of emetics, followed by rehydration.[10] Sutton, a Kentish doctor, used the term to describe the delirium he had observed in local sailors who, on occasions, smuggled gin and rum into England. Although he did not recognize delirium tremens as a product of heavy drinking, Sutton, unlike his professional colleagues, had little time for blood-letting as an effective treatment, and proposed the administration of opium and laudanum in its place.

The failure of the likes of Sutton to establish a direct link between abuse of strong alcohol and symptoms such as those described above opened the door to a blunter, more didactic approach. Macnish, in his popular work *Anatomy of Drunkenness*, published in 1836, saw alcohol as the cause of almost all human pathology.[11] He placed particular emphasis on liver damage, claiming that wine alone had no effect upon the organ (the English unfortunately drank wines fortified with brandy). One by one he reviewed other organs affected: stomach, brain, kidneys, bladder, skin, eyes; one's blood turned black and one's nose crimson – 'the hallmark of a Bacchanalian tendency'. In addition, there were accidents associated with delirium tremens, not to mention sterility, gout and epilepsy. Drinkers of spirits grew thin, whereas those preferring wine put on weight; all, however, succumbed to premature old age and dementia. In spite of all this, Macnish vehemently rejected the notion of complete abstinence, claiming that during the Napoleonic wars the English and Dutch, who drank schnapps at Walcheren, survived fevers that killed others. In similar vein, he cited the rash of deaths that followed a breakdown in liquor supplies at Niagara during the Anglo-American war of 1812–14.

It is this refusal to accept total abstinence *per se* that explains the ambivalence of Macnish and those like him towards the temperance organizations. These groups had mounted a huge propaganda exercise during the 1780s. J. C. Lettsom, for example, published a print that was later to be imitated by Rush in America, where it achieved great popularity. The picture showed a thermometer demonstrating the degrees of damage a drinker could expect to inflict upon himself: vices, varying from idleness to suicide; ill health, ranging from simple malaise to untimely death; misfortune, extending from debt to the gallows. Only if men were sober would they generate health and wealth.

The English followed the example of the Americans and a first temperance society was formed in 1817, although its life was short.[12] From the outset, the organization was plagued by the fundamental issue that continues to divide such groups today: should the message preached be one of complete abstinence, or could the reformed drinker limit himself to an occasional drink? A Methodist organization founded in 1830 followed Wesley and forbade only distilled liquor; later, in 1841, one of its members demanded total abstinence. During the same era, a secular group developed 'teetotalism', the emblem of the group being the letter 'T'. In Leeds, a Mrs Carbell and the Revd Tuncliffe founded the National Temperance League which, with 'hope groups', set out to educate first children, then adults.

A spectacular campaign was conducted by an Irish priest, to whose memory a statue was erected in Cork. After unrewarding attempts to promote temperance amongst his local whiskey- and beer-drinking parishioners, Father Theobald Matthew (1790–1856) was eventually persuaded by William Martin, himself a Quaker, to preach abstinence. He travelled throughout England and Ireland collecting names for his cause, setting up reading-rooms to compete with the taverns, and organizing temperance rallies. He eventually landed up in a debtor's prison, from which he was freed by the proceeds of a public collection. Following his compatriots to the United States, where they had been driven by the potato famine, he enjoyed considerable success, despite being a Roman Catholic.

George Cruikshank (1792–1878) was another colourful character. Engraver, book illustrator, caricaturist and a former drinker himself, he led a vigorous campaign for abstinence. In 1847, he wrote an abysmal family melodrama, *The Bottle*, which was a great popular success. The play ran concurrently at eight theatres (a popularity never enjoyed by the play adapted from Zola's *L'Assommoir*), was also sold as a cheap novel and provided motifs for china plates. Charles Dickens, a friend of Cruikshank, did not think much of the drama, but this mattered little, since it made its mark with the audiences. Cruikshank, however, was an extremist in all he did, and his mission developed into a violent obsession. His tracts lost their conviction and he quarrelled with Dickens.

The public (or at least the upper and business classes) appear by 1841 to have been well aware of the dangers of drink. This year saw the establishment of the first life assurance company to deal solely with non-drinkers: contemporary awareness of the increased longevity enjoyed by those abstaining from alcohol was reflected in lower premiums.[13]

It is conceivable that the English were drinking less in the mid-eighteenth century than a hundred years earlier. The sales of gin fell sharply and less beer apparently was being drunk (18 gallons per head in 1830 as opposed to 36 gallons in 1722).[14] Whether consumption was reduced or not, the temperance movement had at least been effective in stirring up public opinion. The Victorians, however, were not going to be satisfied with a partial and possibly temporary success of this kind.

ALCOHOLISM IN GERMANY

German research into alcohol-related problems was strongly influenced by contemporary developments in England. In Germany, however, alcoholism interested only the medical community, possibly because political ideas did not spread easily from one state to the next. Many German doctors seemed to agree with the ideas put forward by Trotter, whose works were translated into German and Swedish, and many regarded alcoholism as an illness.[15] In 1802, Hufeland (1762–1836) took a staunchly medical view of the problem and concentrated principally on the question of treatment, dismissing mesmerism and homeopathy, and reserving the full force of his criticism for Brownism, which was enjoying a vogue in Germany and Italy. This movement, founded by Dr John Brown (1735–88), classed all diseases as arising either from an excess or a lack of excitability (sthenia or asthenia); alcoholism fell into the latter category and as such was to be treated with stimulants – namely, alcohol itself and opium. Such a therapy struck Hufeland, the founder of the first German temperance society, as absurd.[16] In its place he recommended abstinence from spirits, but permitted wine and beer, if drunk in moderation.

Brühl-Cramer, a German doctor practising in Moscow, also considered heavy drinking to be a disease and used the psychiatric term 'dipsomania' to describe the disorder: 'Those affected have an abnormal, all-consuming and elemental need for alcohol.'[17] The destruction of their moral judgement was a consequence, and not the cause, of their sickness. Will-power alone could provide a cure.

Statistical evidence for the effects of alcohol was produced for the first time by Lippich (1799–1845).[18] His life illustrates the mobility enjoyed by Austrian citizens at this time: born in Bohemia, he studied in Budapest and Vienna, ran a private practice in Ljubljuana, where his original and clear-sighted work earned him such a reputation that he was asked to teach in Padua, before finally retiring to Vienna. Lippich followed up two hundred drinkers for four years and established that their lives were shorter and that they had fewer children, who were more prone to illness than those of patients who did not drink.

Rösch (1808–66) was well known in France for his work on cretinism, and in 1838 he published *De l'abus des boissons spiritueuses* (On the abuse of strong liquor). Having performed numerous autopsies, he came to the conclusion that alcoholism was a mental illness leading to subsequent physical degeneration. In his opinion, authoritarian measures were needed to prevent the indulgence of an inclination for drink and subsequent dipsomania.

A different approach was taken by Fuchs, a professor at Gottingen University, who adopted a toxicological approach to alcoholic excess. In 1845, he compared the symptoms of heavy drinkers with those of patients consuming other poisons. By analogy with the terms 'arsenicism', 'mercurialism' and 'ergotism', he created 'methylism' to denote addiction to alcohol. (This was a misguided venture, since alcoholic drink contains ethanol and not methanol, which is highly toxic.)

These German studies provide a background to the works of Magnus Huss, the Swede who in the mid-nineteenth century provided a crucial turning-point in the history of heavy drinking. As a result of his travels in France, Huss (and his fellow countrymen) followed developments in contemporary medicine closely, and he was clearly influenced by them. He considered Rösch's work 'the most important treatise on alcohol ever published'. Like so many innovators and reformers, Huss drew on the ideas of his predecessors.

PIONEER AMERICA

The early colonizers of America had left Europe to inhabit a continent about which they knew little. What they found to eat and drink there differed considerably from their native diet, although they prepared the food in the way they had been accustomed to do so at home. It is interesting to note that English colonial society began to protest against the drunkenness of its members later than had been the case on the other side of the Atlantic. A further feature that renders the American campaign for temperance remarkable is that it was conducted in a particularly charged moral and political environment.[19]

The seventeenth-century settlers in New England were subsistence farmers who, with the grain they harvested, brewed a dark beer resembling the beer drunk throughout Britain. Home-brewing was the norm and the brews varied from one farm to the next. Wine would have been too expensive to import and anyway, as we have seen, it was only drunk by the wealthier echelons of English society, who were poorly represented in the New World. Attempts were made by the French Huguenots to plant vineyards in Virginia, but these were soon replaced by fields of tobacco, which brought greater returns.

Gin was never very popular in America, even though in some towns it formed part of the day-labourer's wage. Every home had its own still and other spirits soon appeared: beer was 'boiled'; cider (well-loved in Maine and Vermont) was used to make apple-jack; fruits – pears, berries and Floridan peaches (legacies of Spanish occupation) – found their way to the alembic, as did grain crops like rye; potatoes were distilled in America long before they were introduced into Britain. Slave-ships returned from the Caribbean laden with rum; they also brought molasses and the first distillery opened in Boston in 1700 to turn it into alcohol.

The first half of the nineteenth century seems to have been a time of heavy drinking. Strong (or 'hot') waters were fashionable. Every event, whether family or public – elections (frequent in the British colonies), the opening of a town hall, the building of a church or school – was celebrated with a drink. The same was true of religious occasions – the departure of one priest, the arrival of his successor, ordinations, episcopal visits – all were feted with alcohol (the drunken habits of the clergy were frowned upon by many). Alcohol was needed to fight malaria, exhaustion, the difficulties of childbirth and the general trauma of the rough colonial existence. One popular poem considered it 'one of the Lord's creations'.

Alcohol was the white man's right; others could only drink when allowed and according to his rules. Its pleasures were denied to Indians and blacks alike. A slave who drank did not work hard and the effects of alcohol sometimes provoked him to rebel against his lot. Although taverns remained closed to slaves, even after emancipation, some masters distributed alcohol amongst their workforce to promote good-will. As for the Indians, a commonly held view was that they could not tolerate alcohol and it was an offence to sell it to them. Indians had been familiar with fermented drink long before the appearance of the white man in America and it was for this reason that they were attracted to more potent liquor. So it was that, eluding their chief's watchful eye, they began to buy. The whites paid little heed to the ban on selling liquor and in many ways it was instrumental in their westward progress: trappers used it as payment when trading furs and it soon accompanied any business or agricultural transaction.

In addition to the Calvinist minority in New England who regarded drinking as a sin, there were those who spoke out against the unruliness it provoked. The authorities in most towns, whatever their religious denomination, were strict with those found drunk in the street, particularly if they had been involved in brawls, and punishments varied from fines to spells in prison and, occasionally, brief exclusion from church. Repeated convictions were common and for a time the town of Boston appointed alcohol inspectors to some family homes.

The distinction made between distilled and fermented liquor (the former being supposedly the more toxic) crops up again in 1735, when a law was passed in Georgia forbidding the drinking of whiskey, brandy and other spirits; good English beer was recommended in their place. Few heeded the legislation and the law was repealed seven years later.

The Quakers and Methodists continued to speak out, and the abundant rhetoric and pamphleteering of the 1760s shows the relative ardour and puritanism of the northern colonies, when compared with the aristocratic south, which was more sympathetic to the ways of Charles I and his Cavaliers.

In 1776, speaking before the Connecticut General Assembly, a priest maintained that those who indulged in alcoholic excess lost their human dignity and became no better than animals.[20] A more patriotic argument also existed, namely that abuse of this kind was an attempt to imitate the decadent and dissolute behaviour of the English.

The War of Independence was to have its effect on drinking habits. With the breaking of commercial links with the West Indies, which remained under British jurisdiction, there was demand for substitutes for rum. The new domains to the west of the Appalachians produced whiskey from their growing yields of maize; rye whiskey became more popular and a large estate in Kentucky began to make Bourbon.

The temperance lobby continued to condemn the various faces of alcoholism, whether acute, occasional or public, until Benjamin Rush (1745–1813, a revolutionary hero, chief army medical officer and a physician of repute) published an influential work in 1784. *An Inquiry into the Effects of Ardent Spirits on the Human Mind and Body* dealt for the first time with the mental and physical dangers associated with alcoholic abuse.[21] Rush's political and educational work over a period of thirty years was to make him the father of American psychiatry. He demonstrated the considerable effects of alcohol on the mind and body of the heavy drinker: 'Strong liquor is more destructive than the sword. The destruction of war is periodic whereas alcohol exerts its influence upon human life at all times and in all seasons.' He was the first to raise the argument, voiced on many occasions since, that 'a nation corrupted by alcohol can never be free'.

Rush and Trotter were contemporaries. However, where the Englishman focused his attention upon the organic problems of alcohol, the American leaned towards more psychological arguments – arguments the French alienist Pinel would have termed 'moral': 'Drunkenness is the result of a loss of willpower. Initially drinking is purely a matter of choice. It becomes a habit and then a necessity.' This notion, which sees the drinker as dependent upon his poison, is well-founded, but the treatment Rush considered necessary to effect a cure – cold baths and total abstinence – was ill conceived and gave only disappointing results. Since it proved almost impossible for Rush to impose his radical therapy in everyday surroundings, he proposed the construction of detoxification establishments, asylums and 'sober houses', where regular offenders would be shut up until cured.

Rush's arguments were well constructed, but shot through with moral and social considerations. Drunkenness leads to poverty, disorderliness and civil disobedience; in other words, it is unpatriotic or 'anti-republican'. Many of Rush's supporters continued the propagation of these ideas and produced tracts, posters and popular pictures and, although his action had little effect upon the drinking habits of Americans as a whole, it had considerable influence in religious and political spheres and in certain other sections of society. The bourgeoisie and educated classes, judges and intellectuals in America took a far greater interest in the fight against alcoholic excess than elsewhere. Drunkenness was the cause of all violence and unleashed vile behaviour of the worst kind; consumption of distilled liquor led to poverty, ruin, domestic strife, unemployment and any other social problems in existence.

Far-fetched and naive as it was to blame alcohol for all evils, the idea seems to have caught on. The first group of those opposed to distilled liquor met in 1808 at Moreau in New York State and, although it soon disbanded, many other similar societies were formed at this time (a trend imitated subsequently in England). In 1813 Samuel Dexter, an ardent publicist, founded the Massachusetts Society for the Suppression of Intemperance. A pamphlet published by the Greene and Delaware Moral Society proclaimed 'we are becoming a nation of drunkards'.[22] The organization that was to become the National Temperance Society was formed in 1826 and had sections in several states.

All forms of propaganda were exploited to the full: posters appeared, there were street demonstrations, and novels, poems and emotive autobiographies were written. Religion became implicated: in 1813, the Society for the Promotion of Morals was founded to combat the vices springing from alcoholic excess, to fight against the neglect of religion in everyday life, and to rekindle respect for the Sabbath. Most of the Protestant churches, fearing the increasing power of lay organizations, took up the cause and the theme of drunkenness became increasingly popular with preachers. Six sermons on the subject were published by Pastor L. Beecher and were used as models by his colleagues.

By the 1830s the temperance associations had a combined membership of over 500,000.[23] Some were short-lived, as was the Washington Temperance Society, which was founded at the Chase Tavern, Baltimore in 1840 by six former drinkers. Their avowed aim was to cure hardened drinkers and they helped to set up asylums along the lines proposed by Rush. Financial difficulties, however, led to their dissolution. Some societies were for men or women only; some admitted only whites, others only blacks; others were linked to religious denominations; some such as the Good Templars (founded in 1848 as the Jericho Society) were semi-secret organizations, whereas others dealt only with immigrants from given countries; some even had their own insignia and uniforms.[24]

Politics also became involved: a good American was a sober American. Neorepublicanism expected leaders to be sober men of integrity, respecting family life, keeping the Sabbath and Protestant too, if possible. God's blessing would then fall on the land.

Such fervent activity led to spectacular success. The report of the American Temperance Society in 1831 heralded victory: almost two million people had renounced strong liquor; there were over 800 temperance societies with a combined membership of 1.5 million, at least 4,000 distilleries had closed down and more than 8,000 suppliers had stopped selling liquor; more than 12,000 ships' captains refused to carry spirits; and over 12,000 former drinkers had renounced alcohol entirely.

Father Matthew, the Irish priest, was a star in several states. A complete abstainer, he preached on many occasions to Protestants in addition to his own Catholic congregations, and he even delivered a speech in the Senate House in Washington. The concrete result of all this was the introduction of legislation in several states: in 1846 a law was passed in Maine forbidding the sale of 'alcoholic' (meaning distilled) drink – a law whose powers were strengthened in 1851. In the course of four years, twelve states and two bordering Canadian provinces had introduced similar legislation.

Such victories over alcoholic excess were short-lived, however, because they neither had the support of the general public, nor were they the result of a concerted, united campaign. The temperance organizations quarrelled and could not agree on their aims. Thus, lay organizations were criticized for their very laity by those with a more religious leaning; some groups only forbade consumption of spirits, whereas others banned the use of all fermented drink; some were ferociously teetotal, whereas others were content with sobriety. The ambiguity of their position resembled that of Rush: they considered the heavy drinker to be, on the one hand, sick and, on the other, guilty of committing a moral sin.

It was the rich and educated who dominated the Council of States; although they passed laws that satisfied their pretensions to morality and respectability, they rented taverns as venues for electoral meetings and were not averse to organizing free hand-outs of beer and whiskey to buy votes. The conquest of the west and the domination of the Indians and the deserts were achieved in a climate scarcely conducive to sobriety. The new frontier towns were built by ranchers, miners and gold prospectors. They were places where gambling, brawls and fighting were commonplace, and where the message of the prohibitionists fell on deaf ears.

The population of the United States was changing rapidly and with it, drinking habits. The Irish, who were in the main impoverished and Catholic, congregated in the east, where they were looked down upon because they kept taverns and were heavy drinkers – they maintained their cohesion as a community by drinking whiskey together. The Germans achieved more rapid prosperity by importing their light 'lager' beer, and it was not long before each state had its own German brewery. For all new settlers, irrespective of nationality, drink in whatever guise formed a part of their community, and the right to drink was one of the liberties granted the individual under the Constitution. Accordingly, they considered any attempt at prohibition, however anodyne, to be an infringement of their civil rights. The decision to drink or not to drink was a matter for the individual. The political parties were as divided on these matters as the temperance organizations: the arguments of the 'dry' prohibitionists were as debatable as those of their 'wet' counter-parts.

In 1850, two factors led to the alcohol question being pushed into the background. First, there was the indisputable fact that the supposedly 'dry' states had been unable to implement the legislation banning drink; as a consequence the laws fell into disuse. (The United States failed to learn from this experience and embarked on the same futile experiment a century later.) In addition, the slavery question was very much the issue of the day. (One party that tried to combine 'abolitionism' with 'prohibition' – that is, freedom from slavery with freedom from alcohol – experienced a disastrous election result.) Abolitionism involved all sections of society and the dramas of the War of Secession made the virtuous struggle for temperance seem trivial in comparison.

It will be noted that doctors (with the exception of men like Rush), unlike religious leaders, had little role to play in the fight against alcohol in the United States. Medicine was by no means as well organized as it was in England; qualified doctors were few and far between, and there was no consensus on alcohol. It would appear that the majority did not welcome prohibition. Whatever the case, their contributions to the identification of alcohol-related disease were slight in comparison with their European colleagues. J. Eberle was an exception to this rule. In 1833, he published a paper on the effects of alcohol in the foetus: 'The majority of children born to mothers who are heavy drinkers are weak and sickly and few of them reach adolescence'.[25] His conclusion was to ban the drinking of spirits in pregnancy. Despite Eberle's poor statistical method, he had nevertheless raised a fundamental issue which today is still a source of constant debate.

The struggle against alcohol abuse was by no means over and once again it became a major issue with the return of peace to the United States. Times may have changed, but the issues remained the same: a mixture of morality, religion and a little medicine.

THE BIRTH OF PUBLIC HEALTH IN FRANCE

In eighteenth-century France the problems of alcoholic excess did not awaken the same interest as they had in the English-speaking world. Such excess certainly existed, but its presence was probably less obtrusive: drinking habits were different and the drinking of spirits was far less common. Just as the spoken word is easier to interpret than silence, so it is easier to find historical explanations for situations where factual data exist than it is in those where it does not. Thus an explanation of alcoholism and the phenomena that gave rise to it in France is necessarily complex.

The Bourbon era paid scant attention to the problems of drinking. Political writers of the eighteenth century made only the occasional reference to alcoholic excess amongst the peasantry. They were far more concerned with the organization of the state and with the distribution of food to the populace in times of scarcity; the distribution of wine did not pose the same problems – water could always be drunk in its place. Physiocrats, amongst them Quesnay, who was himself a doctor, were interested solely in agriculture, and concerned themselves with fertilizers, yields and the growing of potatoes. Wine-growing areas witnessed the loss in value of their produce and lamented the current vogue for champagne. Excessive consumption was criticized by no one. In France there were no Trotters or Rushes, nobody stopped to wonder whether drunkenness was an illness, a vice or a sin, and preachers were restrained on the subject.

Nevertheless heavy drinkers did exist, a fact that is borne out by contemporary police reports. Among the working classes, labourers who were found drunk on several occasions were sacked, and those who were repeatedly drunk and disorderly were sent to prison or the *hôpital général*; if found in the harbour areas, drunkards were frequently sent to the galleys or the colonies. The upper classes despatched their incurable drinkers (those who spent their family fortunes and destroyed the family) to the same establishments that housed aristocratic lunatics, idiots and teenage delinquents. One such establishment was at Charenton but others existed elsewhere.[26]

A qualitative picture of the alcoholization of any country can be built up from the types and quantities of drink available and in the sixteenth century both factors were on the increase. Since the rule of Henri III, the *cabarets* had been open to all, even to those living close by, and the only restriction placed upon them was that they closed during certain church services. This regulation was intended to instil a respect for religion in the populace, but served only to oppose Church and tavern in the minds of the people.

Anyone could start up a *cabaret*, if granted permission; they were places where people came to eat and drink. Beer or wine was drunk, depending on the area, and eau-de-vie was available everywhere. Taverns were frequented by all social classes, but were never the haunts of honest women. With the introduction of coffee into France by Francesco Procopio in 1669, the word '*café*' came to designate a drinking place where, for many years, only coffee, chocolate or herbal infusions were consumed. The distinction between the *café* and the *cabaret* disappeared, however, during the early nineteenth century.

Cabarets were meeting places, places where the clientele could keep warm and win drinks playing dice, darts, *boules* and traditional games; wandering entertainers would dance, play instruments, perhaps bring in performing animals; in the classier establishments, there were newspapers to discuss, and billiards tables. Official business – meetings, assizes, judgements – was transacted there for want of better premises and they were often the base of corporations, guilds and associations.[27] Less salubrious social activities such as prostitution, illegal gaming sessions, fights and brawls, which often warranted police intervention, were also conducted within their confines.

In a country on the verge of revolution, political thinkers freely admitted that the *guinguettes* of the Parisian suburbs made an indispensable contribution to the physical and mental well-being of the capital's poorer classes. It could be said that the turmoil of early July 1789 originated in these haunts. Historians have more or less neglected this fact, but those in power during the century that followed did not, and always looked after the interests of the proprietors.

The preceding 150 years had seen the establishment of many *guinguettes* (the word seems to be of Flemish origin) around the outskirts of the city and it was here that the workers came to eat and drink. There was no tax on the cheap wines sold in these areas, whereas in the city duty was levied, irrespective of the quality of the fare. However, at the beginning of 1784 the municipality decided to increase its income by building a new city wall (*l'enceinte 'des fermiers généraux'*), which would enclose many of the *guinguettes*, particularly to the north and east of Paris. Workers would be faced with the prospect of not being able to afford a drink, since it would be rendered too expensive by new taxes; owners would lose their clientele; and even if new establishments were to open beyond the wall, the distance between them and their custom would be too great. Work on the project was suspended when, spurred on by traffickers, smugglers and the innkeepers themselves, the workers of the Faubourg St Antoine, Montmartre and Belleville attacked and set fire to the half-finished buildings that were to make up the wall. These riots took place in early July and were a prelude to the storming of the Bastille on 14 July. Wine had sparked off the revolution and was destined never to be absent from the events that ensued. The role of famine and the lack of bread have rightly been cited as a cause of the 'patriotic' riots, but historians have minimized the part played by the price of drink and people's thirst for wine. Marie-Antoinette's 'let them eat cake' (*brioche* actually) and *le boulanger et son petit mitron*, made in reference to the starving mothers of Paris, are well known, whereas no such famous quotation has been set down by historians to evoke the plight of the *cabaretiers*, who resorted to violence to protect their livelihood.

After the laxity of the revolutionary era, Napoleon brought the *cabarets* under tighter control by restricting their opening hours. The need for tax revenues, however, led to a relaxation of this measure and the number of taverns continued to increase: in Lille, where in 1765 there had been 300 establishments catering for 58,000 people, in 1829 there were 400 for a population of 65,000. Throughout the nineteenth century this sequence was repeated by successive governments, obliged, on the one hand, to reduce the number of taverns because of the policing problems they created and, on the other, needing to allow the trade to develop for fiscal reasons.

The health of the nation did not figure amongst such considerations, and between 1788 and 1862 the consumption of eau-de-vie in France rose from 169,000 to 2.7 million hectolitres (300,000 to 475 million gallons). An increase of this magnitude was attributable not just to the growing number of *cabarets*, but also to greater production and lower prices. With the development of the chemical industry in France and the blockade, which reduced imports of rum from the West Indies, the *'bouilleurs'* (literally, boilers and hence distillers) were given a free rein; they progressed from the more traditional 'raw materials' (grape pressings – *marc* – cider or perry) to the use of starch (*faules*) beet, chestnuts and all kinds of fruit. A few modifications to the domestic still at this time suddenly made industrial distillation a reality.

Doctors undoubtedly had to treat patients whose ailments were the result of chronic alcohol poisoning, but neither they nor contemporary pathologists appear to have made the connection between cause and effect. Following Hippocrates, they were willing only to accept that chronic alcohol abuse predisposed an individual to certain complaints, amongst which were dropsy, gout and apoplexy, a fact that is not disputed today. When Laennec described a case of hepatic atrophy in a patient who had died of tuberculosis and named the condition 'cirrhosis', he also failed to make the link between the organic change and the dead man's alcoholic excesses.[28]

Progress was being made, however, in the field of nervous and mental disease. The term 'delirium tremens' was rapidly accepted in France, and in 1819 Rayer implicated alcohol abuse as the consistent causative factor in the condition. He spoke of the unfortunate need for alcohol as *'œnomanie'* (wine mania), classifying it amongst the manias of the insane. In 1826, Dupuytren failed to recognize delirium tremens as the true cause of a 'nervous delirium' seen in patients admitted to the Hôtel-Dieu who had been involved in accidents.[29] Franco-German collaboration, together with Blake in Edinburgh and Ware (1831) in Boston, soon resulted in a full clinical and symptomatological classification of the condition.

Since the beginning of the nineteenth century, alcohol had been considered a plausible cause of mental disturbance in the same manner as trauma, intestinal worms, syphilis and menstrual upsets. Pinel was of this view, but saw abnormal behaviour as just that and not the result of the action of a toxin on the brain. Esquirol went a little further and, in doing so, had much in common with Brühl-Cramer and his notion of 'periodic dipsomania'.[30] Esquirol believed that alcoholism was involuntary, a form of monomania, and that it was a symptom (or rather a syndrome), not the cause of disease. In his book on the drinker's madness ('*la folie des ivrognes*'), Léveillé, a doctor who practised at the Hôtel-Dieu and the Parisian prisons, writes in the same vein: the madness driving patients to drink should be treated by isolation, by a careful watch on their fluid intake and by use of the straitjacket in cases of resistance or violent agitation.[31] Léveillé used other, supposedly simple, methods, either individually or in combination: expectoration (advocated by Esquirol), irritation with mustard plasters (a method Esquirol did not recommend), evacuation by blood-letting and with emetics (disapproved of by Sutton), stimulation with alcohol (recommended by Chomel), sedation with opium (put forward by Cullen and others), refrigeration by immersion in cold water or by application of cold cloths to the head (a treatment inflicted upon all maniacs). Unfortunately Léveillé could not follow up his patients over a long period of time and, although he probably managed to break their habit, he gave no figures as to the likelihood of relapse. The summary of his treatments shows a methodological approach, which was rare at the time in the therapy of mental disorders.

Doctors showed no professional interest in alcohol abuse and the subject had no place in the realm of pathological study. Indeed, alcohol was an important therapeutic agent in the vast pharmacopoeia at their disposal. Despite the fact that its cost was equal to that of the combined salaries of the staff, wine was provided in hospital, since it formed part of the patients' everyday diet;[32] furthermore, many doctors, in town and country alike, were known to be heavy drinkers.[33]

Doctors were ignorant and therefore so was the general public. One popular book of home medicine stated: 'Intemperance always damages the human constitution. It impairs digestion, slackens the nerves, upsets the patterns of secretion, blackens the mood and is the cause of countless maladies.'[34] It would be anachronistic to assume that in this passage intemperance was synonymous with heavy drinking. Were this the case, then much of what is being said would be correct; the fact that intemperance has a rather different meaning in this context becomes clear in the following quote: 'Intemperance knows no bounds and drunkards, gluttons, and debauchees rarely come to a standstill before dwindling fortunes or failing health forces them to do so.' Dictionaries of the time define intemperance as a word applicable to all forms of sensual excess. Thus, although excessive consumption of alcohol entailed risks, these were the same risks encountered by those indulging in gluttony or sexual excesses, and as such they were entirely non-specific.

In certain areas there circulated at this time a quaint rumour on the subject of spontaneous combustion, which must have provoked many a conversation and inspired greater moderation in drinking habits in those hearing it. It was said that some cases had occurred where a drunkard of many years' standing had caught fire on approaching the slightest of flames and had gone up in smoke, leaving the merest trace of greasy soot on the surrounding objects, which remained otherwise undamaged. The victims of these stories were almost always fat women.

Scientists had reasons to doubt such tales. Experience of cremation showed that a considerable amount of heat was needed to burn a human body. Furthermore, if the tale was true, how was it that the generation of such heat had not set fire to furniture or whole houses at a time? In 1847, a police investigation led by Bischoff and the chemist von Liebig in Darmstadt provided an answer to this thermodynamic riddle. The Countess of Görlitz had disappeared when sitting by her fire and a careful analysis demonstrated the sheer impossibility of spontaneous combustion having carried her off; the manservant who had strangled her confessed to having tried to dispose of the body by burning it on the fire. The myth propagated by journalists and the credulous had been exploded and was pronounced dead by Tardieu, a forensic pathologist: 'The spontaneous combustion hypothesis is pure invention.' It nevertheless survived in folklore and was exploited by Zola some forty years later in his novel *Le Docteur Pascal*, published in 1893.[35] An old drunkard Macquart has fallen asleep, and in his lap his discarded pipe still burns; suddenly he is gone and all that remains is a pile of dust, which is carried into oblivion by a breeze through the open window.

Villermé was the first to draw the attention of the money-conscious wealthy classes of the July monarchy to the issue of alcohol. He was a well-known doctor with an interest in demography, and had published one study in 1828 on relative mortality in the richer and poorer classes of society, and a second in 1832, during the cholera epidemic, when he had compared the number of victims in the crowded St Antoine district with those in the Faubourg St Germain. A member of the recently re-formed Academy of Moral and Political Science (Académie des sciences morales et politiques), he was commissioned to conduct a survey of the physical and moral condition of the working classes.

This was a time of great industrial upsurge in France and a huge labour force had been drawn to the towns to work in chemical plants, cotton mills, foundries, mines and in the construction industry. The workers were paid subsistence wages, were badly housed and poorly fed, and the job market was plagued by unfair dismissals and absenteeism. Gradually governments became aware that grossly overcrowded city areas existed, that they were difficult to police and that they harboured a disturbing degree of poverty. Suddenly there was a 'social problem', and Louis Napoleon Bonaparte's reputation for generosity originated in his avowed intention to combat it with a plan to 'abolish pauperism'.

Villermé travelled the length and breadth of France, studying the working conditions and life-style of the workers. On drinking matters, he observed that wine was drunk exclusively in the south, but only in moderation. The rest of the French workforce, it appeared, drank water at meal times, and if they did not drink beer and eau-de-vie at their workplace, then it would seem that on every other occasion they did. Villermé spent one Sunday in the silk-weaving area (*canuts*) of the Saint-Croix district in Lyon, observing what was drunk and the manner in which it was drunk. A sociologist before the word existed, he presented his *Picture of the Moral and Physical Condition of the Workers Employed in the Wool, Cotton and Silk Industries* to the Academy in 1840.[36] His audience was impressed with what it heard and the newspapers gave him enormous publicity.

If Villermé is to be believed, heavy drinking was common almost everywhere amongst the working classes. The stance he adopts is a purely social and moral one: 'The drinker is incapable of saving money, fails to bring up his children as he should and ruins his family's happiness ... he becomes lazy, argumentative, unruly and gambles. Drinking degrades and coarsens; it is harmful to the health; it often shortens life; it knows no manners, provokes social unrest and leads to crime... It is the curse of the working class and if we can prevent it or reduce its incidence, then the workers will not only be better off, they will be better people.' Amongst the remedies he proposes, Villermé suggests prevention of idleness, educating the public in the evils of alcohol, and the issue of 'reprimands by priest, mayor and other public figures'.

It was in France during this period, a time of social flux when new classes that were still uncertain of their precise status were merging, that the notion of public health was born. There is no way of knowing what kind of influence Villermé had on the governors, intellectuals, politicians and doctors who were becoming increasingly interested in 'public hygiene'. It is curious, however, that, despite being a doctor, his arguments are based on considerations of social morality and are never couched in terms of disease and cure. Not once in the *Annales d'hygiène publique* does he consider the effects of alcohol on the human body.[37] For him, drink is a curse on society and a sin in the individual. The idea of the drinker as a sinner who should be treated as such is one that was to influence medicine for the next hundred years. However, where Villermé proposed that drink led to poverty, others were suggesting that poverty led to drink; certainly both arguments have an element of truth.

In France, there were only a few hundred highly educated people who showed any interest in the new notions of public health and 'social medicine'. For the most part, doctors and the general public knew nothing about these matters. Drinking problems in any case were scarcely a major issue for the public health movement, concerned as it was with installing running water, improving living conditions, fighting poverty, educating the masses and increasing food supplies. Attitudes to drinking in France differed from those prevalent in England or the United States; it was not a preoccupation and there were no public campaigns nor temperance organizations. Those who worked in asylums remarked on the numbers of heavy drinkers amongst their patients, but they never went so far as to suggest that they should be housed in special hospitals, nor did they propose any specific treatment for them. All this was destined to change in years to come.

PART II

ALCOHOLISM: VICE OR MALADY?

DURING the mid-nineteenth century knowledge about the effects of alcohol on the human body was fragmentary and varied from country to country. A Swedish doctor, Magnus Huss, drew together these diverse findings and systematized their study. He called the condition chronic alcoholism. It was established that this new disease, in forms that took the same guise, affected all countries and all classes of society; it interested not only doctors, but also governments, economists and moralists. For a century, alcoholism was to be considered a discrete medical entity and the concept was to prove satisfactory until around 1950, when certain ambiguities became apparent in the term.

The history of alcoholization and the means proposed to remedy, reduce or prevent it is inevitably complex. In their fight against alcoholism, doctors were to call upon the resources of new experimental medicine, which was based on reason and the tenets of rationalism; nevertheless they also worked under the influence of erroneous convictions, which they shared with the rest of society. Politicians vacillated between imposing new legislation and the need to respect the citizen; they were both fearful of infringing personal liberties and wary of the outcome of new laws. For their part, men of religion condemned sin and vice, but their preaching stirred up congregations to violence.

Interpretation of such contradictory attitudes in different countries is necessarily complicated. In order to clarify the available socio-historical data a thematic and chronological approach is required, even though this has the disadvantage of creating artificial divisions in what is a complex human phenomenon.

4
Magnus Huss and Alcoholism, 1807–1890

MAGNUS Huss, the doctor who first coined the expression alcoholism, was born in 1807 in Sweden, a Protestant country which produced no wine of its own. Sweden's first still was operational in 1469. It belonged to a certain Berend, who needed alcohol to manufacture gun-powder. By 1498, *bränwin* was on sale in Stockholm. It is probable that once the drink became popular, the prohibitive cost of wine forced distillers to look for other sources of alcohol, and from the seventeenth century Swedish farms produced their own, using grains, maple syrup and, later, potatoes. Initially, tax on alcohol was only levied in the towns, but the legislation was extended to include the provinces in 1731. In 1756, there were 180,000 stills in the country; measures were taken to prohibit their use, but the reform was quickly withdrawn in the face of threatened peasant revolt. The parliamentary representatives of the Swedish states were divided between two parties: the 'hats' and the 'bonnets'. Although they took a different stand on the subject of distilling, their principal concern was not with the problem of alcoholism, but rather with the fact that the taxes levied on alcohol served only to increase the power of King Gustave III, whose enlightened rule already verged on absolutism. In 1775, Gustave was short of money; he again attempted to prohibit home distilling and set up state distilleries in its place. The *bränwin* these produced was not popular; thus private stills were once again legalized and the king's factories eventually closed.

Huss was later to acknowledge the work of those who had expressed concern for the danger that alcohol posed to the Swedish nation in the early days of distillation. Among these earlier observers were Linnaeus, who wrote several books on the subject of spirits, Westerdahl, Hagström, and Bergius; the last-mentioned submitted a medical thesis on the subject at the University of Uppsala in 1764.[1] Aquavit and schnapps had become a part of daily life and were drunk by all; in the countryside, they formed a portion of the labourers' wages with different amounts being allocated to men, women and children. The first half of the nineteenth century was a period of heavy alcoholization in Sweden. In

1830, the country's 3 million inhabitants drank 22 million gallons of alcohol (today 8 million Swedes drink 11 million gallons of alcohol and 20 million gallons of wine every year).[2] Possibly as a result of events witnessed in England, some people began to worry about alcoholism; it was seen as the root of declining moral standards, poverty and crime. Swedish industrialization had given rise to poorly housed workers and in the countryside there was still an impoverished peasantry. Under such conditions, a temperance movement was born that had great success with the masses.

In 1818, Pastor Wieselgren founded the first temperance society at Wäxjo. His example was soon copied, and by 1848 there were 420 such associations, numbering more than 100,000 members. Their message was essentially pietist, counselling moderate use of alcohol, and their adherents came from all classes. They also enjoyed the support of the royal court; King Charles XIV drank wine in moderation and disliked schnapps, as did his son, Oscar I, who refused to countenance the spirit at table.

Magnus Huss was born in 1807 in central Sweden.[3] His father was a pastor in the Lutheran church, owned a large farm and had industrial interests in the manufacture of iron. Magnus and his brothers grew up in a cultivated, bourgeois atmosphere, having links with both rural and business life. The austere education he received as a child was to mark him throughout his life, and the ideas of duty and vocation were to inspire all his later actions. Initially he embarked on a military career, but his interests turned to literature and he wrote a dissertation on Greek mythology. He was then attracted to botany and wrote a Latin thesis on a Linnaean theme. Finally, he chose medicine and attended the University of Uppsala, but later, drawn by the dynamism of the recently formed Karolinska Institute, he transferred to Stockholm. The medical thesis he submitted there in 1835 was one of the first to break with medieval tradition; it was written in Swedish rather than Latin. In this he followed his father, who had translated a Latin prayer-book into Swedish for the benefit of his illiterate peasants and workers. The quality of Huss's work won him the approval of his superiors and he was appointed to a position in a hospital founded by a religious brotherhood, the order of the Seraphim. After a few years he was put in charge of the hospital. His reputation grew and he became physician to Charles XIV and, later, to Oscar I.

In a period of convalescence after a bout of typhus, Huss travelled in Germany and France, staying in Berlin, Vienna, Halle and Paris.

Inspired by this experience, he subsequently made several more trips to Europe, during which he paid visits to various medical schools, where he became familiar with new medical techniques being developed at the time and where he acquired a working knowledge of German and French. On his return, the experience he had gained was transmitted to the Swedish medical establishment in a number of works, including his book, *Typhus and Typhoid*. In 1849, he collected and expanded several articles he had written on drinking. These were published as his book on alcoholismus chronicus. In the period that followed he was extremely productive. Now renowned in both Europe and America (where he was referred to as an 'eminent public benefactor'), he was able to execute numerous projects in Sweden. As Professor of Medicine at the Karolinska Institute, he reformed teaching methods and was himself responsible for many students. He was an able fund-raiser and oversaw the building of a new general hospital in Stockholm and the establishment of a hospital for the children of the poor, named after the Crown Princess Lovisa; he reorganized the country's psychiatric hospitals, stimulated reform in the dental profession, championed the fight against alcoholism, published several works and gave numerous lectures. In his struggle for educational and humanitarian reform, he made use of the administrative posts he held as municipal counsellor for Stockholm, as a member of parliament and, later, as the country's Director General of Asylums and Hospitals. He was a member of numerous Swedish and foreign medical associations, and various charitable and anti-alcoholic organizations. He was also a high-ranking freemason. Late in life, he married a rich young widow from a noble family, was made a noble in his own right, became very rich and retired to a large estate close to Stockholm, where he died the object of universal veneration at the age of 83. The king himself attended the funeral service.

Huss is best known outside Sweden for his studies on alcoholism. It is said that two incidents from his life account for this interest: as a young soldier, he had been appalled to receive a portion of his salary in *bränvin* and, as a student in Uppsala, he was once so ill after a night of carousing that he swore never to drink to excess again. A more plausible reason for his concern with alcoholism may have been that the subject was highly topical amongst his peers. Furthermore, as a good doctor, he had observed the damage done by drink among the charity cases he treated at the Seraphim hospital.

The fact that in 1849 Huss wrote his major work in Swedish cannot be overemphasized. Although Latin was being used less frequently in

Swedish scientific circles, he could have written in German. In the nineteenth century, Sweden had close economic and commercial ties with Germany, the prime northern European power of the day. During his travels Huss had spent more time there than in France and, had he chosen to write in German, he would immediately have had an international audience. Instead, he chose to write for Swedish speakers: the Norwegians, who lived under the Swedish Crown; the Finns, for whom Swedish was the language of the educated; and the Swedes themselves. His vocation since childhood had been to serve his own people. Translated into English the title of the 1849 work reads: *Alcoholismus Chronicus, or Chronic Alcoholic Illness. A Contribution to the Study of Dyscrasias Based on my Personal Experience and the Experience of Others.*[4] The work attracted the attention of a doctor from Bremen, Van dem Busch, who, in collaboration with Huss, produced a revised German edition containing further clinical observations. In 1852, the book appeared simultaneously in Leipzig and Stockholm. It was to secure Huss's reputation throughout the West.[5]

The title merits closer analysis. The word 'dyscrasia', defined by Littré in his medical dictionary as a 'poor constitution', is no longer used. Practically speaking, this vague term was used to describe symptoms and organic lesions ascribable to a given cause and potentially distributed throughout the body. Its usage reflects Huss's holistic approach to his work.

'Alcoholism' was a new expression. The choice of the prefix 'alcohol' was the direct result of his own medical observations. Huss had concerned himself with the effects of distilled drinks and he discovered that, independent of the type of spirit being drunk, both the poor and needy he treated at the Seraphim hospital and his richer patients exhibited the same symptoms. It is hard to criticize Huss for this emphasis on distilled drinks because, at the time, it was commonly believed that fermented drinks were harmless. His new word, 'alcoholism', was succinct and supplanted the German term, 'methylism', which was not only obscure, but chemically incorrect. It was common scientific usage to use the suffix '-ism' in the description of diseases, especially poisoning: 'ergotism', for the effects of the ergot parasite in rye, and 'saturnism', for lead poisoning. Throughout the work, Huss took the view that alcoholism was one form of poisoning to be ranged alongside others. He followed Linnaeus in his desire to systematize and classify; in inventing a new disease, he was obliged to place it within a known family. '-Ism' was a suffix also used for the cumbersome systems of medical thought that were a hangover from the Enlightenment. By Huss's time, 'broussaisism' had been abandoned in France, but 'brownism' was still current in Germany and Huss was also familiar, if somewhat sceptical, of the doctrines of 'animal magnetism' and 'hypnotism'.[6] In alcoholism, he proposed a unifying theory, a new way of viewing problems that formerly had defied classification.

In the German edition, the 'dyscrasia' of the original title is replaced by 'intoxication', and the author's intentions are made clear from the start: 'By intoxication I understand certain cumulative pathological psychic, motor and sensory symptoms which develop in those who have consumed excessive quantities of alcohol over many years. These symptoms may or may not be related to other changes in the central or peripheral nervous system which may be pathognomonic of other disease.' This definition excludes the symptoms of alcoholic inebriation, but allows for the discussion of phenomena such as delirium tremens which, though itself an acute crisis, only occurs in chronic drinkers.

It was not the first time that many of the physical and mental symptoms discussed by Huss had been described, and he paid tribute to the clinicians who had identified various gastric problems and mental disorders before him. The importance of his work lay in the fact that he was the first to classify systematically damage that was attributable to alcohol. The book also demonstrates the knowledge he had gained in Europe and shows how he was influenced by his stay in France with Andral in the attention he pays to anatomo-pathology, which would have it that medical observations must correspond to clinical findings and anatomical changes. Huss constantly reiterates the point, however, that his findings at autopsy were non-specific and that the changes he observed in brain, intestinal tract, heart, liver and blood might be attributable to causes other than alcohol. In Paris, Louis's numerical method had been in vogue and because Huss became conversant with it, he was able to use his long hospital experience to good effect in support of his findings. In a later work on pneumonia, he noted that 3,000 people had been treated under his care in fifteen years.

Huss himself admitted that he felt ill at ease in the realm of psychiatry. Although he had had no experience of mental patients during his time at the Seraphim hospital, he did learn a great deal during his stays in France between 1849 and 1852. On this basis he argued that, in the same way as physical damage, mental problems observed in alcoholics were non-specific and could equally be found in non-alcoholic patients. Only in the case of patients for whom the sole pathological antecedent had been excessive long-term drinking did he hold alcohol to be uniquely responsible for insanity. Those of his subjects who could not restrain themselves from drinking Huss classed as 'dipsomaniacs', but his interest lay in any physical symptoms they might exhibit and not in the reasons that lay behind their mania for drink.

Huss's emphasis on organic lesions and the necessity for a long period of intoxication led him to believe that chronic alcoholism was not hereditary and could be explained by other factors, such as poor housing conditions, bad parental example, drinking without eating and harsh climate. Unlike other doctors, who would continue to debate the subject for decades, Huss himself formulated no firm hypotheses, because of the lack of relevant statistics.

Although it would serve no purpose to review in detail the faults in Huss's work, there are some drawbacks: his use of statistics would not satisfy today's more rigorous mathematical requirements; he was wrong in certain cases to argue the non-specificity of damage for which we now know alcohol to be entirely responsible; and there are certain omissions, which make his list incomplete. In comparison with his achievement, these are minor issues. His book created a new diagnostic entity and gathered together all the medical findings on intemperance. From this time forth, doctors had to face up to the problems of drinking: alcohol-ism was now an integral part of medical knowledge, to be consolidated upon and expanded. But is alcoholism uniquely a medical problem? In Huss's opinion, it was ultimately the individual who was responsible for his own behaviour and therefore the question was also a matter of personal morality. Thus Huss's teaching was both moral and technical, and it was this dual emphasis that made it so influential, not only in Sweden, but in Western medicine as a whole.

Huss remained active until the end of his life and his reputation assured him of a wide audience. In Sweden he had educational and administra-tive resources at his disposal, which facilitated communication of his message. In 1855, the government passed a law banning domestic distillation and reformed the alcohol trade, reducing the number of sales outlets. Propaganda activity against alcohol increased, tracts and posters were produced, and Huss lent his support to the temperance leagues and to anti-alcohol meetings. For those with drink problems, he established special clinics that were distinct from the asylums, and the forms of treatment on offer included hypnotism. In 1882 he published a pam-phlet, *The Consequences of Drinking on the Individual, the Family, the City and the State,* in which he deplored the decline in moral standards that resulted from excessive consumption of schnapps. He was a moralist rather than a moralizer and, although he forgot neither the strict education he had received from his father, nor his days at the pietist University of Halle, he never condemned alcoholic patients in his care.

In the last decades of the nineteenth century, it was widely believed that alcoholism represented a state of degeneration. Huss was himself influenced by this idea and argued that drinking threatened Swedish manhood, a charge he illustrated with statistics allegedly demonstrating that Swedes were shrinking. In his old age, it seems, he had lost the statistical rigour of his youth, but, despite this lapse late in his life, Huss's work had been responsible for a profound change in attitudes towards alcoholics. In his own lifetime, he had the satisfaction of seeing them come to be treated as though they were ill rather than simply criminals. There was also a drop in levels of aquavit consumption. The law of 1855 was not readily accepted in the countryside, but, as communication networks were extended to rural areas, peasants were able to market their grain and their standard of living increased. Rather than producing their own spirits, this made it possible for them to buy the state *bränwin*, which had improved in quality, and as a result they drank less. Huss also played a role in the development of new systems of tenant farming for the production and sale of *bränwin* in certain towns. These pioneering reforms are at the origin of regulatory measures that are still in force in some countries. Outside Sweden, the German translation of Huss's book meant that the concept of alcoholism became widely accepted. He became well known in Germany and the United States, and his work provided doctors and politicians with a better understanding of the phenomenon.

In France, his work became known through a review of the book published in a medical journal by Renaudin, who was director at the Maréville asylum, near Nancy, which Huss himself had visited.[7] The 28-page review was recognized as an important medical event. In 1853, R. Huss was nominated for and awarded the Monthyon prize. Among his proposers was Andral. Several authors have mentioned a curious anecdote arising from the Academy's discussion of the work. One speaker reportedly announced that the book was to be commended, but that there were no alcoholics in France. There is no record of such a remark; the nearest to it is the statement of one of the book's nominees, possibly Andral: 'Magnus Huss has collected a great deal of material relating to chronic alcoholism, a condition rarely seen in France.'[8] Huss had therefore drawn the attention of his colleagues abroad to phenomena of which they had hitherto been ignorant.

Renaudin concluded his otherwise favourable review on a cautionary note: 'We must leave it to the reader to assess the undoubted merits of the book. Even if the author's opinions are not shared, his intelligent method and careful observations are an example to us all.' The lesson was taken to heart; in the decades that followed, a chapter concerning the clinical aspects of alcoholism was included in all French medical textbooks, and French doctors added several new items to the pathologies described by Huss.

Renaudin added: 'In order to fully understand his objective and the limits he set himself, it is necessary to remember that Dr Magnus Huss is a Swede and writes for Sweden with aquavit in mind. It is this writer's opinion that if he had also considered fermented drinks, his understanding of this interesting subject would have been even greater.' The last sentence points to a blind spot in Huss's work, which he came to acknowledge in subsequent years, and in Sweden regulations governing aquavit were extended to cover other drinks such as wine and beer. In considering fermented and distilled drinks together, Renaudin was ahead of his time in France. Several decades were to pass before French doctors agreed that all forms of alcohol had the same harmful effect on the human body: Renaudin's experience as a doctor in the beer-drinking region of Lorraine led him to recognize this.

5
Drinking Habits

THE preceding chapters have demonstrated how difficult it was, prior to Huss's definition of alcoholism, to assess the numbers of excessive drinkers in any given country. They also serve to highlight the inability within the medical profession to describe adequately the damage caused by alcohol within a population. For the period 1850–1950, we might expect the situation to have improved. Doctors had a clearer understanding of the problem, and administrators and those in power were in the habit of recording statistics. Unfortunately, however, examination of the statistical evidence they gathered is complicated by ambiguities in the precise definition of alcoholism and their failure to establish the exact nature of the relationship between alcohol intake and organic lesions.

In assessing the levels of alcoholism within a population, or attempting to compare the statistics available for different countries, methodological problems arise that, even with the aid of computers, remain unsolved. It is no easy task to establish the toxic level of alcohol for any given individual, and the figure varies from person to person. As a result, gross indicators such as population statistics are hard to interpret and even though higher levels of alcoholism might be expected in countries with high alcohol consumption, a necessary distinction must be made between the two concepts. There is no precise relationship between a country's alcohol production and the consumption of its inhabitants: the product is both exported and used in the chemical industry. Furthermore, in many countries there is a certain amount of domestic distillation, legal or otherwise, about which little is known. All statistical work therefore deals in approximations, which make it difficult to establish the exact links between production, consumption and the role played by alcohol within society.

The passage from producer to consumer is a complicated one. As a result, the information relating to the alcohol trade is located in a variety of archives. Inevitably this leads to problems for the historian: different agencies record different aspects of the trade; only occasionally do we have a long statistical series at our disposal. In France, for example, we find that the figures furnished by the Ministry of Agriculture differ from those issued by the Ministry of Finance. Similar problems are encountered elsewhere.[1] None the less, in countries where attention is given to the systematic collection of statistics, collective consumption is easier to establish than the amounts drunk by individuals who, in routine clinical situations, have a tendency to understate their consumption.

OTHER PEOPLE'S ALCOHOLISM

When we look at the drinking habits of other nationalities prejudice often colours our judgement; only too often are foreigners considered irredeemable drunkards. The moment we enter into particularities, however, general statements that may be put forward are unmasked as simple approximations, worth little more than the prejudice out of which they grew. The spread of distillation in Europe after the seventeenth century and its disruptive influence on traditional drinking habits has already been discussed, but levels of alcohol consumption are also determined by specific agricultural and cultural traditions and evolve in response to sociological and historical events. At the end of the eighteenth century, for example, the breakdown in commercial links between the British West Indies and the newly independent American colonies resulted in a decrease in American rum consumption and an increasing preference for locally produced whiskeys. Similarly, the nineteenth-century wave of German immigrants into the USA explains the development of breweries in the Mid-West, and the French immigration to California accounts for the wine industry in that state. The influence of such events is substantiated by quantitative studies.

Tradition and cost also influence drinking patterns – every population has its favourite drink and its own rhythms of consumption. Until the 1950s, Scandinavians were great Saturday-night drinkers of schnapps, restricting themselves to milk for the rest of the week. In contrast, the French drank wine every day. Periodic festive drinking differs from daily consumption, but if repeated to excess on a regular basis, the harm it will do to the human body will doubtless be the same. In the nineteenth century, however, it was widely believed that intermittent drunkenness was less dangerous than regular drinking. Today it would appear that both modes of consumption are equally detrimental to the drinker's health and family life. Even this assumption is speculative, while we remain ignorant of the mechanisms whereby the body stores and eliminates alcohol.

The rituals surrounding drinking vary both between and within countries. Social groups common in Western Europe in the period

1850–1950 – brotherhoods, associations, unions, clubs, guilds and societies – all had their own attitudes towards alcohol; their consumption varied, as did the drinks they favoured.[2] For this reason, comparison between them is meaningless; the drinking habits of a group of Prussian cavalry officers bears little relation to the behaviour at a meeting of shareholders in Victorian England. Focusing at the level of the group also masks the presence of individuals who are themselves habitual drinkers, and only on occasion is it possible to state how many excessive drinkers – those who cannot escape an irrepressible desire to drink – are present. Equally, although injuries resulting from drink depend on individual tolerance, they are also related to the alcoholic product in question and the general pattern of drinking. This makes it impossible to deduce the number of people who have suffered physical damage because of alcohol, but, as a general proposition, it is true to suggest that the greater the consumption of alcohol, the greater the number of individuals afflicted by delirium, cirrhosis or cancer in any group or population (a relationship again brought out by quantitative studies). On the whole, drinking patterns are so varied that no single model of consumption adequately accounts for the range of behaviour observed in a single society. This means that we are here concerned with micro-sociology – separate models are necessary for different social groups. Whatever the exact nature of the group, the patterns of drinking they adopt invariably comply with their own attitudes and aspirations rather than those of society at large.

A CASE STUDY: FRANCE

The period 1850–1950 has been the subject of considerable research.[3] Here we will only cover the salient points, shedding light on the development of alcoholism in France and the ways in which it has been represented. As might be expected, numerous events combined to influence patterns of drinking. The complexity of French history makes isolation of the various phenomena at work in the country a complicated procedure, and we must never lose sight of the fact that a single influence can have different effects, depending on the context. Patterns of drinking are influenced by so many different factors that any campaign of reform cannot be based solely on simple solutions.

In 1850, drinking habits and the quantities consumed varied greatly throughout France: the inhabitants of Bordeaux drank 196 litres (43 gallons) of wine per person per year, but at the other end of the scale in Caen the equivalent figure was only 12 litres (2.5 gallons). Such a comparison does not take into account other alcoholic drinks. The people of Caen no longer seem quite as abstemious when we know they each consumed 245 litres (54 gallons) of drink each year, but even this is no match for the inhabitants of Rennes (440 litres/96 gallons annually). Such figures illustrate that beer was still a more popular drink than wine, even in what are now centres of wine production such as Dijon.[4] Furthermore, when compared to contemporary patterns of consumption, these differences prove that the majority of the French still drank water, even in the big cities. Many different factors came into play to change the situation. Drinking habits became more uniform as differences between north and south, and town and country were eliminated, and the poorer classes came to adopt the behaviour of the rich.

With the industrialization of France under the Second Empire (1852–70), manufacturing industry, large-scale construction work and the building of railways increased the flow of people from rural into urban areas, and this swelled the developing working-class districts. Standards of living improved and the change was reflected in food and drink. The new urban classes began to drink wine, initially with meals and then as a pleasure for its own sake. The development of roads, canals and railways introduced wine-drinking to new areas and its consumption grew accordingly.

This rise in the fortunes of the wine-growers was not to last indefinitely. In the 1870s, a vine mould, oidium, was to strike at their livelihoods. This blow was followed by the ravages of a parasitic insect, phylloxera, and within two decades all the vines in France were affected. Only with the introduction of insecticides and tougher, more resistant vine stocks did French viticulture begin to recover and to benefit from new developments, such as Pasteur's revolutionary work on food preservation and improvements in wine production, storage and transport.[5]

This fraught period for the growers had affected drinking habits considerably. The derisory yields of affected vines resulted in wine shortages in the regions north of the Loire. The demand for wine had to be satisfied by other means and people soon discovered a replacement in spirits. In the decade 1870–80, distilled drinks grew markedly in popularity and became widespread, even in areas where beer-drinking was customary. Other factors also fuelled the uptake of spirit-drinking, notably the development of high-yielding industrial distilleries and the low cost of drink relative to other food products. In *L'Assommoir*, Zola portrays the increased popularity of spirits, doubtless an accurate view of the *cabarets* in 1876, the time at which the book was written, but anachronistic in that the work is set during the Second Empire.[6]

The plagues of oidium and phylloxera resulted in the redistribution of France's vineyards. Those with a low or mediocre yield were abandoned when they became diseased, whereas in other areas vines were planted for the first time. In Languedoc, for example, even the plains were given over to wine production and by the end of the nineteenth century the *département* of Aude was the biggest producer in France.[7] New methods and techniques meant that although the area under cultivation was reduced, yields increased. This was a double-edged blessing. Grape yields are notoriously unpredictable and a good harvest can flood the market, causing a slump in prices. An occurrence of this nature led to the peasant uprisings in the Hérault and Aude during the early years of the twentieth century, when the left-wing government of the day was obliged to send in the troops to quell the unrest. Table 5.1 illustrates the fluctuations in the area cultivated and wine production.

Table 5.1 Wine in France, 1850–1950

Year	French vineyards in thousands of hectares	Millions of hectolitres produced in France	Millions of hectolitres imported from Algeria
1850	2182	45.3	00.2
1860	2205	39.6	00.1
1870	2238	54.5	07.2
1880	2209	29.7	10.8
1890	1817	27.4	05.2
1900	1609	68.5	08.0
1910	1630	28.7	05.4
1920	1516	59.3	13.4
1930	1527	45.6	09.6
1940	1470	49.4	12.0
1950	1453	65.1	

Source: S. Ledermann, *op. cit.* vol. I, figures supplied by the Ministry of Agriculture.

The growing popularity of wine and better methods of distribution increased the temptation to alter its composition. The practice of blending and other forms of adulteration came to the attention of the authorities and a monitoring service was established to check wines on sale. In 1884, the municipal laboratory of Paris submitted a report which gives some indication of the scale of abuse. Out of a total of 3,361 samples examined, 11 per cent were declared 'good', 32 per cent 'passable', 51 per cent 'bad without being harmful' and 6 per cent 'harmful'. Given that 40,000 hectolitres (875,000 gallons) of wine were subject to the city toll annually, these figures can only give a poor idea of the quality of wine drunk by Parisians. In the case of beer and cider,

Alcoholism: Vice or Malady?

Table 5.2 Consumption per head of population of beer, cider, wines and spirits in the UK between 1900 and 1986

Year ending 31 March	Pints per head		Consumption (litres per head)			
	Beer	Cider	Beer	Cider	Wines	Spirits[b]
1899/1900[a]	259.1	. .	147.2	. .	1.9	3.1
1909/10[a]	216.6	. .	123.1	. .	1.2	1.5
1920/1[a]	229.0	. .	130.1	. .	1.3	1.2
1929/30	165.9	. .	94.3	. .	1.8	0.7
1939/40	156.3	. .	88.8	. .	2.0	0.6
1949/50	153.3	3.6	87.1	2.1	1.1	0.5
1959/60	147.7	3.2	83.9	1.8	2.0	0.7
1960/61	151.2	2.9	85.9	1.6	2.4	0.8
1961/62	156.2	3.0	88.8	1.7	2.4	0.8
1962/63	153.0	2.7	86.9	1.6	2.5	0.8
1963/64	158.3	2.7	90.0	1.6	2.9	0.9
1964/65	159.5	2.8	90.7	1.6	3.1	0.9
1965/66	160.9	2.9	91.4	1.7	3.1	0.8
1966/67	164.9	3.3	93.7	1.8	3.1	0.8
1967/68	165.2	3.6	93.9	2.1	3.7	0.9
1968/69	168.0	3.7	95.5	2.1	3.8	0.8
1969/70	173.8	4.1	98.7	2.4	3.5	0.8
1970/71	180.8	4.5	102.7	2.6	4.0	0.9
1971/72	185.8	4.5	105.6	2.6	4.5	1.0
1972/73	188.1	4.5	106.9	2.6	5.3	1.1
1973/74	200.9	4.9	114.1	2.8	6.8	1.5
1974/75	200.3	5.0	113.8	2.8	6.4	1.5
1975/76	202.1	5.8	114.8	3.3	6.0	1.5
1976/77	209.3	6.8	118.9	3.8	6.6	1.6
1977/78	209.8	6.4	119.2	3.6	6.6	1.5
1978/79	210.0	6.5	119.3	3.7	7.7	1.9
1979/80	215.7	6.7	122.6	3.8	8.5	2.0
1980/81	204.7	6.6	116.3	3.8	8.0	1.8
1981/82	190.7	7.2	108.4	4.1	8.6	1.6
1982/83	191.2	8.5	108.6	4.8	8.8	1.5
1983/84	195.1	9.5	110.8	5.4	9.1	1.7
1984/85	192.5	9.4	109.4	5.4	11.2	1.6
1985/86	190.9	9.1	108.5	5.2	10.7	1.7

[a] Includes all of Ireland.
[b] 100% alcohol.

Sources: HM Customs and Excise, Office of Population Censuses and Surveys; *The Brewers' Society Statistical Handbook, 1986*.

testing was not as extensive, but it does suggest, at least for beer, that quality was higher.[8]

When wine became freely available once more in the 1890s, former drinking habits did not return. Rather than making a choice between wines and spirits the people now drank both – in fact they drank as much of both as in the days when only one or other had been available. The end of the nineteenth century was thus marked by a considerable

Drinking Habits

Drinking Habits   57

Table 5.3 Total consumption and average per adult of pure alcohol contained in alcoholic drinks in France (wines, beer, cider and spirits)

Year	Total consumption of pure alcohol (10³ hl)	Average consumption of adults aged 20 and over (l per adult)	Average consumption per adult aged 15 or more[a] (l per adult)
1970	8499	25.0	22.3
1971	8681	25.2	22.5
1972	8763	25.2	22.5
1973	8921	25.3	22.6
1974	8766	24.6	22.0
1975	8841	24.7	22.1
1976	8874	24.5	22.0
1977	8790	24.1	21.6
1978	8530	23.2	20.8
1979	8419	22.7	20.3
1980	8603	23.0	20.6
1981	8325	22.0	19.7
1982	8287	21.7	19.5
1983	8199	21.3	19.1
1984	7827	20.1	18.1
1985	7820	19.9	18.0
1986	7779	19.7	17.8

[a] Most countries in the EEC calculate the alcohol consumption of adults aged 15 or over; we think it is useful to include this statistic.

Source: INSEE.

increase in alcohol consumption, and by the turn of the century drinking amongst the French had reached its highest level ever. Figure 5.1 shows the consumption of pure alcohol per head in France between 1830 and 1899, according to Mayet, a doctor in Lyons.[9] It is interesting to note that although he himself was aware of the dangers presented by all forms of alcohol, the figures he quotes refer only to the consumption of distilled drinks.

It is impossible to deduce the numbers of excessive drinkers solely on the basis of an understanding of a population's drinking habits. A study conducted by Camille Lian, while he served in the French army in 1915, is instructive in that it considers individual drinkers, albeit in a small sample. Lian, who was to become one of the most eminent French clinicians of the inter-war period, examined and questioned 150 members of the French territorial army stationed outside the combat zone. Of comparable age, 42 or 43 years old, the soldiers in all probability came from modest backgrounds.[10] Lian ranked the men's drinking habits on a scale that ranged from 'sober' – those drinking less than 1 litre of wine per day and abstaining from aperitifs, spirits and liqueurs – to 'very heavy drinkers' – those drinking at least 3 litres of wine and four to six

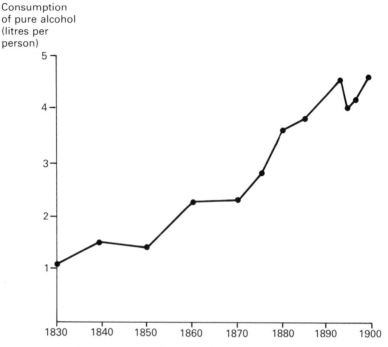

Figure 5.1   Annual consumption of pure alcohol per head of population in France, 1830–1900

aperitifs or small spirits on a daily basis. By today's standards more than half of his sample would be classified as excessive drinkers. Even if his choice of subjects is not necessarily representative of the French people as a whole, this proportion of excessive drinkers is strikingly high.

Whatever the nature of drinking amongst the troops, the First World War resulted in a generalized decline in the consumption and production of alcohol. After hostilities had ceased, drinking habits of the pre-war period reasserted themselves, but consumption did not return to the same high levels. The Second World War also witnessed a decrease in levels of alcohol consumption that were soon reversed once peace returned.

Figure 5.2 shows the total consumption of pure alcohol, including fermented drink, in France between 1831 and 1960. Adaptation of Ledermann's statistics shows that French adults drank 14.6 litres of pure alcohol per person annually in the period 1831–3. By 1931–2, the figure had more than doubled to 31.1 litres, but it fell to 28.8 litres in 1954–5.

Regional studies indicate that these levels of consumption were by no

Total consumption
of pure alcohol
(10^3 hl)

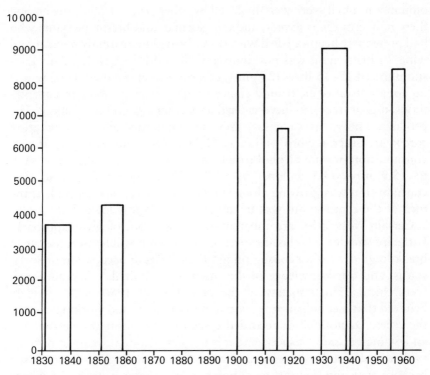

Figure 5.2   Total consumption of pure alcohol in France, 1830–1960

means uniform throughout France. In Alsace, there was no tradition of wine-drinking in rural areas and beer remained the most popular drink. Despite a constant increase in demand for wine during the nineteenth century, a similar situation was seen in the town of Valenciennes.[11] (In comparison with Germany, however, levels of beer consumption were low.[12] For the Germans, wine was reserved for special occasions and beer was the beverage associated with meals and relaxation.[13]) Western France, still considered to be an area of high alcohol intake, exemplifies the phenomena that contributed towards increasing alcohol consumption during the nineteenth century: towns were growing in size and the increasing purchasing power of their inhabitants brought alcohol within reach of the majority. As transport improved, the wines of Languedoc, Burgundy and Cher arrived by rail; those from Bordeaux and Algeria by sea; and between 1878 and 1893 maritime imports of wine, rum and other spirits quadrupled.

In the French interior, poor-quality vines that had fallen victim to oidium and phylloxera were replaced by other crops. A favourite among these new crops was apples, and the Norman and Breton peasants who had previously been satisfied with water turned increasingly to cider and wine. In Brittany, it was not unusual to find drinkers with a daily consumption of 12–15 litres (25 pints) of strong cider. Frequently there was no apparent rationale behind choice of apple variety, and consequently thousands of trees produced cider that was only good for distilling. The product, known as calvados, grew in popularity and its reputation spread to other regions of France. In the Eure, for example, annual consumption of pure alcohol rose from 3.7 litres (0.81 gallons) in 1850 to 15.9 litres (3.5 gallons) in 1890.[14] Throughout France alcohol consumption was growing along similar lines; it reached its peak at the turn of the century, but was to stabilize at a slightly lower level.

Certain difficulties are inherent in a more sociological approach. Different modes of classification make it impossible to produce a breakdown of alcohol consumption on the basis of occupation or social status, and our knowledge of the situation is limited.[15] In traditional, hierarchical French society of the period 1850–1950, it was widely believed that alcoholism was restricted to the poor and working class of the cities. Doctors alone recorded cases of alcoholism among the men and women of *salon* society, and it is to them also that we must turn for evidence of drunkenness in rural areas. Their findings were dismissed because they ran counter to popular opinion, which held that it was healthier to work the land. This dogma was later to have repercussions on trade union attitudes towards the fight against alcoholism. Doctors also noticed that many of the alcoholics they treated had either served in the army or were members of guilds: in both military and professional life initiation ceremonies were accompanied by heavy drinking. A third and related finding made by doctors in France and elsewhere was the increased incidence of alcoholism in waiters, café owners, hotel keepers, wine merchants and other groups involved in the retail of alcohol. In these cases, alcohol was always available and the desire to drink was greater than the will to abstain.

Problems are even greater when drinking habits are compared internationally within the Western world: we encounter variation in tax regulations, an absence of customs agreements, and different systems of weights and measures. The agricultural and financial concerns of

Table 5.4 Annual consumption of pure alcohol in
different countries

Country	Year	Alcohol consumed (litres per person)
France	1950–4	30.0
Italy	1951	14.2
Switzerland	1950–4	12.0
Belgium	1951	8.2
USA		8.8
Great Britain		8.5
BRD		5.1
Sweden		5.1
Denmark		4.9
Finland	1953	4.8
Norway	1954	3.0
Netherlands	1946–8	1.8

individual nations were not the same and definitions, even of what constituted alcoholic drink, did not coincide. Ledermann, a cautious statistician, acknowledges such difficulties and only makes international comparisons for the period after 1950 (table 5.4).

Lentz published statistics for the alcohol trade in Belgium from the first year of independence in 1831 until the outbreak of war in 1913.[16] His figures represent the volume of pure alcohol consumed and show an increase of roughly 350 per cent over the period: from 121,061 hectolitres (2.66 million gallons) to 422,401 hectolitres (9.3 million gallons). This growth is not regular and the author argues that any small decreases are the short-term result of administrative measures such as increased taxes or alterations in regulations governing alcohol sales. He adds that because the figures do not take account of the unknown quantity of home distillation, they cannot be viewed as exhaustive.

Available statistics for Britain are inconsistent in that information from Wales and Scotland is sometimes omitted. Purely on the basis of convictions for drunk and disorderly behaviour, it would seem that the Scots drink more than the Welsh and English. Unfortunately such a comparison is of doubtful validity, since the exact relation between public disorder and alcohol remains to be established.[17]

In the USA, the administrative, social and political organization of the country altered radically during the period 1850–1950. This has made comparisons between successive years and between different states difficult. Furthermore, administration in some states was rudimentary and tax returns are an unreliable guide to consumption. On the basis of the fragmentary information available, however, it would seem that levels of alcohol consumption in the USA were at their peak at the end of the nineteenth century.

The development of industrial distillation in the nineteenth century did not, as might be expected, bring about a decline in domestic distillation in rural areas. Family stills had been in existence for too long for the practice simply to be abandoned, and the centuries had lent it a variety and richness reflected in the array of spirits to be found. Liberal in their choice of raw materials, the distillers by no means restricted themselves to wine; the distillation of cider was certainly taking place in areas of western France as early as 1589 and such experimentation was not unique to this region. Throughout the French countryside a vast range of distilled drinks were produced.

From the time of Louis XIV (1638–1715) until the Revolution, commerce in spirits was taxed at the same rate as the wine trade. Everybody was entitled to operate a still, if they so wished, and it was not until the Revolution that attempts were made to restrict this right, attempts which ended once Napoleon came to power.

The ratio of domestic to industrial production, however, has been in constant decline. For the period 1830–9, domestic distillation accounted for 4,340,000 gallons of spirits and industrial processes for 9,868,700 gallons. By 1950, domestic production stood at 9,474,800 gallons, compared with an industrial production of 122,647,700 gallons. There was also a change in the products used in distillation. Between 1840 and 1850, 91 per cent of the alcohol produced was made from wine, cider or fruit, but this figure fell dramatically to 27 per cent by 1950–4, when molasses and sugar beet became increasingly popular. (Potatoes or grain have only been used to a limited extent for distilling purposes.[18])

The freedom of the domestic distillers lasted for a long time. The agents of the treasury, and later those of the state-controlled *Régie des alcools*, a body established to deal with the alcohol trade, faced a difficult task. They were unable to estimate how much alcohol was produced per alembic and although they knew about the authorized stills, there were others whose existence was kept secret by their owners. Even with the assistance of mounted police, the agents still had considerable problems unearthing frauds. Later, Thiers (1797–1877), in an attempt to pay off the war indemnity demanded by the Prussians, decreed that home distillers who were suspected of defrauding the state were to be taxed at higher rates than the more easily monitored industrial concerns. Nevertheless, the relative freedom enjoyed by rural areas helped to fuel the rivalry between industrial and domestic production. Based in rural areas, home distillers catered directly for village merchants and the agricultural population. Their clandestine trade in spirits escaped surveillance and avoided both state taxes and tolls imposed on goods entering towns; this greatly annoyed drink wholesalers and retailers, who could not avoid making such payments on their merchandise. Urban dwellers with country homes would also purchase the spirits they required from the home distillers and urban-based traders were forever complaining about unfair competition. Such concerns were purely financial, but in some quarters people showed disquiet at the damage done by alcoholism. For half a century tax authorities, municipal councils, doctors and politicians campaigned against home distillation; between 1879 and 1900, no less than 14 bills and 18 *projets d'initiatives* on the subject were rejected by Parliament.[19]

The home distillers were not without their own arguments. They pointed out that their detractors could come to no agreement regarding the scale of alleged fraud. Farmers in Normandy justly claimed that the increasing quantities of home-produced liquor were the result of better apple varieties, more precise methods of distillation and the discipline imposed by agricultural societies and trade unions. Despite a general upward trend in yields from orchards and vineyards, it was nevertheless argued that their dependence on the weather meant that they experienced considerable fluctuations in output. (Available figures support this: for example, 13,670 gallons of spirits were produced in the Lower Seine in 1886, but in 1890 this figure had fallen to 3,390 gallons.) The lobby for the home distillers insisted further that they were no more to blame for alcoholism than their industrial counterparts, and that any controls or bans on their activities would be an infringement of constitutional rights.

The 1875 law regulating the rights of 480,000 home distillers survived for some considerable time because of these protracted arguments. In the *Chambre des Députés*, industrial interests opposed the farmers, and *députés* who had trained as doctors were torn between loyalty to voters and concern with alcoholism. The question divided parties and home distillation enjoyed support on both left and right of the political spectrum. After one debate in the *Chambre*, Péguy exclaimed: 'There are only two true parties, two sincere and deeply-rooted parties, two real parties: one in favour of home distilling and one against.'[20] Nevertheless, a law passed in 1900 included a new and restricted definition of the term 'home distiller', created new penalties for any infringements and reduced the tax on 'hygienic' beverages (fermented drinks).

Prior to the First World War the debate lost its intensity and in 1916 a law banned the creation of new stills, restricted rights to operate those already in existence and made such rights non-transferable. With the return of peace these restrictions were relaxed, but changes were again made in 1935 and these remained in force until 1960, when the measures of 1916 were reintroduced. At present there are 2.5 million home distillers in France. The trade is well organized and has its own co-operatives and professional press. In Parliament attempts are still made periodically to reanimate debate.[21]

The history of home distillation in France illustrates the ambivalence exhibited by all governments when confronted with activities detrimental to public health, but beneficial to the exchequer. The products of domestic distillation are no more responsible for alcoholism than other forms of ethanol. In France, attempts to control home distillation by restricting the number of licences have led to clandestine production rather than abstinence. All efforts to combat potential illegalities by prohibition are doomed to failure. In Russia, despite severe repressive measures, Soviet peasants continue to distil their own alcohol, and stills have even been discovered in the rooms of Moscow students. They can be found on the high plateaux of the Andes; in Sweden, they are reappearing in rural areas, mirroring the situation in the eighteenth century. Governments fight a losing battle, and yet, if they are to be effective in combatting excessive consumption, they must be relentless in their struggle against clandestine alcohol production.

FRENCH TAVERNS AND BARS

Drinking establishments vary in appearance and social role – their character reflects both the part they play in communal life and the status of their clientele.[22] As history transforms society, so the changes are seen in institutions catering for the demand for alcohol; the dingy grog-shops, gentlemen's clubs and brothels of the nineteenth century have now been replaced by a panoply of new drinking places. Governments continue to monitor taverns and bars, both in the interests of public order and state finance, but their influence on levels of alcoholism and alcohol consumption is difficult to assess. Instinct tells us that if a product such as alcohol is freely available, then it will be consumed in greater quantities. This would seem to implicate bars, taverns and cafés in the growth of alcoholism in countries such as France. The issue, however, must be examined more closely.

Until the mid-nineteenth century, when there were 331,000 *cabarets* in France, trade was largely unrestricted: to open a *cabaret*, one simply had to inform the police.[23] In 1851, after his *coup d'état*, Louis Bonaparte, fearful of conspiracy, issued a decree suspending rights to sell drink for consumption on the premises without special government authorization. The number of *cabarets* duly fell to 291,000 by 1855. Gradually the regime became more liberal and authorizations were granted more freely, causing the number of *cabarets* to rise to 351,000 in the next decade. With the exception of a fall in numbers following the loss of Alsace-Lorraine, this figure rose steadily until 1914.

At the end of the nineteenth century, consumption was increasing and the anti-alcohol movement had grown more vocal. The *cabaret* was to feel the effects of both phenomena. In rural areas, all agreements concerning the sale of livestock, grains or forage, and the hiring of labour took place in the café. The local fairs that developed during this epoch meant busy days for café owners. In towns, the establishments became increasingly part of the world of work: every workshop and factory had an adjoining café, where workers drank before and after work; where they were recruited; and where they were paid (sometimes even in the form of tokens to be used at the bar – a great source of profit to the tenant[24]). Under these conditions the trade union movement was born and bars became the venue for political discussion. Electoral meetings were held in back-rooms and the animation of debate was often more closely related to drink sales than genuine political sentiment.

As the social role of the bars grew, they became increasingly the target of active anti-alcohol campaigns inspired by the medical establishment. One doctor coined the term '*cabaretism*' to designate the various illnesses and vices contracted from frequentation of these establishments. Although the term itself was only used in medical circles, the attacks on drinking places went much further. The *cabaret* was held responsible for all the harm done by excessive alcohol consumption: immorality, theft and crime. Such arguments were advanced at all social levels. *Le Grand Almanach des Familles*, a work aimed at the masses, contained the following extract in 1885: '*Départements* with a small number of *cabarets* have very few drunkards and, in consequence, fewer convicts and destitute people. The relationship is a mathematical one.' This assertion is supported by statistics from various *départements*. In the Seine and the Rhône – two of the most densely populated *départements* – the large number of *cabarets* and the high incidence of crime and pauperism contrast with the 'honest, hard-working' inhabitants of the Creuse, a region with far fewer *cabarets*.[25]

Alcohol was not restricted to the *cabarets*; it was also to be found in the dining-rooms of big hotels and high-society lounges. Doctors on occasion abused medicinal alcohol. A contribution to *La Revue des Deux Mondes* (Two Worlds Review) of 1886 illustrates the attitude of the educated classes toward the *cabarets*.[26] The author, Rochard, maintains that 'alcohol filters through society like rain through soil' (a fact which the upper classes can witness for themselves by simply observing workers and peasants) and draws attention to the political power of alcohol: 'When a nation is called upon to choose its representatives, alcohol is the great impartial elector which flows for all parties.' He goes on to describe the evils occasioned by drink, but concludes optimistically: 'In a few years it would not surprise me to see public opinion triumph over the tyranny imposed upon us by those who make, sell and drink alcohol.'

The anti-alcohol campaigners were unsuccessful in their efforts to impose restrictive measures on bars and taverns. (Although the laws of 1871 and 1873, which were designed to reduce public drunkenness, were aimed in part at drinking establishments, the law of 1880 abrogated the decree of 1851 and facilitated the creation of new *cabarets*, a source of profit to the state and the trade's middlemen.) Within a few years the number of *cabarets* on the small Île de Sein quadrupled.[27] In France as a whole, the number of wine outlets grew from 380,000 in 1880 to 480,000 in 1910, despite the opposition of the wealthy classes, who remained convinced that the workers alone were victims of alcoholism.[28]

During the First World War several measures were to affect trade in alcohol: laws passed in 1915, 1917 and 1919 forbade the opening of new *cabarets*, banned alcoholic drinks from the workplace and increased licence tariffs. In reality, these laws were less effective in controlling the trade than the war; many bar-keepers were killed in battle and the number of *cabarets* fell to 410,000 in 1918. The figure, however, rose again to 450,000 within four years and it was in the 1920s that Charles Richet, Nobel laureate for medicine in 1913, proposed energetic measures against the 'merchants of death', the *cabaretiers*: 'They should cultivate wheat, or go to the Colonies'.[29] The government followed a policy of compromise in alcohol-related issues: the intention was to keep tax revenues at a level acceptable to consumers, but which did not encourage excessive consumption. Current

French codes governing alcohol sales date from the inter-war period, when the opening of a new outlet was made conditional on another falling vacant; thus in theory the number of cafés remains constant (except in special circumstances, such as unforeseen population growth). Four types of licence, based on the types of drink sold, were created and exclusion zones were introduced in the vicinity of certain institutions such as schools, hospitals and churches (bars that had existed in these exclusion zones for a certain length of time retained their licences). The Second World War and the statutory orders and laws introduced by the Vichy government had the same effect as the 1914–18 period, and the Fourth Republic adopted similar measures to that of the Third in respect of alcohol: an initial period of close control was followed by a more relaxed approach. Overall the number of outlets fell from 509,000 in 1937 to no more than 439,000 by 1953 (280,000 outlets for consumption on the premises, 18,000 hotel–restaurants and 141,000 off-licences[30]). At this time French citizens were the best provisioned in Europe, with one café for every 97 inhabitants, as against one for every 273 in Federal Germany and one for every 425 in England.

The French authorities experienced the same difficulties in their dealings with bars, cafés and *cabarets* as they had in their struggle with the domestic distillers. Both cases called for a balanced approach, which ignored neither social responsibilities nor fiscal returns.

In France, anti-alcohol campaigns did not on the whole stir up public passions, nor were they accompanied by violence; few truly wished the activists any success. In nineteenth-century Britain, there was an increase in the number of public houses, but the regulations governing pubs were stricter than their French counterparts. Another important difference concerns restaurants. The provision of food and alcoholic drinks were not automatically linked. This explains the number of unlicensed hotels and restaurants to be found in Britain – something unimaginable in France. In the United States, it was maintained that bars were places of debauchery. There was some truth in this: in the states and territories of the west, there was an acute shortage of women and prostitution was rife in many saloons, where pictures of scantily-clad females were to be found plastered above bars. At the end of the nineteenth century, the French painter Bouguereau, who had married an American, made a fortune with his buxom odalisques, which adorned the walls of the classiest clubs. This association of drink and sex animated the pious women of the anti-saloon leagues, who sacked bars and attacked saloon-keepers with canes and pokers.

It seems unlikely that a ban on the sale of alcoholic drinks would rid humanity of alcoholism. Cafés and bars facilitate drinking and certainly require some form of regulation. At the beginning of the twentieth century Jack London wrote in *John Barleycorn*, a popular work among the American temperance organizations, that wherever men came together to exchange ideas, joke, relax and forget the monotonous labour of the day, they invariably found themselves before a glass of alcohol.[31] He likened the bar to a primitive camp-fire. From Neolithic times, he argues, men have needed this sort of establishment – alcohol is perhaps not indispensable, but it seems inevitable and bars, lit for most of the night, welcoming and noisy, are more tempting and more visible to the solitary person in search of company than the Salvation Army refuge or the hostels of the YMCA.

Several countries have created temperance houses, but these have soon closed through lack of interest. Radical attempts at prohibition have always failed. Bans on brothels in France changed the pattern of prostitution without changing sexual needs and there is no reason to suggest that similar measures against alcohol would fare any better. Social drinking differs profoundly from alcoholism, and the bar can scarcely be blamed for the ravages of excessive alcohol consumption.

6

Alcoholism and Medicine

THE term 'alcoholism' arrived in France and from 1852–3 was incorporated into medical parlance, finding its way in subsequent years into medical dictionaries, papers and textbooks. As a concept, alcoholism slotted easily into contemporary medical thinking, having affinity, on the one hand, with other forms of intoxication such as ergotism and, on the other, with recognized multi-system diseases like rheumatism.

Medical literature of the period 1850–1950 abounds in works, articles and reflections relating to the subject. The fact that there was widespread interest in this field before 1890 is witnessed by discussion in provincial and departmental reviews, debates at the Académie de Médecine and books published at the time. Between 1891 and 1900, twenty-three theses on the psychiatric problems of alcoholism alone were submitted.[1] Such enthusiasm waned at the outset of the twentieth century, probably because doctors became discouraged at their failure to bring about a change in drinking habits: however successful they were with the numerous temperance organizations, they found it impossible, whether by legislation or in their practice, to lower the incidence of alcoholism in their patients. During the First World War, medical passion for the cause flared up once more and support from the government resulted in certain measures being taken, only to be dropped when peace returned. Between the wars doctors attempted to place the study of the organic change caused by alcohol on a more scientific plane, and the coming of the Second World War heralded once again a campaign against excessive consumption.

With the exception of times of war and privation, it is impossible to trace the development of alcoholic pathology. However, there were undoubtedly waves of interest in the problem; it would seem that the degree of concern shown bore little relation to the real danger of alcoholism, but depended largely on other, less specific emotional, political and economic considerations. Movements of this kind were not limited to any one Western country, but followed a pattern consistent with the particular climate of the day.

Medical pronouncement on the subject during the period leaves something to be desired. In general, doctors, enjoying the prestige of their position in society, speak with authority, even where their understanding of a subject is poor, and leave it to subsequent generations to prove their findings wrong. Consequently, the lack of precision and rigour seen in works emanating from reputedly serious-minded establishments is striking. Only rarely were analysts of the problem careful and scrupulous in their work, and men such as Lucien Mayet (who came to question confidently-presented statistical data and the proposed causal relationships that were glibly said to exist between a given pathological finding and excessive alcohol intake) were exceptions to the rule.

Imprecision of this kind continued until the mid-twentieth century and should perhaps not be criticized too harshly. Doctors have never completely adhered to the mathematical principles set out in 1840 by Louis in his '*médecine numérique*' (numerical medicine); they have always veered towards the subjective and have based their observations on groups of patients that were too small to be representative. Their beliefs were those of the society in which they lived and in denouncing peremptorily evils whose causes they could guess at, but not prove, they meant well.

ORGANIC DAMAGE

Doctors of the mid-nineteenth century considered alcohol to be harmful to almost all organs in the body. As from 1865, one hundred pages of Dechambre's dictionary (which, in its hundred volumes, summarizes medical knowledge at the end of the nineteenth century) were dedicated to the discussion of alcoholism.[2] Lancereaux, responsible for this section on alcoholism, follows Huss in defining the term:

By chronic alcoholism we understand a condition caused by prolonged use of spirits which develops slowly and progressively. Anatomically it is characterized by specific, non-suppurative inflammation and fatty degeneration of the organs; its symptoms are primarily those of disturbed function, notably of the nervous and gastrointestinal systems.

Lancereaux was a distinguished and respected professor, but his views were by no means shared by all his French colleagues. His definition reflected personal opinions and he admitted that it was not beyond criticism; a few decades later he would probably have written something different. Take, for example, his reference to alcoholism being caused only by spirits. Such a view was widespread until the early twentieth century and is reflected in the grouping together of fermented drinks such as wine, cider and beer under the heading 'hygienic'. By the 1890s, however, a few voices began to speak out against excessive drinking of wine: the first criticisms were directed at white wine, which was said to lack the fortifying qualities of red wine and to be more toxic. By 1906 Mayet was writing timidly: 'Fermented drinks are infinitely less harmful than spirits and yet perhaps they do not entirely deserve to be described as "hygienic", as has been the custom.' The First World War meant that doctors examined almost the entire adult male population of France, and they were obliged to relent in the face of the clinical evidence that alcoholic damage to organs was as prevalent in those who drank 'hygienic' fermented liquor as it was in drinkers of spirits. By 1920, the issue had been settled and it was accepted that the medical distinction made between fermented and distilled drink was spurious and had no pathological basis; of sole importance was the quantity of alcohol ingested.

Having defined his terms, Lancereaux proceeds to list the organic lesions attributable to alcoholism: hypertrophy of the mucosae of the tongue and larynx (here he raises the possibility of synergism with tobacco); vomiting; stomach ulcers; cirrhosis of the liver; dropsy; tuberculous granulomata in the lung; phlebitis of the portal vein; aortic atheroma; cardiac damage; hypertrophy of the spleen; serious exudates around the optic disc, resulting in visual impairment; fatty change in the kidneys; testicular atrophy. The apocalyptic list did not end here and the items enumerated were reiterated time and time again by authors in subsequent decades, who took each other to task for the slightest omission. So much medical literature exists on this subject that a complete bibliography would be impossible to collate. Amongst the many writers on the subject, Pepin chose a banking metaphor to express his opinions: 'alcoholism is a loan taken out by the worker against the surety of his health; sooner or later his body will go bankrupt.'[3] In 1888, by taking into consideration not only the amount spent on alcohol, but also the additional expense to society (days of work lost; medical treatment; unemployment; asylums; suicide and accidental death; periods of time spent in prison), Rochard estimated that 1,555,757,296 francs were being needlessly spent each year.[4] Rochard's calculation was by no means the last of its kind; similar attempts to put a price on alcohol were made well into the twentieth century.[5]

The problem of causality in alcoholism remains a difficult one. Lesions of the liver or heart can occur in drinkers and non-drinkers:

alcohol is thus not essential to the development of the lesion, but it may facilitate the disease process. Even today, with advanced statistical and experimental techniques, the exact nature of this facilitatory role is difficult to define. Furthermore, the notion of causality – the relationship of cause and effect – raises philosophical problems of the kind that have never really interested doctors; even today medicine pays little heed to such issues, which should form the basis of all therapeutics.

In his definition, Lancereaux mentions liver cirrhosis and pulmonary tuberculosis, two conditions that have provoked great controversy over the years. In his analysis of cirrhosis, he mentions the English writers who reported the phenomenon of 'gin-drinker's liver' and he also refers to Magnus Huss. He furthermore reminds his readers that writers like himself and Andral accepted that excessive consumption of alcohol could play a determining role in the aetiology of cirrhosis (a condition in which the liver can either be small, hard and nodular or hypertrophic, as a result of fatty degeneration). Only in the early twentieth century were French clinicians to accept that alcohol was an important, but by no means exclusive aetiological factor in hepatic cirrhosis; a further twenty or thirty years were to pass before they came to acknowledge that both wine and eaux-de-vie could lead to the condition.[6]

The investigation of cirrhosis thus involves establishing the action of a poison (ethanol) on the cells of the liver. Greater difficulties are encountered in pulmonary tuberculosis, where study involves differentiation of the effects of chronic alcoholism from those of ongoing microbial disease. What effect does alcohol have on the progress of tuberculosis? Hippocrates believed the two forces to be interrelated, whereas Galen did not. Similarly, since the Middle Ages thought has been divided on the matter: some doctors recommended alcohol for its fortifying qualities, which supposedly protected against tropical disease and debilitating chronic conditions such as consumption; others disagreed. In 1770 Didelot in the Vosges and in 1782 Brieulle in the Auvergne mentioned that consumption was rife amongst peasants who were addicted to eaux-de-vie.[7] In 1859, Bell in New York dismissed as fanciful the notion that alcohol protected against consumption.[8] In his conclusion on the matter, Lancereaux was guarded: 'In some cases the development of miliary tuberculosis is undoubtedly influenced by alcoholic abuse.' Caution of this kind, however, did not characterize the pronouncements of the following years. In 1909, Lancereaux himself wrote that alcoholism played a major role in 56 per cent of all cases of tuberculosis. Laudouzy spoke for specialists in the field in the inter-war period, when he stated 'tuberculosis is caught at the bar'. 'Alcoholic tuberculosis syndrome' was the term then applied to cases that proved resistant to medical and surgical treatment.[9] Even today, where intensive antibiotic therapy is used to combat the Koch bacillus, it is noticeable that pulmonary tuberculosis is slower to respond in heavy drinkers.

The difficulty of establishing causality in medicine is complicated beyond that of establishing a simple relationship between toxin and micro-organism by other, less specific influences. The progress of pulmonary tuberculosis, for example, is more rapid where there is malnutrition and poverty, where living conditions are cramped and unhygienic. Furthermore, heavy drinkers are often capricious and undisciplined in their behaviour (traits acknowledged by sanitorium doctors and which might result in alcoholic tendencies, rather than vice versa). As a consequence, they tend to comply as poorly with therapeutic regimens (rest cures and drugs) as they do with the dictates of normal social etiquette.

One relatively simple way to measure the effects of alcoholism involves comparison of alcoholic patients with those presenting from the general population. Until 1950 studies of this kind were rendered impossible by the lack of valid statistics, and even today the extraction of statistics from medical records is far from straightforward. Also problematic is the scrutiny of death registers to establish the numbers who die as a result of alcoholism. The classification of the cause of death remains unsatisfactory even in developed countries, where obligatory declaration of such causes has been a relatively recent phenomenon. Thus, retrospective studies for periods prior to 1950 are almost impossible, and even the most astute statisticians can only be reserved in their conclusions. Ledermann found that in Bavaria between 1869 and 1913, in Prussia between 1875 and 1927, in France between 1840 and 1958, and in Italy since 1927 there was a significant increase in male mortality as compared to female, which correlated with increases in excessive drinking habits.[10] Following a similar line of study, it might be thought that the files of insurance companies that offer special premiums to the temperate would be a valuable statistical source, and when Ledermann came to study them, he indeed found that they demonstrated reduced longevity in drinkers.[11] Unfortunately, however, the records give considerable reason to suspect the authenticity of clients' declarations, on the one hand, and the good faith of the insurers, on the other.

Medical science was thus unable to provide incontrovertible evidence reinforced by statistics as to the exact consequences of varying alcoholic consumption. Accordingly, scientists turned to laboratory studies, which during the flourishing years of experimental medicine – when

Claude Bernard was teaching at the Collège de France in the 1850s and 1860s – and provided clinicians and researchers with a less subjective approach to the problem. Such studies allow the investigation of the effects of a given substance on a given organ in an environment in which other extraneous influences can be carefully controlled; they presuppose only that the physiology of the animal model resembles that of man.

At the Académie des Sciences, Claude Bernard himself presented a paper by Pupier that reported the effects of alcohol intoxication in chickens force-fed on absinthe and red and white wine. Magnan (a doctor whose work will be discussed later) studied postural and nervous disorders and hepatic disease in a variety of species (dogs, cats, rabbits, rats, guinea pigs and birds) subjected regularly to alcohol. Some years later, Dujardin-Beaumetz conducted similar experiments on pigs (the tissue make-up of this animal closely resembles that of man). Just as the species of animal was varied, so too was the type of alcohol tested: thus both the 'superior' products distilled in traditional ways and the less 'natural', more 'dangerous' industrial alcohols came under the scrutiny of organic chemists, as did liqueurs, aperitifs and aromatic flavourings. New monitoring techniques were developed at this time to provide visual records of experimental data, which were easily verifiable by other researchers. Mechanography registered respiratory patterns and the opening and closing of the heart valves, while sphygmography, developed by Marey, measured the arterial pulse; these techniques led Magnan to impute the existence of high levels of vascular atheroma in cases of chronic alcoholism and senile dementia.

The results of such experiments are of little value today. They lack rigour, fail to take the relative weights of their subjects into consideration and, in addition, do not seem to have been performed in the awareness that effects witnessed in chickens and pigs force-fed on alcohol cannot be assumed to be the same in agricultural or industrial workers drinking several litres of wine or cider during their labours. Furthermore, our understanding of the electro-chemical effects of alcohol on human nervous tissue is today not such that century-old data from research on guinea-pigs might prove useful. Similarly, Magnan's claims as to the effects of alcohol on the vascular system could never be substantiated: the group he studied was far too small for any conclusion about atheroma – an extremely widespread condition – to be reached.

In the light of present-day biochemical and experimental knowledge, the research of the mid-nineteenth century appears extremely crude. However, it was conducted by well-known public figures and as such had considerable influence on drinking habits for the next hundred years. The data that appeared were taken up and used not only by temperance organizations, but also by politicians and compilers of almanacs, both of whom were concerned with the promotion of public health.

ABSINTHE

Events leading to the ban on absinthe in France in 1915 provide a good illustration of moral and legislative mechanisms at work within society. A commission from the canton of Vaud in Switzerland defines absinthe as

a strong liquor; its high alcohol content allows numerous flavoured essences to dissolve within it, amongst them absinth (wormwood), aniseed, fennel and hyssop such that the addition of a few drops of water transforms the whole into a cloudy suspension. Absinthe can be prepared either by crushing the necessary herbs in alcohol and distilling the mixture or simply by blending a sweetened green alcohol flavoured with the same herbs with alcohol at 70 per cent.[12]

Invented in Switzerland, absinthe came to Pontarlier in France with Pernod in 1805 and became popular in subsequent years. When the nineteenth-century writer Alfred de Musset was repeatedly absent from the editorial sessions of the *Dictionnaire de l'Académie Française*, he was said to be 'absinthe a little too often'. Cafés and *cabarets* in Paris, irrespective of the status of their clientele, were peopled equally by male and female drinkers of the 'green fairy' ('fée verte'). Drinking was a ritual in itself and involved the addition of water to the spirit – which was sometimes as strong as 72 per cent proof – through a strainer containing sugar to sweeten a concoction that was otherwise undrink-able; the whole process of preparation and consumption thus had its own particular rhythm. Absinthe was produced throughout France and distributed throughout Europe. It facilitated French colonial campaigns, particularly in Algeria, where it boosted courage and sanitized drinking water. Consumption was further increased when phylloxera wreaked havoc in the vineyards. So commonplace were absinthe drinkers that they found their way into the sketchbooks and paintings of Monet, Degas, Picasso, Rops and others.

Such popularity could only lead to jealousy in other quarters; the general public, however, had become so accustomed to the enormous variety of absinthes on the market that resentment from competitors was voiced relatively late. Only in the first years of the twentieth century, when viticulture flourished once more in Languedoc, did wine-growers begin to blame absinthe for the poor sales of their own product.

Worries on the grounds of public health had been expressed before this: in 1859 Motet presented a thesis that dealt with the general effects of alcohol and, more specifically, with the toxicity of absinthe;[13] Jolly performed a study on the combined effects of alcohol and tobacco, and published his findings in 1875;[14] and the 1890s saw a veritable, if unco-ordinated, onslaught on the spirit.

From their experimental work, doctors claimed that of all the essences used in the flavouring of absinthe only thuja was truly toxic. As such it was held responsible for the large part of the nervous disorders and convulsions observed in chronic alcoholics grouped together under the newly-coined medical term 'absinthism'.[15] These nervous conditions were attributed in other quarters to 'impurities' incorporated in the manufacturing process either when the herbs were picked or during the more traditional of the distilling processes.

An anti-absinthe movement gradually came into being: the Académie de Médecine demanded a ban in 1903, and other scientific groups and temperance organizations supported the cause; Galliéni, who had been Governor General of Madagascar, where absinthe was greatly appreci-ated, pleaded for its suppression; and in 1907, d'Arsonval, the eminent physicist, led a demonstration on similar grounds at the Trocadéro. Activities of this kind failed to prevent further increases in consumption, which reached record levels in 1913. Some 239,000 hectolitres (5.25 million gallons) were drunk during this year; nevertheless this repre-sented only a small proportion of total alcohol intake.

Concern was expressed in other countries and Belgium was the first to take action: absinthe was banned in the Congo in 1898, and in Belgium itself ten years later. Other governments followed suit: Switzerland after a referendum in 1908 and Italy in 1913; in Morocco, proconsul Lyautey took similar action in 1914. Finally, in March 1915, wartime shortages in France led to the passing of legislation prohibiting the manufacture, sale and distribution of absinthe and similar spirits (this occurred despite estimated losses of more than 11 million francs in revenue to the ex-chequer). This law pertained to all flavoured spirits; however, legislation directed specifically at those termed '*anisés*' (flavoured with aniseed) was passed in 1922, 1940 and 1951, when their sale was permitted, prohibited and then finally once again freed from restraint. Today, Britain, where absinthe is not considered to present any great risk to the population, is alone amongst European countries to allow its sale.

It is difficult to understand why absinthe fell into such disfavour. The experimental protocols employed in the testing of the vegetable essences used to flavour alcoholic liquor at the end of the nineteenth century are not available for scrutiny today, but it is probable that they lacked scientific rigour – indeed such a claim was made at the time.[16] Furthermore, neat absinthe, as dispensed in the cafés, had an alcohol content that varied between 45 per cent and 60 per cent proof, and it is difficult to see how doctors were able to attribute their patients' convulsions, delirium and fits to herbal flavourings rather than to the sheer quantity of alcohol consumed. With the benefit of a hundred years' hindsight, it would seem today that absinthe became the scapegoat for damage done by alcohol. Whatever the reason, it is now evident that the twenty-year-long anti-absinthe campaign, which culminated in prohibition in numerous countries, had no scientific basis. In France, the legacy of such measures has been such that absinthe has been superseded by other forms of alcohol to such an extent that few would dream of campaigning for its reintroduction and legalization.

In the nineteenth century, clinical anatomists and the somatic school of medicine – namely those expressing interest only in organic disease – attributed many lesions to overindulgence in alcohol that were shown later to have a different aetiology.[17] In spite of this, they were right to show alarm at the damage done. With time their observations became more precise and they described conditions throughout the human body which are still thought to be induced by alcohol; descriptions which substantiated Huss's pioneering work. In 1865, Lancereaux described the flaccid, atrophic muscles, reduced reflexes and cramps of alcoholic polyneuropathy. In 1881, Gayet and Wernicke identified an encephalopathy characterized by nervous paralysis of the eyes and limbs, motor disorders resulting from cerebellar damage, speech difficulties and, on occasions, delirium. In 1881, Korsakoff described mental changes characterized by disorientation, amnesia and anxiety terminating in apathy, which were later attributed by Gamper (1928) and Neubürger (1931) to atrophic sclerosis in certain areas of the brain. In 1898, alcoholism was linked with a necrosis of the corpus callosium, which in health allows vital communication between the cerebral hemispheres. Activities of this kind continued in the twentieth century: in 1901, Uthoff confirmed visual disturbances resulting from optic-nerve atrophy that had already been noted by Galezowski in 1871. In the same year, Huchard presented work on cardiac problems in heavy drinkers which, in 1908, was completed by Bauer and Bollinger in Munich with a description of 'alcoholic myocarditis' (inflammation of the heart muscle). In 1915, Lian examined 150 soldiers in the territorial army and discovered that 48 per cent of the heavy drinkers amongst them were hypertensive, compared with 8 per cent of their more abstemious colleagues.[18] Lian's study failed to attract any attention when it was published – only recently have its findings been confirmed and has medicine come to accept that alcohol predisposes to raised arterial blood pressure.

Not only did clinicians unmask the aetiology of numerous organic lesions, but they also began to discover alcoholism amongst sections of society where it had been thought previously not to exist. Doctors at the time saw alcohol as a vice of the lower classes, a view that is still held by the more affluent classes in France today. In their textbook of medicine, published in 1925, Roger, Widal and Teissier maintained that 'alcoholic excess is less common amongst the affluent and educated; here, over-indulgence in wine is usually accompanied with overindulgence at the table and thus only occurs intermittently.'[19]

As a phenomenon, alcoholism was far less visible amongst the bourgeoisie, where it was shrouded in silence and hidden from view. Appearances proved deceptive, as is shown by the numbers of patients from this class of society who were treated by urban doctors. Babinski described one such patient, a woman with an alcoholic polyneuropathy stemming from the solace she sought in champagne after a series of difficult labours. In 1921, at the Académie de Médecine, Guillain presented a paper entitled '*L'Alcoolisme mondain*' ('Alcoholism in the Upper Classes'), in which he listed the constituents of the most popular cocktails and lamented the harm they cause.

Although doctors throughout most of rural France believed the contrary, it was a widely held view that alcoholism was an urban phenomenon. In attempting to put their case, the same doctors came up against a second myth, namely that the peasants lived healthy lives as opposed to their cousins in the cities, where squalor, overpopulation and malnutrition prevailed. This myth was conferred upon eaux-de-vie of provincial origin, which were considered less harmful than those produced by industrial methods. In 1866, members of the *Sénat* sought the opinion of doctors in psychiatric asylums and were almost unanimous in 'the harmlessness of natural eaux-de-vie, especially those made from marc and cider'.[20] Some doctors were of similar opinion: Roché, whose practice was at Toucy-sur-Yonne, maintained in 1898 that there was a higher incidence of liver cirrhosis in the towns, that it was rarer in wine-drinkers and that chronic alcoholism was less common amongst heavy drinkers of traditionally prepared eaux-de-vie than it was amongst those drinking 'poor-quality spirits and commercial aperitifs'.[21] These ill-founded claims were based on the results of a questionnaire completed by forty-two doctors in the Yonne district, which did not include a single urban centre. They reflect above all the poor clinical acumen, if not the poor education, of doctors in rural districts; although they show an awareness of contemporary social issues – the opposition of town and country, of industry and traditional production methods – they are completely devoid of rational thought and statistical rigour. In contrast, doctors working in mental establishments (whose preoccupation was therefore not principally confined to organic disturbance) demonstrated that amongst their alcoholic patients those from the country greatly outnumbered those from the cities.

Alcoholism amongst women had already been brought to light by Villermé and, although its existence was not denied at this time, the subject has always received less attention and been the object of greater disapproval than alcoholism amongst men. Drunkenness in women, the custodians of domestic virtue and the moral educators of the young, has always been considered more culpable than it has in men. Eonnet was one of the few to consider the problem in women and reported in 1889 to the Académie de Médecine the prevalence of alcoholism in women of the 'wealthier and better-educated classes' of the Morbihan district.[22]

More serious were the possible effects that maternal alcoholism might have on children. The notion of hereditary alcoholism will be considered at a later stage; the concern here is one voiced by contemporary doctors, namely that dependency on alcohol was encouraged in the breast-fed infant. Reboul, a surgeon from Nîmes, described in 1878 cases of infants who fitted when fed the milk of alcoholic wet nurses and failed to convulse when given milk from other sources.[23] There is no mention made of the number of cases in which such a phenomenon occurred; the alcoholization of babies, however, whether breast- or bottle-fed, whether in urban or rural environments, was well recognized at the time.[24] Naturally enough, as infants grew up, they came to mimic their parents' eating and drinking habits, which was not without ill effect on their growth and general behaviour.[25] Like adults, they were prone to acute inebriation and might suffer delirium tremens.

Proof as to the toxic effects of alcohol came during the First and Second World Wars and was particularly apparent after the imposition of food-rationing in the period 1939–45. Restrictions placed on the sale of alcohol and on agricultural produce used in its manufacture led to an abrupt fall in the nation's alcoholization: patients with cirrhosis were no longer seen in hospitals and admissions to psychiatric establishments for reasons connected with alcohol were few and far between. Furthermore, if we are to believe Armand-Delille, a paediatrician at the University of

Paris, the health of children in the provinces who were deprived of wine and eaux-de-vie improved significantly.[26]

During the period 1850–1950, the medical profession did not concern itself solely with the visible effects of chronic alcoholism. Interest was also aroused by those heavy drinkers who drank without ever becoming drunk; it was ascertained, however, that the prognosis for this group (which was always difficult to identify, for obvious reasons) was equally as poor as for those who showed the normal signs of inebriation.[27] Other circumstances also served to bring to light alcoholics who would otherwise have escaped notice. Following on from Lecœur, who in 1858 considered the question of surgery in alcoholics, Verneuil declared in 1870 that the outlook for recovery from accidental injury was 'exceptionally poor among those whose lives were tainted by alcoholism'.[28] Similar opinions have been expressed by surgeons ever since and such was the conclusion of a French conference convened in 1960 to discuss the matter.

Ever since Huss drew his colleagues' attention to the widespread damage caused by chronic alcohol abuse, doctors have been preoccupied by the subject. Indeed, they have damaged their credibility by describing the phenomenon as catastrophic for the human race in times when general health has not ceased to improve; in reality, alcoholism is just one illness amongst many. Medical education has also contributed to a certain confusion in the profession and its message concerning alcoholism has been received differently by different practitioners. Some innovations in diagnosis and treatment may gain widespread acceptance in a matter of years, others require generations. The latter proved to be the case with alcoholism and explains to a large extent the variation in medical pronouncements on the subject.

MENTAL PROBLEMS

By his own admission Huss was no psychiatrist. In his book, however, he did record a number of mental disturbances, which he associated with chronic alcoholism, but wisely did not attribute exclusively to alcohol. He also referred his readers to earlier works by English and German colleagues, which had first alerted him to these clinical conditions. In Huss's day, no distinction was made between neurology (the study of the nervous system and its disorders) and psychiatry (the study of mental illness); psychological disturbance was considered a part of nervous disease.[29]

In France, a law was passed in 1838 obliging all *départements* to build mental asylums and within a few decades the country was well supplied with specialist hospitals. Old medieval prejudices prevailed and these establishments were mainly situated in the countryside, as the towns refused to tolerate 'madmen' in their vicinity. The institutions were staffed by doctors who all had medical qualifications (the same could not be said of every medical practitioner at this time), but who were none the less not fully versed in a discipline still in its advent and still in the throes of developing its own methodology and language.

Between 1850 and 1950 research into alcoholism was hampered in France by the subdivision of alcoholic patients into categories, according to the nature of their disease and to where they lived. Most doctors in the large urban and university hospitals were interested in organic disease and described, for example, the different types of cirrhosis and tendon reflex, whereas the alienists, most of whom worked outside the towns (the St Anne hospitals in Paris and Charenton being exceptions to this rule), worked with long-term psychiatric patients, used different terminology and found it difficult to combine their findings with those of others.

Doctors in the asylums were never able to give a categorical picture of the links that existed between mental illness and excessive consumption of alcohol. Good medical practice should have caused them to formulate a number of hypotheses to explain this relationship; only one such theory was entertained, however, and this gained acceptance without being verified. This was the notion that alcohol led to mental disturbance and that admission to mental institutions could be avoided through abstinence. Other hypotheses did not come under serious consideration until the mid-twentieth century, when the possibilities that alcohol might conceal mental disorders or indeed that mental disease predisposed to alcoholism were examined. Although it is certain that not all alienists were of the opinion that the majority of their patients had been admitted because they were alcoholics, their writings were interpreted as if this was indeed what they felt. The public believed implicitly in this simple notion of causality and much of the alienists' work was quoted by those involved in anti-alcohol campaigns.

The psychiatry of alcoholism in France was dominated for a century by Magnan, who worked in the asylums of the Seine district. His inaugural thesis, 'On alcoholism, the different types of alcoholic delirium and their treatment', appeared in 1874 and for several decades he observed patients and taught generations of students.[30] Magnan rightly criticized Huss's system of classification and the latter's description of six forms of 'delirium': 'a careful appraisal of the facts leads us to the conclusion that they might just as easily be grouped in two or three categories'. The first of these forms included symptoms of acute alcoholic episodes and delirium tremens. In a second group, Magnan placed patients who were slow to recover and quick to relapse, many of whom had suicidal tendencies. A third category consisted again of those with alcoholic delirium who frequently relapsed, but whose convalescence was marked by delusional ideas; some of these patients eventually failed to respond to any form of treatment and ended their lives in a state of 'generalized paralysis'. Magnan's classification was thus made according to symptomatological and prognostic criteria and, although it was more systematic than that attempted by Huss, its terminology was no more precise: 'generalized paralysis', for example, with its connotation of combined intellectual decline and dementia, was used between the wars with specific reference to syphilis.

In 1903 Papadaki, a Greek doctor working in Swiss asylums, proposed a better system of classification.[31] He chose to divide patients into two groups, namely, those for whom alcohol was an occasional cause of dementia (amongst them epileptics and generalized paralytics) and those for whom alcohol played a direct causative role in the development of acute or chronic psychosis. Papadaki's paper, although open to criticism, seems to have been largely ignored in France.

French alienists in general did not apply themselves to the questions posed by toxicomania, but contented themselves rather with listing symptoms and clinical manifestations, suicidal tendencies, bouts of rage, amnesia, subacute alcoholic confusion and hallucinations. Such a list was lengthened considerably by the contributions made by Charcot in the 1880s and Laignel-Lavastine in the 1930s. Similarly, only a few specialists, amongst them Lancereaux and Dromard, addressed the question: why do people drink? For them, alcoholism was the loss of freedom that allows the individual to choose not to drink. They went on to make a distinction between neurotic and social alcoholism and, since manias were fashionable at the time, invented the term 'dipsomania' to describe a condition involving the compulsive and uncontrolled drinking of any alcohol (including eau-de-cologne). Dipsomania differed therefore from 'potomania' – where patients experienced the compulsion to drink any liquid, especially water – and also from neurological disorders such as polydipsia, which were attributable to brain lesions. Wright, an American alienist from Ohio, made the transition from mental to organic pathology while studying 'oenomania' (wine mania) in the late nineteenth century and became convinced that alcoholism was a physical disorder, a nervous condition and as such did not allow for a distinction between the heavy drinker and the dipsomaniac.[32]

The clinical spectrum represented by alcoholics admitted to mental institutions was so wide that the alienists were scarcely to blame for their rather confused attempts at classification. Some patients were admitted because they had lost all social awareness and were unstable and unpredictable, both at work and at home; others were violent, liable to murderous aggression and were a danger to friends and family; others were in confusional states and utterly disorientated in time and space. Clinical pictures such as these were highly variable and dramatic episodes were interspersed with long intervals of apparent normality, during which patients were kept busy with building work, in the gardens and in the workshops. Furthermore, similar patterns of behaviour were to be observed amongst patients who did not drink (chronic alcoholism did not give rise to a specific clinical picture), and any distinction between alcoholic and non-alcoholic symptomatology was necessarily subjective, unless specific organic manifestation such as liver cirrhosis or Korsakoff's syndrome were also present. Alienists found it difficult not to speak of alcoholism in moral terms; Dromard spoke of 'perversion', which led to drinking habits and dependency, but like other doctors of his day he made no effort to identify the mental mechanism that, as he observed, might drive members of any social class to drink. This issue was to remain ignored until the mid-twentieth century.

Statistical records, on the other hand, were considered important by those working in the asylums and demonstrate the numbers of patients admitted to hospital with alcohol-related disorders. Unfortunately their interest to the modern researcher is limited by their lack of detail; no information is given about the duration or frequency of admissions to hospital, the rates of relapse or the social circumstances of the patients. It would seem that contemporary medicine considered such matters irrelevant. Even in clinical matters statistical method was to prove disappointing: some authors wrote up individual case-histories that they considered particularly interesting, but their lack of a coherent system of nomenclature at the time means that it has proved impossible to estimate the incidence of the common pathological states. Such is the complaint of the medical historian; the lack of rigour in the collection of epidemiological data was to be found in all Western countries and problems of classification in psychiatry have always existed.[33]

Studies of alcoholism were conducted throughout France: Magnan collated the number of suicides in the asylums of the Seine between 1870

Alcoholism: Vice or Malady?

Table 6.1   Number of alcoholic patients admitted to mental institutions in nineteen French health districts

Health districts	1936	1939	1942	1943	1944
Lille	3	6	0.9	0.5	0.13
Laon	7	6	1	0.5	
Rouen	8	9	2	1	
Paris	10	11	1.5	1	1.7
Châlons-sur-Marne	8	12	1	0.6	0.25
Nancy	7	10	1	1.1	
Besançon	5	6	1	2.2	1.7
Orléans	9	10	2	1.5	
Rennes	7	11	5	2.5	
Nantes	11	18	3	3.4	
Poitiers	7	10	3	3.1	4.2
Bordeaux	22	17	2	0.7	
Limoges	2	3	1	0.5	
Clermont-Ferrand	4	4	0.6	1.8	2.8
Lyon	10	10	2	1.6	
Montpellier	3	1	3	2.5	1.4
Grenoble	4	4	1	1.3	
Marseille	4	3	2	1.1	
Toulouse	7	6	2	3.1	

Source: J. Perrin, 'L'Alcoolisme; Problèmes médicaux et sociaux, Problèmes économiques', *Expansion scientifique*, Paris, 1950, p. 89.

and 1871, while Lardier in 1893 and Baudin in 1902 reported on the situations in the Vosges and Doubs respectively. Most striking, however, was the number of medical papers on the subject that originated in western France, and especially Normandy. Although it would be wrong to correlate the prevalence of such studies with the alcoholization of the population in the areas where they are conducted, other information provided by doctors who spent their entire working lives often in a single asylum helps to plot the emergence of the 'alcoholic' class of patient. Works of this kind – long statistical series plotted over several decades – exist for the Auge, Calvados, Manche and Eure districts, the most notable of all being the record kept at the Bon-Sauveur asylum near Caen between 1838 and 1925;[34] Magnon and Fillassier followed patients in the Seine district from 1867 until 1912.

These medical reports were supplemented by others commissioned by *préfets* and parliamentarians: in 1887, the Gadaud report on alcohol and insanity was presented to the *Chambre des Députés*; and Claude, representing the Vosges in the *Sénat*, published a paper on the consumption of alcohol. Numerous other papers appeared at about this time and the conclusions reached by all authors were unequivocal: alcoholism was responsible for a large proportion of patients being admitted to asylums and, furthermore, the problem was on the increase. Of Magnan's patients, 14 per cent in 1860 had been hospitalized for alcohol-related disorders, 25 per cent in 1870, 27 per cent in 1871 and 33 per cent in 1899.[35] Legrain, who took over from Magnan in the struggle against alcohol, estimated that a quarter of the 80,000 mental patients confined to care in France were admitted for reasons attributable to alcoholism, and the figure rose to 40 per cent in Normandy.[36] Other authors were less specific, speaking of alcohol in terms of 'national catastrophe' or stating, even more bluntly, that 'all workers are alcoholics'.

The number of suicides was equally distressing. Magnan quotes Brierre de Boismont, who recorded 530 cases in 4,595 alcoholics (11.5 per cent), and the German alienist Casper, who claimed that over a nine-year period a quarter of those committing suicide in Berlin had been dependent on alcohol. In his own practice, Magnan encountered twenty-four attempted suicides (8.2 per cent) and eighty-four murders (29.2 per cent) in 291 patients. Readers are reminded here that in view of the shame and distress experienced by the families of those deemed to have killed themselves, notifications of suicide have, until recently, been less frequent than the event itself.

At the turn of the twentieth century there appears to have been a decline in events of this kind and during the First World War alcohol consumption fell dramatically. The balance was redressed in the post-war years such that in 1925 the politician and statesman, Edouard Herriot felt obliged to request the Académie de Médecine to research into 'the real causes of the recrudescence of alcoholism'. In the 1930s, the medical journals once again showed concern at the incidence of cirrhosis of the liver and mental disturbance in drinkers, conditions which again declined in number between 1939 and 1945. In 1942, Pagniez and Plichet established a proven link between 'the reduced incidence of acute alcoholic confusion and restrictions imposed on the consumption of alcohol'.[37] This link was confirmed by Lhermitte in his work in asylums and hospices for the elderly; he emphasized 'the role played by alcohol in the aetiology of mental disease'.[38]

Vallery-Radot, Loeper and Laroche confirmed the reduced incidence of alcoholic cirrhosis during the Second World War. It was estimated that deaths attributable to alcohol fell fourfold during this period, whereas those attributable to liver disease fell by 70 per cent in France as a whole (but by only 53 per cent in Normandy and Brittany).[39] Unfortunately trends such as these were to be short lived.

The statistical work of this period lacks precision and is difficult to verify; indeed comparison of the numerous studies often proves unfruitful.

Problems such as these arise when doctors are confronted by new pathological phenomena, which present in a wide range of different ways. Alcoholism is just such a phenomenon and although today the statistical studies discussed in this chapter hold relatively little interest, they were to influence and stimulate many readers when they first appeared.

THE RELATIONSHIP BETWEEN ALCOHOL AND CREATIVITY

A question that aroused the interest of numerous nineteenth-century doctors and thinkers concerned the relationship between 'madness' and artistic creation. If the question 'does madness contribute to artistic creation?' is a valid one, then the relationship between alcohol and creativity is also worthy of consideration. Enachescu conducted an appraisal of this relationship in his essay, 'Alcoholism and literary creation: a psychopathological evaluation of alcoholic writers'.[40]

Few sculptors seem to have been heavy drinkers, possibly because alcoholic 'shakes' are incompatible with skilled manipulation of the tools of the trade. There were, however, painters who drank heavily. Rossetti appears to have abused both morphine and alcohol and experienced numerous bouts of delirium tremens. Van Gogh was apparently highly sensitive to the effects of alcohol, claiming in 1888, 'One small glass of cognac is enough to get me drunk.' He reproached himself for drinking and smoking too much and yet, every time he was allowed out of the Saint-Rémy asylum, he would go drinking in the local bars.[41] It has also been conjectured that Van Gogh abused digitalis (which was used at this time in the treatment of epilepsy); toxic levels of this drug cause a disturbance of colour vision, which might account for the artist's preference for yellow, beige and ochre.[42] Alcoholism was prevalent amongst the artists of Montmartre and Montparnasse in the early years of the twentieth century and during the inter-war period; Suzanne Valadon and Utrillo were the most notorious offenders in this respect.[43]

For reasons similar to those applicable to sculptors, practising musicians are less prone to alcoholism than composers. Beethoven died at the age of 57 of hepatic cirrhosis with jaundice and dropsy. Among his ancestors were both musicians and wine merchants; he frequented taverns, enjoyed drinking contests and his ninth symphony was a bacchic celebration; 'wine is both necessary and good for me', he said in 1804.[44] To assert that Beethoven was an alcoholic is not to detract from his genius; none the less, some regard this as a slur upon his character and attribute his cirrhosis to a bout of acute hepatitis suffered several decades before his death. This alternative hypothesis is medically plausible, but naturally cannot be verified, as is usual, by microscopic examination of the composer's liver. More obscure is the pathological sequence leading to the death of Mussorgsky at the age of 42. He had been prone to manic depressive episodes since adolescence and was known to have attacks of delirium, referred to by his brother as delirium tremens. It is certain also that Mussorgsky used alcohol, especially towards the end of his life, as a means of calming his hyperexcitable tendencies and of overcoming depression. It was not unknown for him to arrive drunk at appointments with patrons of the arts. In the end he was said to have succumbed in 1881 to erysipelas, a bacterial infection that overcame the weakened defences of a body that had progressed to a state of near-emaciation in the months before his death.[45]

The links between alcoholism and literary output are so numerous that it would be impossible to make an exhaustive study of the subject. This analysis will restrict itself to certain questions raised by the phenomenon and to the most illustrative examples thereof.[46]

Is alcohol a source of inspiration to authors or do they write in spite of its effects? Writers may dissipate their *angst* either by writing or by drinking. In all probability, alcohol both hinders and helps the process of literary creation, calming troubled thoughts, but also leading to their exacerbation. Sophocles reproached Aeschylus for only being able to write when drunk,[47] and in more recent times Verlaine and his companions are known to have spent much of their time in bars – a habit alluded to in Verlaine's 'Ballade de la Mauvaise Réputation' and in the portrait of the poet seated before a glass of absinthe.[48]

Leaving aside the Dionysian and hedonistic in literature, we can turn our attention to more subtle literary manifestations of acute or chronic alcoholism. The nineteenth-century German writer E. T. A. Hoffmann was a heavy drinker and has been retrospectively diagnosed as an alcoholic by some and as a schizophrenic by others. His psychopathological state may indeed represent a synthesis of the two conditions, a notion reinforced by the *angst* and hallucinations incorporated into his *Tales of the Fantastic*.

Psychiatrists have also taken great interest in Edgar Allen Poe. The frequent phenomenon of coexistent alcoholism and tuberculosis was not unknown amongst Poe's family and friends; he himself was not only an alcoholic, but also abused opiates and died during an episode of delirium tremens at the age of 40. Poe's tales almost certainly describe visions of the fantastic experienced either while under the influence of alcohol or during attempts to withdraw from it (at one time he was a sworn member of the 'Sons of Temperance'). 'The Crow', for example, has been interpreted as an expression of the threatening and terrifying hallucinations of animals (or 'zoopsies'), experienced by those in a state of alcoholic delirium.[49]

Americans figure highly amongst alcoholic writers of the twentieth century, and amongst them names such as London, Fitzgerald, Sinclair, Lewis, Faulkner, Hemingway, Chandler, Hammet and Kerouac come readily to mind. It should be remembered that the absence of evidence of chronic alcoholism in a novel does not necessarily prove an absence of the phenomenon in the population being described: it may just be that the author is not interested in the problem or that he regards it as so 'normal' as to be unworthy of his special attention. Such a premise should be borne in mind when reading Faulkner's descriptions of the deep South, which often deal with characters who are drunk, but rarely with consistently heavy drinkers.

Faulkner himself was associated with alcohol for most of his life. As a youth, he had been sent home from scout camp for being drunk and in later life he underwent numerous detoxification programmes at clinics in Europe and America. The connections between Faulkner's drinking and literary creativity have probably been overemphasized; however, the reports of his drunkenness and intermittent admissions to hospital leave little reason to doubt that he was an alcoholic. His drunken behaviour can have done little for his reputation and one can imagine the reaction in the southern states, when one interviewer interpreted his incoherent and clumsy responses as segregationist. Faulkner's real convictions lay in exactly the opposite direction.[50] His prolific output – short stories, novels, plays and screenplays – was the product of the numerous periods of lucidity in his life and, as with Poe, bouts of intoxication only served to hinder the process of writing. Faulkner did not write because he drank; in drink, as in writing, he sought to dissipate both his *angst* and his inconsolable feelings of loneliness.

Characters in the American novel who are addicted to alcohol are for the most part sinister and closely linked with violence and death. The life of Dick Diver in Fitzgerald's *Tender Is The Night* work unfolds like an endless suicide. Nathan Cass, the narrator of William Styron's *Set This House on Fire* blames alcoholism for his failure as an artist, a situation which is compounded when he kills the vain, manipulative, materialist Mason Flagg.[51]

Feelings of guilt common in Protestant society and amongst alcoholics are often seen to drive writers and characters to self-accusation and suicide. The state of drunkenness resembles suicide in that it frees the drinker from his enslavement to alcohol and the feelings of guilt associated with it, just as suicide gives freedom from life. The hero of Yates's *Revolutionary Road* opts for suicide, joining the ranks who have followed in the footsteps of Fitzgerald, London and Hemingway.[52] Although suicide itself in such cases may appear to be the product of an impulsive decision taken at a time of high alcohol intake, it is in reality the culmination of prolonged feelings of guilt, failure and futility and considerable mental preparation for the act itself.

In one of his poems, Malcolm Lowry wrote 'The only hope is the next drink', and the author has been much studied by 'alcohologists' and psychiatrists.[53] *Under the Volcano* describes the author's own struggle against alcoholism, which only achieved final resolution in suicide.[54] The novel is written from the alcoholic's point of view: feelings of guilt concerning wartime misdemeanours are intermingled with a failed marriage, a failed career, auditory hallucinations and the protagonist's pathetic attempts to hide alcohol from himself. Ultimately the vice-consul chooses a pseudo-voluntary death and is killed after he has assumed a false identity, which he knows will put him at risk. In his preface, Lowry states his intention to write 'a drunkard's story' and the novel reflects his own obsessions, terrors and unresolved feelings of rebellion. Interestingly, his working title had been 'The Valley of the Shadow of Death', and the theme of death is echoed in the title of one of Lowry's collections of poetry, 'For the Love of Dying'.[55] Both author and protagonist experience 'divorce from life' and are prey to such flights of speech and fancy that life becomes 'an extravagant narration'.[56] Lowry's life was truly hellish and his novel became an account 'of the fall of man, of his remorse and of his endless struggle with the weight of the past'.

Alcoholism is an endless journey that allows the drinker to leave behind his dissatisfactions with life and to glimpse a perfect world, a Garden of Eden, a lost Paradise. Such a road can end only in disappointment with life, a disappointment experienced by alcoholic, gambler and user of psychotropic drugs alike. It is impossible to say whether drinking boosts the writer's creative potential or not, because too many individual factors come into play; however, the interplay between alcoholism and the art of writing would seem to correspond to that described by Ey in 1960, when considering the relationship between insanity and artistic creativity in general: 'Madness does not make artists, but artists touched by insanity may continue to be artists'.

ALCOHOL AS A REMEDY AND REMEDIES FOR ALCOHOL

In the nineteenth and early twentieth centuries, doctors were by no means unanimously agreed that alcohol was toxic and that it presented a danger to the human constitution. Consequently the public were not always convinced by medical pronouncements on the subject. Even within the medical profession it was still believed (without any toxicological evidence to prove the matter) that fermented drink was 'hygienic' and that only spirits were dangerous. This notion had been applied to beer and gin consumption by Hogarth, it was supported by Pasteur, who had worked with wine and beer drinkers, and was perpetuated in France by those who saw wine as the country's national product.

The French continue to regard wine as a normal constituent of their diet. Towards the end of the nineteenth century, advances in thermodynamics were applied to the traditional diet and Pasteur expressed the calorific value of a glass of wine in terms of equivalent quantities of milk and meat. Unfortunately, then as now, it was not widely appreciated that calorific equivalents expressed in this way were misleading, since they said nothing about the value of foodstuffs subjected to normal physiological metabolism within the body. Further support for wine-drinking was to appear in the 1930s with the foundation of the 'National Wine Propaganda Committee' and the formation of numerous pseudo-medieval drinking brotherhoods with their own rituals and attire. Doctors also contributed to this move to increase the alcoholization of the nation and in 1933 the first congress of '*Médecins amis du vin*' (Doctors for wine) was held. This organization remains active today.

Similar arguments were advanced by the promoters of distilled alcohol. During the last twenty years of the nineteenth century it was stated repeatedly that the toxicity of eaux-de-vie was due to impurities that accumulated during the production process. Such opinion naturally favoured industrial distillation at the expense of the traditional producers who, it was presumed, would exercise less control over the quality of their product. Thus it was that advances in chemistry would lead to alcohols that would cause no physiological damage. In the interim, however, it was proposed by Desbouvrie to the Académie de Médecine in 1888 that prospective consumers of alcohol should chew a special form of chocolate containing albumin, which would absorb any harmful impurities. Lancereaux, who fortunately recorded the minutes of the meeting, expressed his doubts on the matter.[57]

In 1916, a pamphlet was distributed amongst the French army that attacked the common view that 'alcohol invigorates, warms, sharpens the appetite and eases digestion', and at the same time encouraged the distribution of glasses of wine to the ranks, especially when courage was required. Ambivalence of this kind was common amongst doctors who, like the general public, saw alcohol as a pleasant addition to the diet. One member of the medical profession even wrote a book to protect the 'rights of alcohol', in which he maintained 'Alcohol is a dietary ingredient more important than sugar – it gives twice as much energy to the consumer'.[58]

Such attitudes possibly appear less misguided, if it is borne in mind that doctors valued alcohol as a therapeutic agent and had done so for hundreds of years. In the thirteenth century, Raymond Lulle (1235–1315) attributed alcohol with life-prolonging powers and referred to it as *aquae vitae*. Later, Arnaud de Villeneuve, in his treatise *De conservanda juventute et retardanda senectute*, was to vaunt its qualities. Traditional attitudes such as these had percolated down the centuries and were still prominent in nineteenth-century medical practice.

Alcohol as an external agent remains in general medical use today and is commonly applied to open wounds, which it both dries and disinfects. It was also formerly used at high concentrations as a sclerosant and was injected into the scrotum to cure persistent effusions; it was also injected intracranially into the Gasserian ganglion to relieve facial neuralgia.

The prescription of alcohol to patients for internal use had dangers of which most doctors were apparently unaware until the twentieth century. Its administration as an agent in the physician's traditional pharmacopoeia fell into temporary decline during the twenty-year vogue for Broussaisism in the early nineteenth century. With the discrediting of Broussais's doctrine, the therapeutic use of alcohol again became widespread. Such an upsurge was due in no small measure to the propagandist work of an English doctor, R. B. Todd.[59] Todd maintained that alcohol stimulated the natural healing process, reinforcing the body's defences against disease. He interpreted the work of the German chemist von Liebig in a highly individual fashion, using its scientific argument to uphold his own belief that, since the body metabolized and stored alcohol, it must therefore put it to good use.

Todd's doctrines enjoyed considerable popularity until their proponent's death in 1860, when there was a backlash of polemic against them. Physiologists and chemists in Britain, France and Germany discovered that the majority of alcohol consumed was excreted in the urine and that it consequently had less therapeutic value than had hitherto been believed. The public, however, would have nothing of this and its enthusiasm increased with the discovery that the intoxication of laboratory animals with alcohol led to a fall in their body temperature. Alcohol was thus construed to have useful anti-pyretic qualities, a belief capitalized upon by Béhier, whose marketing campaign for Todd's (highly alcoholic) mixture was hugely successful in France.[60]

Doctors were by now making widespread use of alcohol in both hospital and general practice. It formed the active ingredient of innumerable 'wine tonics', which appeared on the market variously flavoured with coca, gentian, cola, melissa, creosote, scilla or digitalis. Every hospital had its own tonics and every famous professor of medicine his own formulation; the army distributed 'iodotannic syrup' to its soldiers. A manual of practical pharmacy dating from 1893 lists over one hundred medicinal wine tonics. Other quarters simply used rum and Mayet, in 1896, recorded that 23 hospitals (in all probability in the vicinity of Lyons) consumed 34,000 litres (7,500 gallons) of rum; unfortunately, however, he makes no mention of the numbers of patients who received such 'treatment'.

The use of potions was indicated in a wide variety of clinical situations, and alcohol was believed to be efficacious in almost every case, be it haemorrhage, poisoning, fever or infectious disease in the form of cholera, malaria, typhoid or tuberculosis.[61] It was said to invigorate the anaemic and revive paralysed nerves even in alcoholic polyneuropathy, and until recently it was given to alcoholics to relieve symptoms of withdrawal. The quantities of alcohol thus consumed on prescription must have been enormous. Since the qualities of this would-be medicine were so highly praised by medical practitioners, domestic consumption was also considerable and alcohol was given to babies to stop them crying; it was also used as a remedy for period pain and indigestion, and served both as a sedative and a stimulant. Magnan even quotes the case of a woman who was delirious and experienced hallucinations as the direct result of overindulgence in alcoholic tonic, 'eau de mélisse des Carmes', which she used to stimulate her appetite.[62]

At the end of the nineteenth century, in both Britain and France there was considerable controversy in medical circles as to the therapeutic value of alcohol. Disharmony in the profession was also evident in 1919 in the United States, when prohibition was introduced to restrict the sale of any drink with an alcohol content of 2 per cent or more by volume. Doctors who believed in the curative powers of alcohol were suddenly placed in the position where they might not be allowed to prescribe the drug, and if they did, they could not be sure that their patients would be able to obtain it. Already, in 1917, differences in opinion had surfaced during the influenza epidemic, when some patients were treated with alcohol as a first-line remedy. In the same year, the American Medical Association declared itself strongly in favour of prohibition, whereas the American Therapeutics Association still considered alcohol to be of value in the treatment of disease. A survey conducted by the *Journal of the American Medical Association* in 1922 revealed that a small majority of doctors were in favour of keeping whisky on the list of legally prescribable drugs (15,625 doctors voted for and 15,218 doctors against the proposal). Whisky and brandy were to remain in the American pharmacopoeia, even after its revision in 1926.[63]

With the restoration of freedom to consumer and prescriber in the United States, the debate on the question of alcohol in therapeutics began to lose momentum. In Europe, also, the subject seems to have lost its allure, perhaps because it was felt that undue attention had been focused upon it. This general lack of interest was sustained until the mid-twentieth century: the combination of wartime shortages and improvements in the chemical industry meant that less alcohol was available for therapeutic use and that demonstrably better pharmacological agents were to emerge. In the space of a few years, alcohol disappeared from the realm of medical therapeutics.

Between 1850 and 1950, doctors were prone to discuss alcoholism at length without addressing the issue of treatment. Ethanol poisoning, with its dual physical and mental effects, continues to present the clinician with problems, which are often compounded by the reluctance of many individuals to comply with treatment. The therapy available to those with alcohol problems has varied over the years, from the commonsensical to the bizarre.

Magnan stressed the need for caution in the rare forms of delirium tremens that presented with a raised temperature and sometimes proved fatal; other acute symptoms in the alcoholic were relatively easy to manage. For symptoms of acute intoxication, he followed the age-old custom of prescribing emetics, gave ammonia solution in oral preparation or as an enema (*sic*), and recommended coffee in abundance and the application of mustard plasters. Episodes of delirium were treated by the administration of copious fluids, digitalis to maintain cardiac function, purges and enemas for constipation, and regular cold baths. Opinion was divided as to whether sedation in such cases was best induced by opiates, chloral hydrate, hashish or by alcohol itself.

Magnan favoured gradual, rather than abrupt withdrawal from

alcohol and gave his patients a blend of wine and infusions of quassia or gentian. Above all, however, he would admit patients (especially cooks, wine merchants, coachmen and others whose work exposed them to temptation and relapse) so that he could regulate their drinking. To prevent patients doing damage to themselves and to each other, they were obliged to wear special straightjackets, which allowed only limited movements. In the most severe cases, he would recommend cupping to the nape of the neck, a practice barely removed from that of cautery in the Middle Ages and fortunately rarely employed, since the majority of the 'trembling delirious' recovered spontaneously.

Treatment of chronic alcoholic damage to organs and of mental disturbance was far more difficult, as was that of all long-term disease in the late nineteenth century. Physicians drew extensively on the traditional pharmacopoeia in such cases, using, for example, chloral hydrate and bromide as sedatives, and strychnine as a means of reinvigorating the nervous system against polyneuropathy. Magnan made liberal use of wine tonics, which he blended with syrups flavoured with orange peel.

Between 1899 and 1903, a project that used Pasteur's work as a model gave cause for a spark of hope in the fight against alcoholism, a spark which was rapidly extinguished. The experiment was based on the hypothesis that it might be possible to vaccinate against intoxication and that this might prove as effective as vaccination against infectious disease. A horse was accordingly subjected to an alcohol diet and its serum was injected into a second animal, which had been fed in a similar way. It was reported that the serum awakened 'an instinctive defence against, and repulsion for alcohol [which was] induced before a state of dependency had occurred'. The disgust shown by this beast and attributed to the vaccination was probably the result not of a biological reaction against alcohol, but rather of an emotional recoil against the experimenters. Trials in human subjects were inconclusive and the researchers themselves conceded that suggestion probably played an important role in cases where 'immunization' resulted in success. Furthermore, it was clear that 'anti-ethanolic' immunization could only lead to successful results in patients who had hitherto exhibited no sign of visceral or nervous disorder.[64]

Thirty years later, Savy's comprehensive treatise of clinical therapeutics was to contain no separate chapter on alcoholism, and only scant attention was paid to the subject of polyneuropathy.[65] Cirrhosis alone was discussed at length in a tone of absolute pessimism. In reference to the management of alcoholism, the author is of the opinion that, 'irrespective of whether it is taste, illness, heredity, necessity or inclination that has led to a dependence on ethanol ... every possible step must be taken to unlearn the errors of the past'. By this, he means that alcohol in whatever form is to be denied the drinker and that he should, if necessary, be isolated from his normal environment to achieve this. Elsewhere in the work, the combination of cirrhosis and hepatic atrophy is seen to be a terminal complaint, whereas numerous treatments are proposed for oedema and ascites – abdominal drains, diuretics, purges, infusions and liver extracts.

Few other methods of treatment were available in 1950 to Perrin, who had even resorted to intravenous injections of alcohol. Amongst these were the administration of vitamin B_1 (which had recently been discovered and was considered to be the vitamin for nervous disorders), liver extracts to supplement the poor functioning of the cirrhotic liver, and sympathomimetic amines such as benzodine and maxitan to restore nervous function. The latter drugs proved ineffectual in Perrin's patients at Nantes.[66]

Other, more unpleasant regimes proved successful in some cases and accordingly had their advocates amongst doctors. Such regimes involved the use of drugs that induced nausea and vomiting on ingestion of the slightest quantity of alcohol (apomorphine and emetine were used to this end), or that rendered alcohol utterly unpalatable (potassium rhodanate or disulfiram).

Patients who had been hospitalized also received occupational therapy, which not only provided them with something to do, but also helped to restore impaired motor function and stimulated the mind. They were also recommended outdoor activity, saline enemas and mustard footbaths. One regime developed by Kneipp involved the application of warm towels to the large joints for a few days, followed by similar application to the thighs and abdomen, and culminating in a series of frequent baths.

The treatment programmes enumerated in this chapter so far would probably have failed to satisfy most doctors, since they neglected what in the nineteenth century would have been called 'moral', and in the twentieth century 'psychological' aspects of the problem. Encouragement of complete abstinence from alcohol, 'to fight the urge to drink' and 'to develop a moral conscience' was strongly recommended. In their treatise, Triboulet and Mathieu were broadly in agreement with such practice, but went one step further: 'moral advice is often sufficient for the drinker on the slippery slope [to alcoholism; however,] once the stage of alcoholic insanity has been reached, institutionalization is mandatory'.[67] In France, a law passed in 1954 allows for hospitalization 'of patients who represent a danger to themselves and others', thereby facilitating the separation of the drinker from his poison. In the early nineteenth century, Rush proposed the creation of special refuges for drinkers, and the twentieth century has seen the establishment of specialized detoxification units in the United Kingdom, the United States, Germany, Scandinavia and Holland. The French have made no such effort to separate drinkers from other patients with mental disorders.

After the initial period of 'cure', it was further proposed by Navarre in 1898 that patients should be looked after in the protective and watchful environment of 'family colonies', where they would meet former drinking companions in 'temperance cafés and restaurants'.[68] Establishments of this kind had already been created in Britain in the hope of overcoming the problems of maintaining continued abstinence from alcohol. Another French author suggested the creation of 'temperance houses for the people' – a philanthropic, moral and, in France at least, Utopian notion – which would provide the reformed drinker with the opportunity to rest, read, enjoy and educate himself.[69] At a more practical level, however, patients were recommended to join one of the temperance associations.

As is often the case in medicine, when positive cures proved unattainable, doctors turned towards prophylaxis as a second line of attack. The measures introduced since 1850 to prevent patients becoming alcoholics have been social, political and economic, rather than medical in nature. The heterogeneity of these measures demonstrates the growing realization amongst the medical profession that the problems raised by alcoholism extend far beyond its own sphere of influence.

Until the First World War, Western doctors had shown an intense interest in alcoholism and had bombarded their compatriots with literature that was educative and by no means always technical in tone. The French chose to ignore such advice – advice which was taken to heart by other nations. Their reasons for doing so were complex, involving both attitudes within the medical profession and the prevailing social climate.

Doctors are never unanimous on any subject, alcoholism included, and it took many years for them to realize that alcoholism was to be found in all echelons of society and that it put the individual at considerable risk. Furthermore, doctors remained ambivalent to the problem: they belonged to society and shared many commonly held beliefs about alcohol – 'a little of what you fancy doesn't do anyone any harm';

many of their clients worked in the wine trade; and they, like any other member of the general public, have enjoyed the company of heavy drinkers on occasions. Alcoholism was thus a widespread disease, the prevalence and dangers of which were poorly appreciated by society and the medical profession.

Infectious disease, however, was a major preoccupation of both populations and governments at this time. Cholera, typhoid, tuberculosis and measles were real causes for fear during the nineteenth century, not to mention the plague, which resurfaced in the 1890s. The great upsurge of the public health movement was justifiably directed against enemies such as these, as was the spectacularly successful work of Pasteur and other microbiologists. Regrettably, alcoholism was not caused by a particular bacterium, nor could its progress be halted by vaccination.

The French medical profession appears to have lost much of its enthusiasm for the problem of alcoholism after the First World War. There was less discussion at the Académie de Médecine, and fewer articles and letters in the medical journals, in spite of the persistently high incidence of cirrhosis, polyneuropathy and other alcohol-related diseases. Doctors can scarcely have considered the prohibition of absinthe as a conclusive victory over alcohol, since '*anis*' and '*pastis*' were still on the market. It would seem that the decline in their interest in the problem stemmed partly from an increasing and a more generalized lack of interest in French society, and partly from disillusionment at their own failure to treat alcoholism. There were few doctors like Triboulet, who were prepared to declare that 'they [alcoholics] are sick and should be treated like all other patients'. The great majority of doctors, following the rest of society, took refuge in moral condemnation of the unfortunate drinker.

7

Society and Race under Threat

MAN has always sought to understand his environment, but when the answers he seeks are beyond his grasp he turns to divine explanations. Doctors try to adopt a more systematic approach and seek causes, both for reasons of personal satisfaction and professional credibility. Even so, despite the methodological constraints involved, their explanations frequently owe more to prevailing social conditions than to scientific method. This was the case with alcoholism and thus the theory of degeneration came into being.

THE THEORY OF DEGENERATION

Until recently, moral issues influenced all areas of pathological study in Western medicine. In 1857, Morel published his voluminous *Analysis of the Physical, Intellectual and Moral Degeneration of the Human Species.*[1] Some aspects of the title require clarification. In French, the word 'moral' has two senses. Although it was used fifty years earlier by Pinel in a fashion that today would be synonymous with 'psychological', Morel's use of the adjective corresponds to its modern English usage, relating to a person's behaviour with respect to what is widely accepted as the social norm. Morel's preoccupation is not primarily with 'mental' disease; degeneration for him is a process of physical, intellectual and social decline. His book was hugely successful, linking together numerous pathological conditions in what appeared at the time to be the rational concept of degeneration.

Morel trained in the asylums of the Seine and followed in the tradition of Pinel, Esquirol and Royer-Collard, the Parisian school which influenced subsequent generations of doctors and left its mark on modern psychiatry. In 1857, he also published two large volumes of a work treating 'theory and practice in mental illness', and in 1855 he made public a letter he had written to the Archbishop of Chambéry on 'the influence of local conditions on the incidence of cretinism'. In his study of cretinism, Morel followed Villermé, who had already noted that the condition was restricted to certain areas of the Alps.

Morel was already a doctor of some repute when he wrote: 'I believe that many of the patients in our asylums today are simply the representatives of sickly breeds within society; in some cases their condition is beyond redemption. Whatever is at the root of their illness, they all exhibit, in greater or lesser degree, the marks of a degenerative state which, in most cases, is the long-term product of the formidable influence of hereditary predisposition'.[2] In the preface to his *Analysis*, he states, 'degeneration can only occur under an unhealthy influence, whether physical or moral'. He goes on: 'In the human species, degeneration is a pathological deviation of a primitive type... In my opinion, degeneration and pathological deviation from the human norm are one and the same thing.'[3] At the time, the doctrines of Lamarck were in vogue and Morel presented his findings within the framework they provided: the degenerate was a regressive example of the human species. In the years that followed, other doctors identified themselves with Darwinism and thus placed themselves in the paradoxical position of condemning patients to death purely because their 'degenerate condition' ruled out adaptation.[4] Although Morel's book was full of bold assertions, he showed some reluctance to provide exact definitions. Degeneration can be the result of alcoholism, but it may also be its cause. This lack of clarity encouraged other doctors to discover the signs of degeneration everywhere, and physical traits took on diagnostic significance in their eyes; low forehead, diminutive stature, asymmetry of the ears or attachment of the lobes were seen as proof of the condition, as were dental decay and masturbation in the young.[5]

In France, the word 'degenerate' entered common usage, and this was soon followed by other medical expressions such as *avarié*, meaning rotten, which was later reserved for those suffering from venereal disease.[6] A new group of people were identified wandering the streets, *tarés* (defectives), and the word came to describe those of bizarre appearance as well as cheats, swindlers and the immoral – the adjective combined physical ugliness with a moral or social judgement. The educated classes of the day took particular interest in medical matters, and degeneration came to figure as a theme in literature, appearing in the writings of Flaubert, Sainte-Beuve, Renan, About, Gautier, de Maupassant, the Goncourts and Dumas fils; Zola's Rougon-Macquart novels are based on the theory, and one author, Léon Daudet, was inspired to describe his own degeneracy in a novel entitled *L'Hérédo*.[7]

Where Morel, following Lamarck, wrote 'species', the general public understood 'race'. New discoveries made by explorers and conquering colonial armies in far-flung corners of the globe were used to demonstrate the superiority of the white race. Encounters with strange peoples who appeared to exhibit all the symptoms of degeneracy served to confirm that the 'whites' alone were capable of maintaining the integrity of their race. For a century, degeneration was the universal explanation of human misfortune. This sentiment still had echoes in the 1930s, when Jules Romains composed his poem, *Homme Blanc* (White Man), in which the anti-hero resigns himself to drink, thereby betraying his racial superiority and degenerating to the level of the 'lower races'.

Morel's first chapter deals with degeneracy caused by intoxicants. Under this rubric, he includes the 'illness known under the name of chronic alcoholism'. Paying tribute to Huss's work, which had then only been known in France for five years, Morel provides a wide-ranging historical review in which he detects signs of alcoholism in both writings from the ancient world (in Seneca, for example) and the reports of nineteenth-century missionaries working in south-east Asia. He concludes: 'The misery and degeneration observed within populations is directly related to excessive use of spirits.'[8] Morel's preoccupations were those of doctor and moralist; his concern was with the mental and physical welfare of his patients and with problems of social order (the term 'sociologist' did not exist at that time). 'Dangerous occupations, alcoholic excesses, and the decline of morals linked to climatic influences[9] all give rise to signs of degeneration – stunting of the race, weakening of intellectual faculties and general depravity. Affected individuals are to be found in factories,[10] hospices, slums, mental asylums, prisons and reformatories.'

Magnan was the first to apply the general concept of degeneration to alcoholism. Like Morel twenty years before him, he worked in the asylums of the Seine, where he specialized in the treatment of heavy drinkers. Among his many students was Legrain, whose later work was also influential. Magnan believed that many of his patients had become *tarés* (defectives) through excessive alcohol consumption, but his real innovation was to propose a special category of individual 'predisposed' to the condition. Although in other respects the book he wrote in 1874[11] bore the stamp of ideas then influential in the treatment of the insane,[12] he argued that certain patients' overwhelming desire to drink was the product of parental degeneration: 'The inferior cerebral capacity of these patients is inherited.'[13] Observation of patients with family histories of alcoholism, tuberculosis, suicide or madness served to confirm these beliefs. In relation to contemporary understanding of heredity, the examples given by Magnan do not support his assertions, but he did have the merit of attempting to explain why it was that some people were more prone to alcohol abuse than others. For many years alcoholism was linked, either as cause or effect, to the vague concept of degeneration; the relationship was argued by Legrain in 1886 in his thesis on alcoholic insanity, and in 1895 he published a work on degenerates in conjunction with Magnan.[14] In 1902, Dromard proposed that dipsomania was caused by 'a persistent background of mental degeneration.'[15]

Although the concept of degeneration was supported widely by the medical establishment and among the general public, there were nevertheless dissenters who argued that the issue was far from proven. They also pointed out that, should the condition exist, it was not amenable to treatment. With some regret, Magnan and Legrain wrote: 'Despite the rigorous scientific method employed by Morel to enrich the nosography of degenerative states and hereditary insanity, there are still those who disagree. The validity of degeneration is denied by some ... and the creation of a class of degenerates is the object of fierce debate.'[16] It nevertheless remained common practice to classify alcoholics as degenerate and list alcohol as one of the causes of degeneration. For teaching purposes, the two remained linked and as recently as the Second World War, Alexis Carrel listed alcoholism among the degeneracies to be guarded against in the families of potential in-laws.

MORAL DECLINE

Western society in the nineteenth and twentieth centuries would in all probability have come to terms with alcoholism, had it been a disease like any other. Although doctors had no cure for cirrhosis or the mental disturbances observed in heavy drinkers, this was also the case with other diseases and was generally accepted. Alcoholism, however, was more than just a medical condition.

Alcoholics behaved in ways that threatened public morals and their violence, whether directed against themselves or inflicted upon others, had been recognized for millennia. Soon, however, all forms of criminality came to be regarded as products of alcoholism. Drinking establishments were accordingly singled out as responsible and the number of violent crimes in a town or region was compared with the number of *cabarets* – a relationship considered to be mathematical.[17] Famous people put their weight behind these arguments and it was the fight against crime, rather than compassion, which motivated Georges Clémenceau to write the preface for a book by Jacquet that dealt with such relationships.[18] Studies showed that the incidence of homicides and brawls was greatest during holidays, when bars were open. (In Massachusetts, it was estimated that of 600 young offenders in prison, two-thirds came from families in which at least one member was an alcoholic.) More carefully compiled statistics that are now available do not support the view that alcohol is responsible for all crime. At the time, however, those expressing doubt formed a minority.

Sexual offences were also largely attributed to alcoholism. Under this heading were ranged all forms of behaviour deemed morally reprehensible – affronts to honour, rape, incest, prostitution and divorce. Popular anecdotes indicate the belief that alcoholism and immorality were both hereditary and interchangeable: a woman could fall into prostitution as a result of her father's alcoholism, and her children were likely to suffer as a result of her own misdemeanours.

Alcohol endangers the entire social fabric; the ways in which alcoholics behave throw authority into question and undermine the very basis of society, property. Doctors were not interested in alcoholism solely for medical reasons and their attitudes mirrored the concerns of the class from which they came. The physical and mental degradation of the drinker was nothing compared to the threat posed to bourgeois society by a united band of alcoholics. Here, again, the influence of Morel is clear. In 1857, he had written of the 'effects of ignorance and absence of religion on moral and physical degeneration in the human species'.[19] Alcoholism was corrupting Western society. At the turn of the century members of scientific academies and learned societies debated the moral decline they detected around them and related it to drink; idleness, debauchery and selfishness were becoming widespread and social order was collapsing.[20] Legrain published two books dealing explicitly with these themes: *Dégénérescence Sociale et Alcoolisme* (Social Degeneration and Alcoholism) (1895) and *Un Fléau Social: 'L'alcoolisme'* (Alcoholism: A Social Curse) (1896).

In the last decades of the nineteenth century opium enjoyed a brief vogue. Although some doctors spoke out against all forms of intoxicant, it became common in certain literary circles to praise the 'artificial paradises' (the expression belongs to Baudelaire) induced by opium and hashish. Writers were far less inhibited in describing their experiences with these drugs than they had ever been with alcohol, but, although abuse of such intoxicants was never widespread, their addictive properties and the decadent life-styles of those who took them caused them to be associated with drink.[21]

Nineteenth-century France, a country enamoured with order, was deeply shocked by the events of the Paris Commune in May 1871. A

curious juxtaposition was established between revolution and alcoholism, and the fears of the former exacerbated those of the latter. The
repression that followed the popular uprising had largely abated when
Laborde, another asylum doctor, wrote:

Alcohol was everywhere in those fatal times. It was an armed spectre on the
streets and ramparts of the city, near the barracks, in the avenues and
devastated gardens of the suburbs; enthroned in the palace it soiled the
churches, bustled and shouted at public meetings and staggered along under a
filthy tunic, a rifle on its shoulder, belching out fragments of the *Marseillaise*.[22]

The parliamentary inquiry of 1871 had already tried to attribute the
events of the Commune to the effects of wine and eau-de-vie, and similar
reasoning was to appear elsewhere.[23] Linas remarked of the time: 'It
was an example of collective madness ... people driven by a savage fury
to epilepsy and alcoholism were satisfied only with blood, carnage and
destruction.' Lunier maintained that: 'If their profession did not forbid
them to do so, doctors working in the asylums would be able to reveal
that startling numbers of their former patients were among the soldiers
and leaders of the uprising.' In 1872, Maxime du Camp wrote: 'the
Commune was an act of alcoholic pyromania' and, fifteen years later,
Druhen commented in similar vein: 'The bloody orgy called the Commune was no more than an eruption of alcoholism.' Such remarks
abounded at the time.

The explanation offered by Zola in 1892, in his novel *La Débâcle*, is
more enlightened: 'the epidemic of drunkenness spread with the first
siege and was aggravated by the second. With only barrels of wine and
eau-de-vie to sustain them the starving people drank, and from the first
drop they were delirious.' [24] It is possible that there was heavy drinking
in the besieged Paris of spring 1871. Indeed, the *Journal Officiel de la
Commune* (Official Journal of the Commune) includes both a dialogue
between two young recruits who hesitate to join a unit of soldiers who
drink too much and a description of the trial of a unit leader accused of
drunkenness. In times of upheaval, however, such behaviour is frequently
exaggerated and this is probably true for the Commune. Those accusing
the Communards of alcoholic depravity did not do so to plea for
extenuating circumstances; on the contrary, their descriptions served to
justify the severe repressive steps taken against them. Their criticism also
served to confirm the assumption commonly held during the Third
Republic that alcoholism was a working-class problem, likely to provoke behaviour similar to that of the Commune. Since the proletariat,
drunkenness and revolution were seen to be inextricably linked, the

working classes had to be controlled in the interest of society as a whole.

Various attitudes towards alcoholism were reflected in Western literature of the period.[25] Zola incorporates many of the misfortunes that might befall the alcoholic in *L'Assommoir*, which was published in 1877. As a result of his addiction to drink, the main character, Coupeau, allows a friend to sleep with his wife, Gervaise. Following the incident the couple split up and Coupeau dies a lonely death in an asylum, while Gervaise takes to prostitution and drink before her own miserable demise. Zola's real intention was to depict working-class life rather than the ravages of alcoholism. The character of Coupeau is poorly developed; a roofer, handicapped by an accident at work, he is capricious and lazy, working only when he feels like it and spending the pittance he earns at the *cabaret*. No clue is provided as to why Coupeau drinks; in Zola's brand of naturalism, the medical doctrines to which he subscribes are embodied by characters who are largely two-dimensional.

Hardly surprisingly, this portrait was not well received in working-class circles. However, the novel and the play based upon it were successful, demonstrating that the themes broached by Zola corresponded with the educated public's views on alcoholism. The comments of Charles Richet bear this out: 'In Zola's *L'Assommoir* the effects and dangers of alcohol are described in detail and expressed in all their cynical horror: misery, prostitution, debauchery and crime are the fatal consequences of alcoholism and drunkenness. Were it not for the talent of the author the crudity of language employed would have led to the book being branded immoral.'[26]

Dostoevsky's novels are packed with drunken scenes set in hotels and drinking dens where vodka and wine flow freely. The characters come from a variety of social backgrounds, and the drunks are generally described sympathetically as whimsical, gullible and generous – Micha Karamazov, for example. The portrayal of Marmeladov in *Crime and Punishment*, however, is more complex; garrulous and excitable, his moods alternate between pride and remorse, and guilt drives him to self-chastisement for faults he imagines to be his own. When he speaks of Christ's forgiveness for drunks, he combines Russian evangelism with the emotional lability of an alcoholic. In *The Brothers Karamazov* (1879–80), Smerdiakov fits very closely the stereotype of the 'degenerate'. He is the illegitimate son of a lewd and drunken country squire who seduces a simple-minded woman known as the 'stinker' (whence Smerdiakov); he combines epilepsy, deceitfulness, vanity, depravity and jealousy with murder.

The message Dostoevsky addresses to the Russian people is placed in the mouth of the old *staretz* Zossine: 'Drunkenness has made the people rotten and incapable of renouncing their vice; drink leads to cruel abuse of women and children. In factories I've seen nine-year-old children bent-double, debauchery engrained on their frail bodies; a suffocating room, the noise of machines, incessant work, obscene talk and spirits, always spirits.'[27] It is hard to say to what extent such writing was based on personal experience. Dostoevsky was an epileptic and certainly never drank. However, he was a gambler (and must have relied on this in writing his novel of that name) and, although his debts forced him to leave Russia, they did not prevent him losing money in casinos all over Europe. Gambling is in many ways analogous to alcoholism. Like the alcoholic, the gambler loves risk, exposing himself and his family to possible destitution; he lacks self-control and pays no heed to the advice of friends. Confronted by repeated failure, each new hand is a fresh challenge, a possible redemption, but his game with destiny may end in suicide.

In 1883, Pierre Loti's novel *Mon Frère Yves* (My Brother Yves) was published. Loti was a refined naval officer and had smoked opium in the Far East; he was also a homosexual. The book has no great literary merit, but is of interest to the historian because extracts were used for many years in school textbooks and popular almanacs as propaganda against alcoholism; it was in fact only dropped from the school curriculum in 1968. This moral tale set in the navy portrays drunkenness among ordinary ratings from peasant and working-class backgrounds, and supposes officers, the class to which Loti himself belonged, to be free of the vice. It also ascribes to another popular wisdom of the day: namely, that every individual is subject to the influence of hereditary vice, an influence that can be overcome by resolve and will power. Yves, the hero, is the son of an alcoholic. His brothers and sisters all die at an early age; one brother, like their father, dies of drink. Yves joins the navy, but finds it impossible to resist the temptations of drinking in port with his friends. He gets drunk, assaults his superior officers and is thrown in the brig. At sea he is the best of sailors and gains promotion, conditional on future sobriety. Fearful for the future of his children, who might inherit his alcoholic tendencies, he decides to stop drinking and guarantee the happiness of his family.[28]

In Scandinavian literature, similar themes emerge. In Ibsen's *Ghosts* (1881), Oswald is the victim of paternal drunkenness and debauchery. In the prevailing Lutheran environment such degeneracy, as he remarks to his mother, is irredeemable. The Swedish writer Lagerlöf stands out from her contemporaries in that she asks questions about why people drink. She is also less pessimistic than Ibsen in her novel *The Legend of Gösta Berling* (1891). Drinkers are treated more sympathetically and are capable of generosity, humour and selflessness, and the naive young pastor Berling is provided with extenuating circumstances for his drinking. He arrives in the 1820s in a rural northern parish to find that everybody drinks – in winter spirits ward off the cold and in summer they are refreshing. The peasants never stop drinking, so why should the pastor deny himself an occasional glass?[29] Lagerlöf's interest was not specifically historical, but she did rely on authentic documents and memoirs of the period; the atmosphere she describes was one with which the young Huss would have been familiar on his father's farm and it explains Swedish concern with alcohol-related matters. Other works by the same author were more severe in their judgement: drinkers are seen as indecisive, weak, conceited and odious, and her characters were seized upon by the powerful Swedish temperance societies of the day for propaganda.

Whatever their intentions, the above authors share a common message: alcoholics are responsible for their actions and threaten social order. Viewed within this framework, the moral problems raised can only be remedied by social means. Doctors with long experience of alcoholism also reasoned in moral terms and a multitude of preventative programmes were proposed at all levels, from the Académie de Médecine down to popular almanacs. The measures put forward, however, were addressed at disadvantaged members of society and included the promotion of moral awareness and civic responsibility; improvement of workers' accommodation and wages; instruction of women in household management (a good and thrifty housekeeper is more likely to keep her man at home); cultivation of a respect for work, property and family values; increases in sentences for illegal trading in alcohol and public drunkenness; isolation of alcoholics against their will in order to break their dependence; and the funding of temperance houses.

All perspectives – pious, utopian and realist – are represented in these suggestions, the relative merits of which are still disputed in the late twentieth century. Some saw an answer in better household economy and this was reflected in the development of savings banks and friendly societies. Others emphasized the role of the family, which is always a popular recourse in times of social and political crisis. Others, still, reasoned that poverty was responsible for alcoholism and attempted to raise the standard of living of the working population; fiscal measures were introduced to discourage the purchase of alcohol and as a means of increasing state revenues.

1 Copy of Egyptian wall painting depicting wine industry

2 Attic black figure: Dionysus dancing with satyrs and nymphs. Ascribed to potter Amasis and the Amasis painter. Third quarter of 6th century

3   A 16th-century distillery

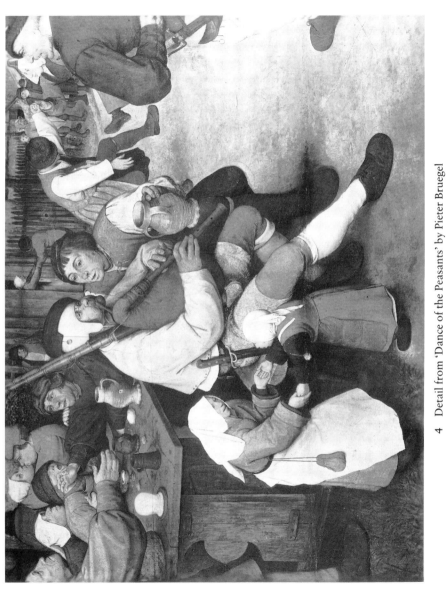

4   Detail from 'Dance of the Peasants' by Pieter Bruegel

5 'The Effects of Intemperance' by Jan Steen. This painting contains warnings against the evils of alcohol. The slumped woman on the left illustrates the saying 'Wine is a mocker', and the boy on her right the proverb 'He throws roses before swine' 1662–3

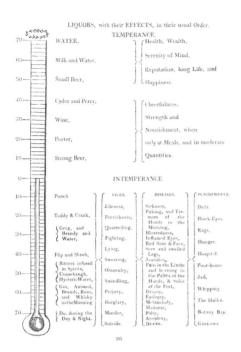

6 Lettsom's Moral and Physical Thermometer: John Coakley Lettsom (1744–1815)

7 Henry Fielding (1707–1754)

8   'Beer Street' by William Hogarth from large engraving 1751
edition in the Mansell Collection

GIN LANE.

Gin cursed Fiend, with Fury fraught,
Makes human Race a Prey;
It enters by a deadly Draught,
And steals our Life away.

Virtue and Truth, driv'n to Despair,
Its Rage compells to fly,
But cherishes with hellish Care,
Theft, Murder, Perjury.

Damn'd Cup! that on the Vitals preys,
That liquid Fire contains,
Which Madness to the Heart conveys,
And rolls it thro' the Veins.

9 'Gin Lane' by William Hogarth from large engraving 1751
edition in the Mansell Collection

10 'The Gin Shop', a drawing by Thomas Rowlandson

11 John Wesley (1703–1791) the founder of Methodism

12 Charles Wesley (1707–1788)

13   'The Gin Shop' by George Cruikshank, from a coloured engraving
in The Mansell Collection, dated 1 November 1829

14 The Bottle: cold, misery and want destroy their youngest child: they console themselves with the bottle. From a series of eight prints by George Cruikshank, 1847

15   George Cruikshank (1792–1878)

16 National Temperance Festival at the Crystal Palace

17   Benjamin Rush (1745–1813)

18 Nineteen-thirties Prohibition in United States of America

Fortunately, not all doctors adopted a moralizing tone towards alcoholics, and it was the view of many that these unfortunates were neither perverts nor delinquents, but patients who should be treated as such, in hospitals, not in prisons or asylums.[30]

THE DESTRUCTION OF THE RACE

Certain moralists maintained that in some cases alcoholics were the victims of parental addiction. This line of argument, which occupied thinkers in many countries, has considerable consequences; not only does the heavy drinker do himself harm, but he also affects the lives of his descendants and therefore endangers the future of his race. In 1794, Erasmus Darwin, grandfather of Charles, wrote that all illness caused by drinking was hereditary and that even with total abstinence its effects might be felt over three or four generations.[31] Morel's work on degeneration had the effect of transforming such hypotheses into certainties.

Triboulet and Mathieu argued that the children of alcoholics had less resistance to alcohol and displayed symptoms of nervousness and neurosis, in time becoming heavy drinkers.[32] In Legrain's view, their bad character led them at an early age to prostitution, dishonesty, insubordination, theft, cheating and vagrancy, while their brutal tendencies involved them in fights and culminated in murder or suicide. He also maintained that such hereditary tendencies might extend through three generations. Medical wisdom held that degeneration was not necessarily passed on directly; it might skip a generation – the drinking of a grandfather might reappear in his grandson. Students were taught to be on their guard for such occurrences and to study the family trees of their patients.

Hereditary alcoholic degeneration did not only produce mental symptoms. Navarre, in 1898, was moved to observe:

Our soldiers are the descendants of the giants who fought the wars of the Republic and Empire and yet from decade to decade they get smaller and smaller. There have never been so many invalids before the military review boards as during the second half of this century. The most frequent reasons given for exemption are poor health, rickets and tuberculosis, the result primarily of hereditary alcoholism.

He concludes: 'This glorious nineteenth century is the century of alcohol.'[33] These remarks represent an anti-alcoholic fantasy, aggravated by worries concerning the declining power of the French army, and bear no relation to anthropological reality. Long-term studies demonstrate that the average size of young men presenting before the review boards increased steadily throughout the nineteenth century. Illiterate recruits, mainly manual workers and peasants, did indeed show some reduction.[34] This finding, however, does not justify the ill-founded views of the day (the physical consequences of a lack of education have nothing to do with 'degeneration', as it was understood).

Fifteen years after the appearance of his first book in 1857, Morel found further evidence among the imprisoned children of the Communards to support his theories:

During a recent visit to Rouen prison I was able to assess the mental condition of one hundred and fifty children aged between ten and seventeen years old... The examination confirmed my theories on the harmful influence of alcohol, not only among those who drink to excess, but also in their children. These precocious assassins and arsonists are the true sons of their fathers and their depraved physiognomy bears the triple imprint of physical, mental and intellectual degeneration. They are unattractive and at times repulsive, their heads have no symmetry or harmony and their height is below average. There were barely ten children in the group who were pleasant to look at. Boys of seventeen looked like fourteen-year-olds and those of fourteen would only with difficulty be taken for ten-year-olds.[35]

Ignoring the moral tenor of his remarks, some of Morel's findings – restricted growth, for example – were indeed correct, but he would have been nearer the truth had he attributed them to poor diet, hygiene and the effects of manual labour, to which children were subjected during the Second Empire.

The doctrine of hereditary degeneration in the children of alcoholics became dogma and many books were written on the subject.[36] Apart from the obvious signs of their condition, the ability of these children to procreate was also judged to be impaired and this gave rise to another popular myth: alcoholism was responsible for depopulation. Legrain stated that the frequency of still-births and rates of infant mortality were highest in the families of alcoholics. The combined curses of syphilis, alcoholism and tuberculosis were putting the entire race in peril.[37]

Not all doctors, however, agreed with such apocalyptic interpretations of the statistics. In 1894, Lannelongue observed that in the *département* of Gers, which had a pure alcohol consumption of 0.164 gallons (0.78 litres) per inhabitant annually, there was a low birth rate; in contrast, the Lower Seine, with consumption in some cantons as high as 8.5 gallons (39 litres), had a high birth rate.[38] Lucien Mayet examined the demographic question with a critical eye and, although he found a relative drop in the growth rate of the French population, he saw no serious statistical reason to attribute this to alcoholism.[39] Despite this and similar opposition, the ideas became firmly fixed in popular consciousness. At the Académie de Médecine, Reynier described the Bretons as a dying race because of their long attachment to alcohol; his vision even extended to the French nation as a whole.[40] These dangers were not restricted to the French alone. Richet applied the same principles in order to excuse 'peoples who have been reduced to servitude or forced to emigrate in order to survive; they are rarely sober, they drink to forget their woes. The Irish and the Poles fall into this category and of all European peoples they are the most highly given to drink.'[41] His views were shared elsewhere. In England, Erasmus Darwin's remarks served as an inspiration to the anti-alcohol leagues, and in Germany doctors were investigating the effects of alcohol on children.[42] In the United States, a report put before the state legislature of Massachusetts indicated that 145 out of the 600 idiots in state care had been born to alcoholic parents.

In countries where population growth was in large part the result of immigration, the theory of degeneration was used to justify policies of selective admission, a procedure that could never be anything but subjective. In Canada, the major concern for the government of the day was the long-term impact of unrestricted immigration; there was fear that the country would be flooded with people unable to support themselves, who would place a serious financial burden on the provinces.[43] Strict immigration controls were introduced. Immigrants who showed signs of alcoholism during their Atlantic crossing were sent home, and habitual drinkers, even after a stay of two years, were liable to be expelled from the country. In 1905, the *Canada Lancet* took an even more extreme line, arguing that degenerate classes – criminals, epileptics, drunks and the feeble-minded – should be prevented from having children, who would undoubtedly prove a burden to the nation.

Governments and doctors of the Western world viewed alcoholism as a blight whose influence extended over several generations. The pitiless Legrain left no room for hope for the unfortunates: 'There are defects in the ancestry of the alcoholic that are magnified in his descendants. Degenerates create drinkers and drinkers create degenerates – a vicious circle maintained by alcohol.'

THE NATION IN DANGER

The climate of revenge that existed in France following the humiliation of the Franco-Prussian war gave the case against alcohol an additional dimension, and some authors attempted to blame the defeat of 1870 entirely on alcoholism. Others, such as Barella, remarked that alcoholism was certainly partially responsible, but they went no further.[44] Bergeron's position, stated at the Académie de Médecine, was clearer, if understated. He suggested that at the beginning of the campaign 'the troops had taken too great an advantage of the populace's eagerness to provide them with wines and spirits'; all in all, it cannot be denied that their resistance to invasion was minimal and their retreat disorderly. Discussing the two sieges of Paris, he concludes: 'Our misfortunes would not have been so great had a part of the population not been inveterate drinkers.'[45]

It is not known whether the French troops drank more than the Prussians and Bavarians. Nevertheless, during the Commune it seems likely that drunkenness was as widespread among the victorious Versaillais forces as among the exhausted Communards. A doctor from Dinan described the triumphant liberation of the city:

When the troops re-entered Paris we witnessed with our own eyes the drunkenness rife in the army. Troops of all descriptions entered the city in an appalling condition; dirty, ragged, drunk and in disarray. Deprivation and exhaustion undoubtedly contributed to their condition, but alcohol was largely responsible. Officers were powerless to impose order on the crush of men, horses, crates and carriages passing through the streets.[46]

Few doctors in the late nineteenth century subscribed to the popular view that alcohol was a source of strength and an aid to the war effort, and many were highly critical of the ways in which army life propagated alcoholism among those 'predisposed' to it.[47] Cases of young recruits being driven to drink by the tedium of barrack life were frequently observed and are cited by Magnan and Legrain: a carpenter who enlisted in the African army and soon became a regular drinker; a soldier who started drinking heavily at the age of 23 in Algeria; another, who drank for the first time in the army, developed symptoms of trembling and vomiting prior to Sebastopol and whose condition deteriorated considerably after Magenta. Strong drink, however, was regarded as a protection against fever. The French consumed enormous quantities of anisette in Africa and Asia during the colonial era and the same was true of the British in India; as early as 1834, generals, in an attempt to combat drunkenness, had asked for the obligatory daily alcohol ration to be replaced by a sum of money.[48] The drinking habits of the colonizers were imitated by the indigenous populations, who developed dangerously high levels of consumption. German maritime expansion contributed considerably to increasing world-wide demand for alcohol, and in 1893 the port of Hamburg exported over six million gallons of distilled drink to Black Africa alone.

Alcoholism in the French land forces was seen as a threat to national strength and caused greater concern than drinking in the navy (in France, defence of land frontiers has always been given greater priority than guarding the coast) or in vital industries, such as mining or road-building. The weakening of military contingents stationed in *départements* that produced large quantities of grain alcohol was seen as a particular threat by the Count of Colbert-Laplace.[49]

The problem of depopulation was frequently couched within this military context. In 1893, Debove noted: 'The population will double in Germany in 98 years, in Sweden in 82 years, in Denmark in 73 years, in England in 63 years, in Austria in 62 years and in Norway in 51 years. In France, however, we will have to wait 334 years for this to happen.' The conclusion of his article was that steps should be taken to reduce the strength of French wines, thereby decreasing the country's alcohol consumption. Debove's underlying fear, however, was the blatant military inferiority of the French army compared with the might of the German army, an imbalance in both number and quality that he ascribed to alcoholism.[50] The military command was evidently aware of these dangers because several attempts were made to control alcohol in barracks and canteens, but as wine made up part of the soldier's daily ration, ways were always found to circumvent new regulations.

The First World War highlighted the inherent contradictions in Western governmental policies towards alcohol. In areas of France outside the combat zones, absinthe and certain other liquors were temporarily banned, and the number of bars and taverns decreased, largely through a lack of tenants. At the front, on the other hand, both wine and rum were freely dispensed with a view to inspiring courage, damping down ill-feeling and preventing revolt.

For many years after the First World War, the French celebrated the virtues of the *pinard de la victoire* (victory tipple) in song, and the *quart du soldat* (soldier's cup) came to symbolize all the gestures of goodwill that had contributed to the patience and endurance of the *poilu* (a term roughly equivalent to the English 'Tommy'). During the Second World War, alcoholism in the French army was no more suppressed than it had been during the First; the period of waiting between September 1939 and May 1940 was spent drinking and playing cards, rather than training. In institutions such as the army, activities like drinking are simply a distorted reflection of behaviour in the society outside. Doubtless alcoholism will continue to plague all armies throughout the world, as it does the countries they serve, and the exact extent to which it does so will remain a well-guarded secret.

Moral condemnation in the military goes beyond the question of discipline and order, and where national security is threatened, alcoholism borders on treason. In extending such reasoning, many countries have come to view alcoholism as essentially anti-patriotic. In the United States, the War of Independence gave the adjective 'republican' a specific meaning synonymous with patriotic. Since the drinker was a slave to alcohol, his addiction interfered with patriotism – a true Republican did not drink.

THE END OF THE 'DEGENERATES'

The survival of an idea depends on how deeply rooted it becomes in the public consciousness and is related to social, economic and political events. The theory of degeneration endured in some circles for a century. Its racist aspects, the alleged superiority of some races over others, made it especially popular among thinkers of the right. In Germany, in 1933, one of the first eugenics laws passed by the Third Reich considered 'hereditary alcoholism' a cause for obligatory sterilization. During the 1920s it was common to interpret history in terms of degeneration. The theory was used with equal felicity to explain the fall of the Roman Empire or the demise of the alcoholic Merovingians in France.[51] A medical thesis written by Lipsky in 1927 went as far as to treat Dostoevsky's *The Brothers Karamazov* as if it were the case history of a family afflicted with hereditary alcoholism.[52] Scientists tried to find a mechanism at the chromasomal level and amongst these d'Heucqueville claimed to have found a Mendelian explanation for hereditary forms of alcoholism, syphilis and tuberculosis.[53]

By the 1950s the theory had disappeared from medical usage – a demise precipitated by its inherent failings and the racist ends to which it had been used. Terms such as 'defective' had also been dropped, and any medical condition transmitted from generation to generation was now referred to by name, with those affected being known as carriers. From time to time, however, elements of the doctrine resurface. In 1952, Professor Lamache of the Faculty of Medicine at Rennes was still able to propose genetic links between dementia praecox and chronic alcoholism at the Académie de Médecine; he claimed a statistical relationship between alcoholic parents and infantile deformity.[54] In 1960, Herzlich and Pierret noted the high incidence of 'alcoholic degenerates' amongst the grandchildren of alcoholics.[55] Similarly, the slogan used in French anti-alcohol propaganda of the same era – 'The children of drinkers become boozers' – is a product of doctrines taught in the pre-1939 period.

Although the term 'degenerate' is no longer used, the hereditary consequences of parental alcoholism are still under study, albeit on a more precise epidemiological basis. Eberle's work of 1833 demonstrated curious cranio-facial deformities in alcoholic women, a fact confirmed by modern scientific methods.[56] In 1968, Lemoine and his colleagues drew attention for the first time in the contemporary period to physical abnormalities in the new-born: excessively domed foreheads, flattened eyebrow arches, a short, trumpet-shaped nose with a collapsed base, a retracted upper lip, ears with detached lobes asymmetrically positioned on the head. The same babies also exhibited a high incidence of visual, cardiac and skeletal deformities and were consistently underweight.[57] From a large sample, the 127 babies exhibiting these features had mothers with a history of chronic alcohol abuse. These physical anomalies are far more precise than the various subjective 'behavioural difficulties' observed by Lemoine's predecessors, but these same children also showed evidence of psycho-motor difficulties. The study, it should be noted, was conducted in the Loire-Atlantic *département*, a region that has always had high levels of alcoholic cirrhosis.

Lemoine's research has since been confirmed on many occasions, notably by Jones, who described the 'foetal alcohol syndrome'.[58] Distinctions between hereditary and congenital factors, which inevitably escaped our predecessors, have become much clearer. The existence of alcohol-related pathological conditions of the embryo and foetus can no longer be denied, although the exact mechanism whereby ethanol affects embryogenesis remains uncertain.[59] The children of mothers who drink to excess during pregnancy can be affected by deformities which appear at birth as congenital defects, but which are not hereditary, since they are not genetic in origin. Such children are incapable of transmitting their deformity to future generations. Contrary to popular belief, nothing is known about the relation between paternal alcoholism and infantile deformity. Nor is it yet clear whether pregnancy alters the metabolism of alcohol within the body. It is possible, but as yet unproven, that the susceptibility of certain body tissues to alcohol is genetically predetermined and therefore truly hereditary.

Degeneration and its pejorative moral overtones may have been largely banished from the medical domain, but they live on elsewhere. Doctors may have stopped blaming alcoholics for their condition, but the world at large has not. The alcoholic remains a target for moral and social condemnation, which inevitably interferes with his or her humane treatment.

8

Virtue in Action

A threat to Western society as grave as alcoholism inevitably provoked reaction and the last years of the eighteenth century saw the formation of the first anti-alcohol groups. The need to fight against drink became as important as the struggle against poverty, tuberculosis and cancer. Alcoholism, however, has not always been regarded as an ordinary illness. In certain quarters it was seen as a form of evil spread on earth by irreligious forces – to do battle with it was to wage a holy war, a crusade, and some temperance societies even adopted the emblem of the cross or modelled themselves upon holy orders of knights from the Middle Ages, in the struggle against this demonic power that was set on destroying humanity.

TEMPERANCE SOCIETIES IN FRANCE[1]

Even with a clear perception of the damage caused by excessive alcohol consumption, the French did not form voluntary organizations until fifty years after the English. At the Académie de Médecine in 1872, Bergeron announced the foundation of the *Association contre l'abus des boissons alcooliques* (Association Against the Abuse of Alcoholic Drinks).[2] Among its first supporters were important figures such as Taine, Louis Pasteur, the chemist Jean-Baptiste Dumas, several asylum doctors, including Lunier and Magnan, Baron Haussmann and many others.[3] The foundation of the organization was favoured by legislation passed in 1871, which had caused a stir in medical circles. In voting new regulations controlling alcohol sales, the government followed the initiative of a doctor from Lozère, Théophile Roussel, who during his forty-year career in parliament championed family and child welfare. Elected to the Académie de Médecine in 1872, he was among the most active of its members in pioneering the cause of public health in the Third Republic.

It was noted at the Académie that a French society against the abuse of tobacco and alcoholic drinks was already in existence.[4] Formed by military doctors garrisoned in Algeria, who had grown alarmed as a result of tobacco and alcohol abuse amongst the troops, this small organization concerned itself largely with tobacco. Despite its lack of famous sponsors, the society produced a number of publications and was successful in drawing the attention of public health workers to the combined dangers of tobacco and alcohol. In the Académie itself, interest focused more on alcohol and tobacco was largely neglected until the 1970s, when statistical studies firmly established the damaging synergistic effects of tobacco and alcohol on the human body.[5]

In 1873, the French Association Against the Abuse of Alcoholic Drinks became the *Société française de tempérance* (French Temperance Society), which was largely made up of doctors and intellectuals directing their efforts at the educated classes. Under the influence of Lunier, its general-secretary until 1885, it waged a tireless campaign: a bulletin, *Tempérance*, was published three times a year; manuals and memoirs were promoted; scientific research was encouraged; and prizes were awarded.[6] In 1873, a new bill on public drunkenness, sponsored by Roussel, was introduced. Organizations that directed their message at society as a whole were soon to emerge: in 1883, the French Blue Cross, a branch of the Swiss society founded in 1877 by Pastor Rochat, was formed; in 1894, Legrain founded the *Société contre l'usage des boissons spiritueuses* (Society for the Abolition of Spirits), which was to become the *Société française antialcoolique* (French Anti-alcohol Union) in 1896. This organization was set up to oppose the elitist tendencies of the French Temperance Society and it united numerous small regional groups; subscriptions were low and efforts were geared towards the poor.

Public awareness of the dangers of alcoholism gradually increased. Zola's *L'Assommoir* was a great success and in 1885 an international congress was held at Anvers, where the expression 'anti-alcoholic' was used for the first time. In 1905, the French Temperance Society and the French Anti-alcohol Union agreed to combine their meagre resources and merged to form the *Ligue nationale contre l'alcoolisme* (National League Against Alcoholism), which widened their influence, but also led to compromise over strategy. The statutes of the French Temperance Society allowed consumption of fermented drink, but other groups were more radical in outlook, often requiring total abstinence. This difference of opinion led to friction between anti-alcohol groups, which affected the treatment provided and, at governmental level, resulted in contradictory regulations. In its wisdom, however, the new organization came to accept that the French people were not ready to abandon alcohol entirely. The fusion of the groups gave the anti-alcohol movement a new lease of life and it began to make new converts.

At the national anti-alcohol congress of 1903 the White Cross, a Catholic equivalent of the Protestant Blue Cross, was formed and a plethora of new groups soon appeared. The message also spread to professional circles, and leagues and federations sprung up amongst teachers, farmers, railwaymen, post-office workers, and in the army and navy. Some of these newly formed groups were short-lived, but others survived the difficulties of the First World War and grew in strength in the 1920s, a period which also saw the formation of associations of ex-drinkers on the American model and marked a change in attitudes towards alcoholics. They were no longer regarded as shameful pariahs, and henceforth former drinkers played an active role in combating alcohol abuse.

In the inter-war period there was a decline in propagandist activity and the Second World War brought about new restrictions, which resulted in a decrease in alcoholism. All anti-alcohol groups faced financial difficulties and witnessed the dispersal of their principal activists.

When peace returned, standards of living improved, agricultural production increased and alcoholism reappeared. To meet this challenge, the statutes of the National League against Alcoholism were redrafted, and in 1949 the *Comité nationale de défense contre l'alcoolisme* (National Defence Committee Against Alcoholism) adopted new strategies.

The activities of the different organizations varied, according to their financial resources and spheres of influence. Members of the French Temperance Society were well placed to influence legislation. Roussel, for example, had promoted effective legislation, although his subsequent efforts to restrict domestic distillation were in vain. Lobbying by doctors and politicans led to higher taxes on alcohol, which it was hoped would reduce consumption. Despite the vigorous anti-absinthe campaign conducted over a period of thirty years, however, it was the First World War that was responsible for the ban imposed on spirits. The Society launched a paper, in 1880, which, it was hoped, would appeal to a large audience, but the venture folded after only six years. Other publications, *La Tempérance* and *L'Alcool*, were produced by associations that were closer to the people and proved longer-lasting. Sobriety was also discussed in articles in mass-circulation daily newspapers and in almanacs, which were especially popular in rural districts. These latter publications were filled with cautionary tales and Mme Legrain's *Almanach de tempérance* included a daily aphorism warning against alcohol. (Legrain himself wrote a small volume of thirty-five pages for use in the army.)

Propagandists saw that sound health education was a priority in the battle against alcoholism, especially amongst the young. As early as the 1870s, Roussel had advocated health education in primary schools and, by the 1890s, the amount of material specially produced for use by teachers and their pupils was considerable. In 1886, a manual was published by Laborde; in 1898, Villette and Lemoine, respectively a teacher and an inspector of schools in the Aisne, published a collection of exercises for use in the classroom; in 1899, the unstinting Legrain wrote a lengthy book on the subject of anti-alcohol education in schools; and in 1901, Laborde added to his opus with a new book of practical advice for young Frenchmen. By 1900, pressure from Roussel had made this form of instruction obligatory in French schools and the standard textbook was edited by J. Baudrillart.[7] The most prodigious example of this genre of literature was a book of over three hundred pages written by Langlois and Blondel;[8] both men worked in education in areas of high alcohol consumption and both were active in local temperance societies. They used every didactic technique: simple medical explanations, diagrams that were easy to complete or copy, essay topics, poetry, songs, cartoons, instructive stories and mathematical problems linked to alcohol consumption or purchase. There were also extracts from Zola and Loti, proverbs describing the dangers of drink and Balzac's comparison of strong drink with cholera. The book also cites famous abstainers, including Charles XII of Sweden and the one-time US president, Harrison.

There were also poster campaigns. Pictures of livers destroyed by alcohol and drunks staggering in the street or beating their children were still to be found in classrooms and soldier's barracks in the 1940s, alongside depictions of the male sexual organs, ulcerated and eaten away by syphilis contracted through extra-marital sex. Whether these terrifying images had any effect on the conduct of young Frenchmen remains in doubt. Similarly, the concerted efforts of the temperance societies between 1880 and 1914 seem to have had no notable impact on drinking habits or public health. In France, the only apparent decline in levels of alcoholism occurred during the two world wars.

There were numerous reasons for this failure. The leagues had no legislative authority and French society did not take the dangers of excessive alcohol consumption seriously. Even the more liberal organizations that preached moderation were ridiculed, as in the Daumier cartoon portraying the 'forty-third toast to the temperance society'.[9] Groups advocating total abstinence met with distrust, if not rejection. Their composition had much to do with this: in France temperance societies were never truly populist, and the intellectual and professional classes that ran them could not communicate with the masses. Although Legrain claimed a membership of 30,000 for the National League at the turn of the century, all the group's organizers came from comfortable backgrounds.

There were periodic debates on alcoholism at the Académie de Médecine. However, although many doctors were involved in the temperance societies, they only represented a minority of the profession. In 1939, Renault argued for the reintroduction of official anti-alcohol programmes in schools, and even called for blood-tests, following brawls and traffic offences, but he did not enjoy the support of the medical establishment.[10] Doctors were as divided on the question as their patients. Like anyone else, they drank and no doubt included in their ranks as many heavy drinkers as other professions. In the *Chambre des députés*, doctors tended to be moderate republicans, elected by the middle classes, and they were more likely to vote with the pro-alcohol lobby. Even those who backed the anti-alcohol movement had divergent views on alcohol abuse and were divided on the question of moderation or total abstinence. Medical training teaches scepticism and many doctors found it impossible to accept the degeneration theorists with their forecasts of doom and destruction which, in any case, were contradicted by their everyday experience: habitual drunkards fathered healthy children and chronic alcoholics lived to a ripe old age. Logically, doctors should champion social reform, but sceptics rarely become crusaders.

The temperance societies during the Third Republic had a certain influence on social attitudes and habitual drinking came to inspire disdain and repulsion. Politicians found it difficult to pass the protectionist measures demanded by the pro-alcohol lobby. The code controlling alcohol sales, which gradually emerged between 1930 and 1950, owes its relative strictness to the activities of the temperance societies. These societies, however, were never powerful enough in France to change drinking habits or dictate government policy.

PROHIBITION OR RATIONING?

Numerous attempts have been made to outlaw the use of alcohol. In 459, the Chinese emperor decreed that drinkers would be decapitated. In Egypt, Caliph Hakim (who ruled from 996 to 1020) forbade all imports of drink and had all vines uprooted in accordance with Koranic strictures. In neither country was the move incorporated into long-standing practice.

Prohibition in the USA

No country in modern times has attempted prohibition on the scale of the United States. During the Civil War, the question of the abolition of slavery was foremost in the American consciousness, but, when peace returned, attention was focused once more on the problems of alcohol.[11] At his inauguration ceremony, Lincoln's successor, Andrew Jackson, delivered a largely incomprehensible address, which his opponents in the revived American Temperance Union attributed to the effects of alcohol and thus he acquired a reputation for drunkenness.[12] The fight against alcoholism was waged along patriotic lines and a well-organized National Prohibition Party was formed with sections in several states. In the elections of 1869 it put up its own presidential candidate, who was unsuccessful, and General Ulysses Grant, the Civil War hero and notorious drinker, was elected. Even during the war Grant's conduct had been criticized, but his detractors were brushed aside by Lincoln, who declared: 'I wish all my generals drank as much and won me as many victories.' Grant was succeeded by R. B. Hayes. The son of a distiller, Hayes himself sided with the prohibitionists (he was possibly influenced by his strong-willed wife), and his stay in the White House marked a period of austerity, when only fruit juice was served at presidential banquets.

In 1874, the Women's Christian Temperance Union (WCTU) was formed. The organization's aim was to rebuild the Republic with emphasis on law and order, enterprise and the family. Mrs Hayes, otherwise known as 'Lemonade Lucy', was one of its most staunch supporters. As first lady, she was highly influential in mobilizing American women in the struggle for prohibition. In a society recovering from the wounds of civil war, engaged in expansion, industrialization and the assimilation of millions of immigrants, these women were the epitome of virtue. The WCTU used all means at its disposal to champion order, patriotism and traditional values. Prime targets in their campaign were immigrants from Europe, who brought their drinking habits with them. Bars represented the evil of drink: disease, prostitution, gambling, corruption, robbery and violence. The women of the WCTU, Bibles in hand, held prayer meetings in the mud outside saloons. They had the support of the clergy and the Archbishop of St Paul was moved to say: 'The American saloon is the mortal enemy of the family, piety, the material and intellectual well-being of the people and the free institutions of the Republic.'

Abstinence was also promoted among America's growing industrial labour force. Nothing could be allowed to interfere with productivity and efficiency; slack or drunken workers were immediately sacked. The great industrialists – Rockefeller, Ford and Hearst – were ardent propagandists for the cause of temperance, but they paid scant attention to the poor housing, low wages and bad working conditions that often pushed their workers to seek consolation in drink. Their influence in the 1880s, combined with that of the clergy and the WCTU, led several states to declare themselves 'dry'. These were the first instances of prohibition in modern times.

The WCTU subsequently increased the scope of its campaign and its members fought for peace, integration of immigrants, votes for women and raising the age of consent. The Union organized rehabilitation programmes for the alcoholics in factories, prisons, hospitals and bars, and formed the 'White Ribbons', a mutual aid group whose members recognized one another by a ribbon worn inside their jackets. Reform Clubs were created for former drinkers.

American doctors were never ardent proponents of prohibition. Like their European counterparts, they recognized the difficulties inherent in a total ban (which would also deprive them of what they considered to be a powerful therapeutic tool). They concerned themselves more with the treatment of alcoholics, and on the East Coast established special centres for the cure and detoxification of patients. These institutions were emulated elsewhere.

The medical profession was poorly regulated at the time and some treatments on offer were the invention of quacks and charlatans. One such remedy, 'double chloride of gold', was launched in 1880 by Keeley, who kept its formula a close secret. Before 'double chloride of gold' was finally discredited it enjoyed a brief vogue and clubs and institutes appeared specializing in its use.

The prohibitionists were highly vocal, but they were not always in agreement concerning total suppression of alcohol, which some considered a threat to individual liberty. American history was rewritten. The famous painting of George Washington, glass in hand, celebrating the founding of the Union was altered: the glass disappeared and the decanter on the table was hidden under a hat. Political parties were placed in a difficult position – saloons played a key role in electoral campaigns and were the venue for debate, vote-buying and even voting itself. Proprietors served as political agents for the two parties and if either were to declare itself in favour of prohibition, it risked losing potential voters.

In the 1890s the political climate was further upset by the launch of the 'Anti-saloon League', which was founded by a Methodist pastor, H. H. Russel. The league proved a great success and was soon receiving substantial financial backing. It only endorsed candidates who were in favour of prohibition, regardless of their party, and accordingly it was able to attract to its ranks groups that had traditionally found no place in the bipartisan American system – the temperance groups, the WCTU and the Prohibition Party. United in this way, the movement for pro-hibition was reinvigorated. Members of the WCTU took to the streets of the large towns in the name of virtue and morality, ransacking bars and attacking their owners. Those pleading for reason and individual rights were powerless in the face of this wave of popular sentiment. New states joined the prohibition bandwagon and by 1913 half of the American population lived in 'dry' areas, apparently to the satisfaction of many citizens.

When America entered the First World War anti-alcoholism became a patriotic issue and drink was viewed with the suspicion otherwise reserved for German immigrants and the banned music of Wagner and Beethoven. Jack London's novel *John Barleycorn*, which depicts the author's struggle with drink, was published at the time and met with popular acclaim. It was under these circumstances that Congress voted in favour of the eighteenth amendment, which came into force under Woodrow Wilson, a man as abstemious as Hayes. The manufacture of alcoholic drinks containing more than 5 per cent alcohol was now forbidden in all states; the 'neo-republican' ideal of national virtue and liberty had been achieved.

For a while the triumph was complete. Alcoholism was no longer considered an illness and proposals were advanced for the exile of those with drink problems to the Aleutian Islands. The world's doctors followed developments closely; never before had such a measure been introduced on so large a scale.[13] The new law dampened the ardour of the prohibitionists. Their battle had been won and now there no longer seemed any need for temperance clubs; the WCTU began to lose members and the Anti-saloon League suspended many of its activities.

It cannot be denied that the early years of prohibition had a positive effect on public health. Studies demonstrated declines in alcohol con-sumption, deaths linked to drink, liver cirrhosis, mental disorders and crime attributable to alcohol in the years 1920 and 1921. Evangeline Booth, daughter of the founder of the Salvation Army, claimed that the number of families broken up by drink was also decreasing. Slowly, however, the figures started to creep up again and by 1930 they had reached pre-war levels.

The drawbacks of prohibition soon became apparent. Violations of the law were so common that courts were placed under great pressure. Judges found it difficult to strike a balance between intolerance and leniency, and by the mid-1920s it was clear that prohibition was a stimulus to all sorts of criminal activity. Actual drinking habits had not changed in any way: those who had been abstemious continued to be so and drinkers continued to buy and consume, albeit in secrecy. Illegal distillation became common and spirits produced in this manner were frequently impure and posed serious health risks.[14] All in all, prohibition had the effect of encouraging consumption of distilled drinks in place of beer.

It was not long before the Association for the Abolition of the Prohibition Act was formed. The organization employed the same arguments as the prohibitionists, but turned them on their heads. On the moral front, they claimed that the law encouraged hypocrisy and immorality; from the economic perspective, they pointed out that alcohol production would provide employment in the difficult years of the 1928–32 depression and that the state itself would also benefit. One-time prohibitionists such as Rockefeller, Dupont and Hearst changed their tune and backed the campaign to have the law repealed.

The Democrats fought the 1932 presidential election on the abrogation ticket and their candidate, R. D. Roosevelt, abstemious though he was, was elected by a large majority over his opponent, Hoover (whom many held responsible for the economic crisis). The eighteenth amendment was annulled in 1933 and responsibility for alcohol legislation was returned to local authorities, as had been the case before 1919.[15] An attempted revival of the Anti-saloon League failed, largely because both the public and political parties were no longer interested. In the first years of Roosevelt's presidency taxes on alcohol brought in $500 million, which was used to finance social programmes. The beer and whisky barons created thousands of new jobs and strove to improve their public image, even to the extent of financing research into alcoholism. Yet, again, no real change was observed in drinking habits. However, there was a renewed tendency to view alcoholics as people who were ill, and in 1932 Alcoholics Anonymous was formed by a group of former drinkers. Out of the old prohibition leagues emerged the modern National Council on Alcohol Problems. Investigation of alcoholism became more rational and scientific. The Federal Health Administration founded the National Institute of Alcohol Abuse and Alcoholism (NIAAA) to collate statistics and conduct research. In 1940, the *Quarterly Journal of Studies on Alcohol* first appeared, and several universities funded their own research groups.

In 1977, at the instigation of the N I A A A, Congress passed a new law aimed at decriminalizing alcohol-related offences and responsibility for offenders was transferred to the social and medical services – this was a far cry from the Republican arguments of earlier decades. In modern America, drink regulations are loosely applied and even in 'dry' states alcohol is often freely available. Alcoholism remains a major health problem in the United States, but at present no further federal involvement is envisaged.

The American experience demonstrates the disadvantages of widespread governmental intervention. It took an active minority three-quarters of a century to implement prohibition in the name of public health and social morality. After only fourteen years this legislation, the product of theoretically sound intentions, was rejected for its intolerance. It was not a flourishing gangster subculture that ended prohibition; the eighteenth amendment had simply failed to stop people drinking.

Canada

Minor differences apart, the history of anti-alcohol campaigning in neighbouring Canada followed a similar course. In 1855 the province of New Brunswick introduced prohibition, which proved impossible to enforce and was withdrawn after a year. In common with their colleagues elsewhere, Canadian doctors had no desire to restrict the use of alcohol, which they valued as a therapeutic agent. A federal law passed in 1874 left responsibility for measures restricting alcohol to local authorities. An investigation into the alcohol trade conducted by a Royal Commission in 1894 showed that doctors were beginning to doubt the medical merits of alcohol and that they favoured temperance. Their position was ambivalent in that they were reluctant to infringe individual rights; like everybody else, they opposed strict controls. However, the prevailing moral climate (one in which women were seen as the guardians of family life) and the upheavals of the First World War led Ontario in 1916 to pass a law banning the sale of drinks with an alcohol content greater than 2.5 per cent that were not destined for medical, sacramental, industrial or scientific use.

The law was extended to cover all provinces in 1918, but for similar reasons the move was to prove even more short-lived than prohibition in the USA. In 1927, it was superseded by a Liquor Control Act allowing local districts that had declared themselves dry in 1877 to remain so; a complex system of licences governing the sale of alcohol elsewhere was introduced. The new Act required that drink should not be on display to the customer, and in some towns and provinces ration books or special permits were introduced. Today these restrictions no longer hold. Ration books and permits were withdrawn in 1961, and since 1969 self-service facilities have operated in larger shops.[16]

Great Britain

In Great Britain the fight against alcoholism was less vigorous and, since it was lacking in patriotic inspiration, less political. Following the foundation of the National Temperance League in the mid-nineteenth century, the Anglican Church set up its own Temperance Society in 1859, a move quickly emulated by the Catholic Church. In 1876, the British Women's Association began campaigning for total abstinence, created recovery houses for female drinkers, and organized tea and coffee stalls at the entrances of factories to counteract the appeal of pubs. (The idea of a temperance café did not seem as strange in England as it had done in France and some of these institutions actually made a profit.[17]) In 1882, the railwaymen formed their own temperance union. Other trades too had their own associations and between 1872 and 1895 they amalgamated to become the United Kingdom Alliance, which favoured total abstinence and lobbied for legal prohibition. The Alliance also drew attention to the immorality, crime and social disruption caused by alcohol and used the press to highlight such cases as that of Jane Cakebread, a London woman who received more than 240 convictions for public drunkenness before being committed finally to an asylum.[18]

In Britain, it had never been customary to interfere directly in the lives of individuals and it was generally believed that legislation could not prevent people drinking. Moreover, brewers and distillers were pillars of the Victorian establishment and were well able to defend their interests. Above all, the message of the propagandists was politically unsound: total abstinence was intolerable to moderates, who formed the majority, and the Alliance collapsed.[19] Some measures, however, were taken against the alcohol trade: in 1883, a law was passed banning the use of pubs for electoral meetings; in 1898, the Inebriates Act was passed; in 1904, licences for those involved in the trade were formalized. In imitation of a Swedish system operating in Göteborg, the government bought up all drink outlets in Carlisle in 1916 and the number of off-licences fell from 100 to 13. This action was repeated in other towns, but it met with opposition and plans were dropped. Today the state plays only a minor role in the campaign against alcohol and local authorities are left to manage regulations governing sales themselves.

Recently, Alcohol Concern, a body of medical and social professionals, was established to provide information on related issues. In Britain, the decision to drink is left to the individual, a policy determined by respect for liberty and British pragmatism.

Sweden

Several Swedish schemes, the product of combined private and governmental initiative, have attracted the attention of other European countries. In 1855, when the government introduced legislation to end domestic distillation and raised tax on alcohol, it was left to individual towns to restrict sales within their jurisdiction. Under what came to be known as the Göteborg system individual municipalities, through the agency of local dignitaries, bought up all alcohol licences and managed the trade themselves. This allowed for control of opening hours, prices and sales, and profits could be channelled into public funds. The system was adopted in other parts of Sweden and, with slight modification, in Norway. By the end of the nineteenth century it operated throughout the two countries. The result was effectively a double monopoly: the state controlled drink production and local companies took care of all aspects of marketing.

For several years these measures proved successful, but in the long term they were ineffective. Public drunkenness became a problem once more and temperance societies regrouped to meet the challenge: the Blue Ribbon Society was formed along American lines; local sections of the Good Templars multiplied and by 1907 had a membership of 200,000; associations for total abstinence were started among schoolchildren, students and teachers; Baptists, Methodists and the Salvationists of the Lutheran state church all preached for the cause. In politics, abstinence became a symbol of personal integrity exploited by politicians from both the newly formed Social Democrats and the Liberals. In working circles abstinence was considered a sign of impartiality and morality; beer, a favourite refreshment amongst the people, also came under attack. Trade union, political party and village celebrations took place in the absence of alcohol and membership of a temperance society facilitated advancement both in administrative and parliamentary circles. Not everybody was interested in forwarding themselves in such a fashion and many eschewed the prestige associated with abstinence and continued to drink. In spite of the Göteborg system, which had increased taxes regularly and made it impossible for individuals to profit from alcohol sales, consumption grew steadily until the beginning of the twentieth century.

The Bratt reform was introduced in Sweden in 1919. Under Bratt's proposals every adult over the age of 21 was issued with a book, known as a *motbook*, in which all alcohol purchases were to be recorded. The shopkeeper was to detail the contents of each bottle in the book and record this separately on a register, along with the buyer's name, the time and date. A married man was initially entitled to 4 litres of aquavit each month, but in 1941 this was reduced to 3 litres. The figure appears large, but the ration was for the whole family; single people received less and married women had no entitlement at all. The sale of wine was not restricted, but all purchases were recorded. Any sale was at the discretion of the shopkeeper, who was obliged not to serve drunks, heavy drinkers, ex-alcoholics, recently released prisoners or anybody suspected of abusing alcohol. Shopkeepers were also authorized to demand and note down customers' profession, especially if they were in state employment. The system was effective and consumption of aquavit fell until the 1940s, when it again began to increase – notably among women and the young – as did alcohol-related offences and cirrhosis of the liver.

The Bratt reform introduced individual rationing, but by giving shop-keepers the power to enquire into the private lives of their customers, it led to forms of policing that Bratt had not envisaged. A simple purchase could only be accomplished after disagreeable waiting and form-filling, and the burdensome bureaucratic aspects of the system made it too expensive to operate.[20] A new solution was required and in 1955 regulations were introduced that remain in force today. As before, the state benefited from all alcohol sales; the joint-stock companies were dropped, but the system remained decentralized, operating through local and regional temperance commissions responsible for measures against alcoholism. Care networks for alcoholics were also developed, providing treatment in specialized establishments and better health education for the public. Ration books were replaced by price controls designed to limit consumption. Taxes were fixed according to alcohol content and the reform was accompanied by the launch of a low-strength beer to compete with stronger traditional brews. Immediate results were encouraging and consumption of spirits dropped consider-ably in favour of beer and wine. Swedes became discriminating drinkers, enjoying good-quality French, Chilean and American wines imported by the state, and temperance societies focused their attention on caring for heavy drinkers rather than legal reform. The situation did not last: production of the new state beer was halted, the Swedes remained avid wine-drinkers and slowly rediscovered their thirst for aquavit.

Current patterns of drinking give cause for concern. Although annual consumption of alcohol per inhabitant has not increased since the days of the Bratt system, the young drink more and at an earlier age, and both the number of convictions for crimes committed under the influence of alcohol and the incidence of drink-related illness have increased. Recent large increases in duty on spirits have led to the re-emergence of illicit distillation, a phenomenon also observed in other countries.

Switzerland

In Switzerland, temperance societies enlisted public support for legislative action. Following his experience of English teetotallers, Pastor Rochat founded the Blue Cross in 1877. The organization was religious in inspiration, but it remained independent of the established churches. Although it demanded abstinence from its members, it merely sought moderation in society as a whole. Towards the end of the nineteenth century many other organizations followed its lead, proliferating at all levels in Catholic and Protestant cantons alike.[21] These groups moved the government to institute a state monopoly over the sale and manufacture of distilled liquor, which, of course, did not include all alcoholic drinks. Today regulations are determined by individual cantons.

Russia

Although fewer statistics are available, alcohol consumption in nineteenth-century Russia was as high as in other European countries. Industrialization came late to this vast agricultural country and alcoholism was viewed as the preserve of the peasant rather than the industrial worker, as it had been in France. Thus the anti-alcohol movement was born in the countryside.

In 1887, the tsarist government attempted to establish small temperance societies in individual parishes, thereby exploiting the moral authority of local priests. The Holy Synod of 1890 recommended that Orthodox priests should set an example by their own abstinence, a stricture which was largely ignored. Efforts were made to control drinking in urban areas and associations were set up in St Petersburg, Moscow, Kiev, Odessa and elsewhere. Markoff, a member of government, was especially concerned about the damage done by alcohol to the nation's agricultural and industrial productivity, and in 1895 he proposed a state monopoly on the manufacture and sale of distilled drinks. He sought to reduce the number of drinking establishments and wine shops in an attempt to curb consumption. His measures were not popular, but were marked by some initial success. The first *dumas* of the twentieth century (a law-making body set up by the tsar in 1905, but disbanded in 1917) viewed the monopoly as an insupportable manifestation of tsarist absolutism and accused the government of encouraging alcoholism in an attempt to increase state revenue. Their opposition led to Markoff's dismissal.[22]

State failure to control alcoholism had led Nicholas II to turn for help to the Orthodox Church, but it was not until the First World War, when Russian military defeats were attributed to alcohol, that he took the drastic step of banning alcohol sales throughout the empire (a move which won him the congratulations of the French Académie de Médecine[23]). The enemies of Nicholas's unpopular regime, however, were not impressed and took the opportunity to stir up discontent among the troops; like so many mutinies and rebellions, the revolution of 1917 was in part stimulated by restrictions on alcohol.

India

Although it is not a Western nation, since its Independence India has experienced many difficulties in regulating drinking behaviour.[24] Almost half the country's 600 million people are vegetarians, and restrictions on meat often extend to tobacco and alcohol. Alcoholism thus represents less of a threat than in European countries. Nevertheless the Indian government has attempted in vain to impose prohibition and the situation now resembles the American pluralist model. Individual states have been largely unable to control production and manufacture of alcoholic drinks, and turn a blind eye to the abuses taking place. Accordingly, the country's alcohol consumption has grown rapidly. Control of illicit trade in alcohol in a country the size of India is impossible, and this further compounds the problem.

Laws governing the production and sale of alcohol vary throughout the twenty-two states. In southern India, the state of Tamil Nadu ostensibly has a rationing system (which does not apply to foreign visitors): local inhabitants must obtain a permit from the administration, which, in practice, restaurateurs rarely demand to see. Furthermore, high alcohol prices mean that the illicit distillation of coconut is common practice and is responsible for many cases of blindness from methanol poisoning. Neighbouring Karnataka limits the hours during which alcohol can be sold and, although a lay state, respects the customs of its Muslim population by banning alcohol sales during Islamic festivals (although exceptions are made on a variety of pretexts). In Goa, the centuries of Portuguese influence have resulted in an absence of restrictions on alcohol, and the wide variety of fruits available in this tropical region gives an equally wide choice of alcoholic drinks – frequently smuggled into the states of Karnataka and Maharashtra.

Conclusion

There are thus different options available to countries wishing to control alcohol consumption: production could be reduced by the creation of a state monopoly, channelling profits into public funds; marketing could also be undertaken by the state; the price of alcohol could be raised; a total ban on production and sales could be imposed. Initially, all such measures have proved effective, but the more radical have been either circumvented or revoked under popular pressure. It would seem that if alcohol is a vice, then virtue is unattractive, and if drinking is a malady, then good health alone is not enough to satisfy man. He is jealous of his liberty, which includes his right to drink. Fortunately, however, moderation is the norm – attempts to reduce consumption by restrictive and punitive measures have little effect on the heavy drinker addicted to alcohol.

ALCOHOL AND RELIGION

Man has always linked substances that alter his perceptions with divinity. The reasons for this are unclear, but such changes in consciousness are frequently viewed as diabolical or divine, the same terms being used to describe drug-induced states and the ecstasies of salvationist religions. Alcohol is frequently associated with the divine repose of the after-life. In *The Republic*, Plato attacks those followers of Orpheus who believed eternal drunkenness to be the reward for the righteous in Hades. Sarcophagi from early Christian times are decorated with Dionysian motifs portraying the revelries of the dead. The Eucharist confers immortality and the Koran depicts a paradise flowing with wine.[25] This fusion of sacred and secular is also seen on Earth: Central American Indians replaced the Host with peyote, when it failed to channel their thoughts in divine directions, and the Aztecs accompanied sacrifices to their gods with libations of pulque. Such ceremonies must not be viewed as corruptions of more religious manifestations or degraded examples of a higher metaphysical state. They all demonstrate a desire to penetrate the ineffable, to comprehend the universe. It is natural, then, that inspirational religions should take an interest in substances that induce a transcendent state. In this context we will examine the relationship between the three major monotheisms of the Western world and alcohol.[26]

Judaism

The Bible provides the earliest record of Jewish history, but it is certain that the Jews drank fermented liquor – both in Egypt, where they lived, and in Babylon, where they were held captive – long before the Bible was written. Noah is the first of many drunkards to be mentioned in the Old Testament. There are many references to wine and strong drink, and the richness of vocabulary employed is remarkable. Wine and the vine are used as symbols of fertility, as are milk and wheat; they are to be respected as gifts from God. The effects of excessive drinking are clearly described: loss of consciousness and a propensity to violence. The Bible and other, later Jewish texts remain equivocal on the subject of wine, recommending it at times and proscribing it at others. The Talmud, which dates from the sixth century, outlines certain rules governing the use of wine in ritual and daily life and its first five chapters, the Pentateuch, even allow for the purchase, sale and consumption of Gentile produce. In the Mishnah, however, wine appears as a symbol of idolatry, debauchery and prostitution, an association that is doubtless a reflection on the pagan Canaanites, who produced their own wines and practised sacred prostitution.[27]

In Judaism wine often accompanies holy ritual: the weekly Sabbath, Easter, marriage, circumcision, commemoration of the destruction of the temple. Rites are performed in the home under the watchful eye of the head of the family, who drinks and passes the cup to other members, children included. The ceremony links members of the household with each other and with God. The use of wine in religious ritual from an early age is often cited as a reason for the traditional sobriety of the Jews. Kant remarked: 'Women, Protestant pastors and Jews do not get drunk'; a century later, in 1893, Lardier, a French doctor from Vosges, claimed that of all peoples it was amongst the Jews that alcohol caused least damage.[28] He attributed this to 'ancestral influence' and the love of family, work and money, and he was so convinced by this explanation that he was drawn to underline the importance of moral arguments in combating alcoholism amongst Christians. His mixture of admiration and aggression, however, is indicative of the moral climate of the day, when French Jewry was under threat from Drumont and his supporters.[29]

Sobriety remains a feature of Jewish society. Statistical studies in the USA have compared Jewish drinking habits with those of the Irish and Protestant communities and found markedly different patterns of consumption, particularly in the young, and reduced incidence of suicide and cirrhosis.[30] In Jewish religious schools even non-Orthodox children drink from the age of 5. Adolescents and young adults tolerate occasional drunkenness, but frown upon repeated lapses; their upbringing would seem to have given them a reasonable, balanced approach to alcohol consumption, although there is some variation in attitudes, according to social origins and degree of orthodoxy.[31] (Sephardic Jews retain from their Hispanic period non-religious poetry extolling wine and the vine, a reflection of the cultural climate of the Mediterranean.) In the contemporary period, however, such differences have become less pronounced and it is difficult to make any generalizations about consumption on the basis of background. In Jewish migrants to America, moderate consumption seems more common than total abstinence. In Israel, migrants from Europe or America drink more readily and with greater frequency than the more ritually-oriented Sephardic Jews from Africa and Asia. The rich and more religious members of the society tend to drink less and, in comparison with European countries or the USA, less alcohol is drunk.[32] Consumption, however, is on the increase, especially among the young.

Judaism neither condemns heavy drinking nor warns of its dangers, but, as a result of the sacramental character of wine, the Jews have developed certain habits of moderation. Whether this non-formalized tendency to temperance is at base religious is uncertain, but it has undoubtedly benefited the Jewish population as a whole.

Christianity

Christianity was greatly influenced by Jewish and Graeco-Latin tradition, and the mystical and symbolic role of wine in worship is part of this inheritance. In Western Europe, Christianity developed in a climate of increasing alcohol consumption. As religious orthodoxy came to be challenged, so the Catholic Church's traditionally relaxed attitudes towards drink were reassessed.

Surviving accounts of life in the high Middle Ages pay greater attention to sexual peccadilloes than dietary habits. St Eligius and his peers condemn lordly concubinage, polygamy and incest, but give the impression that drunkenness was to be expected of those who could afford to drink. God, too, was to turn a blind eye to habitual drunkenness until the Reformation – two centuries after the appearance of distilled drinks – and it was Calvin, not the beer-loving Luther, who was first to condemn strong liquor. In the name of sanctity, Calvinism took up the cudgel against all forms of licentiousness: dancing, gambling, profane music and drink. In the new Reform churches of France, the

Council of Elders demanded sobriety of their pastors and railed against drink. In seventeenth-century Holland, churches resounded with denunciations of bars, beer and gin. Flemish genre painters of the period used their work to educate the people about the dangers of alcohol; their colourful scenes of drunks lying collapsed amid empty bottles and glasses, of peasants and soldiers carousing, and of ragged children fighting may seem Realist in content, but, in fact, they are symbolic representations of Man's sinful excess.[33]

Initially, Protestant England was not as strict as Holland. Many of the ecclesiastical vineyards were retained (some still exist today) and the English never lost their taste for wine and beer.[34] Nash's *Anatomy of Absurdity* took to task intolerant souls who waged a pitiless war on human weakness – debauchery, arrogance, gluttony, lust and drunkenness – but in the mid-seventeenth century the likes of Nash had to face the intransigence of Wesley and the Puritans.[35]

The Anglican Church had relatively little to say on the subject of alcohol and in this resembled the Catholic Church, notably in France, where works published by the Catholic hierarchy to guide priests ranked drunkenness among the more inoffensive of sins. Father Coton, confessor to the French king in 1615, equates gluttony with alcoholic excess.[36] In a similar manual, published some decades later in 1667, meat eaters are especially singled out for the wrath of God, but drunks do not escape His attention: 'It is terrible thing to witness the punishments which await them.' The manual advises potential sinners: 'Consider sincerely the indignity of the vice and beg God to forgive you. Dwell upon the fate of St Louis and of Eve, who succumbed to temptation; avoid the company of drunks and gluttons and turn your mind to the bodily corruption which awaits them.'[37] The moral director of the Invalides in Paris spoke out specifically against bars and drunkenness in 1715.[38]

Works of this genre are purely moral in tone: they state quite simply that it is bad to eat and drink too much, but, beyond allusions to the Day of Judgement, give no reason as to why this should be so. At the end of the nineteenth century reasoning became more eschatological: it was argued that man was a divine creature who, when he drank, lost this essential aspect of his humanity, becoming stupid, a mere animal wrecking his family and damaging his health; it was this which offended the Creator.[39] Few of the many sermons dedicated to the seven deadly sins condemn drunkenness. God's wrath was reserved for the dishonesty of drink-sellers who watered down their wines.[40]

As has been suggested, greed more often than not referred to food rather than drink, and dictionaries indicate similar usage of the word intemperance, which was defined as late as 1881 by Littré simply as the opposite of moderation. Catholic temperance societies did not appear in France until Rochat introduced his Blue Cross in 1877, assisted by Pastor Dieterlen in Montbéliard. Eugène Picard, a minister in the Doubs, won a competition organized by the paper *La Tempérance* to find a work 'capable of giving people advice on the danger of alcoholic abuse and the advantages of temperance'; almost 10,000 copies of the manual were distributed.

Although popular participation was scanty, the more senior members of the Catholic hierarchy were actively involved in the battle against alcoholism. In 1900, Mgr Turinaz wrote a work describing the three scourges of the working classes: violation of the sabbath, alcoholism and poor household hygiene.[41] A longer work by another bishop, Mgr Gibier, was to prove highly successful.[42] As parish priest in Orléans, he had delivered fifty-six lectures and these formed the basis of his book, which went through several editions. The three 'social wounds' he documents differ only from the scourges of Turinaz in that the rural exodus replaces poor household hygiene. Eight sections of his work are dedicated to alcoholism, which he demonstrates successively to weaken the body, to shorten life, to undermine the intelligence, to reduce man to bestiality and to cause the ruin of home, race and nation. He concludes by stressing the responsibility of the individual and the state in protecting against alcoholism and by emphasizing family values.

These arguments reiterate themes developed by doctors, politicians and lay observers of society. A specifically Christian viewpoint did not exist – references to God and Christ are rare. Today the French clergy show little interest in the subject of alcoholism; although they are prepared to run temperance societies, they no longer play an active role in the anti-alcohol movement.

Protestants, especially in the USA, differed entirely in their attitudes. Temperance societies were born in New England in the early nineteenth century and the struggle against alcoholism in America never lost its religious character. Methodists and Quakers considered drinking a sin and, as all sin was considered offensive in the eyes of God, the American temperance leagues tended towards total abstinence. Accordingly, almost all Protestant sects were associated with temperance leagues. In following their example, the Catholic clergy – in particular, Cardinal Gibbons, Mgr Ireland of St Paul and the regional synod in Baltimore – found itself in an awkward position: many German, Irish, Italian and Polish parishioners did not welcome campaigns for prohibition. On the whole, the Church of Rome was conscious of the dangers of alcoholism, which were only too apparent among recently arrived working-class immigrants, but it was unable to take a radical stance. When Russel's Methodist Anti-saloon League came into being in the 1890s, it quickly received the full backing of all Protestant organizations and the Catholic hierarchy was forced to state its position publicly. Compromise was to mark its response: in the eyes of God, the saloon trade was not immoral; it did, however, expose too many people to temptation. Where possible, saloon-keepers should find a living elsewhere.

The Protestant churches continued their activities – indeed, some even ran detoxification centres[43] – until success arrived in the form of the 1919 amendment to the Constitution. (The eighteenth amendment was passed under the presidency of Wilson, whose father was a Presbyterian pastor and who himself was a teetotaller. In matters of faith, he was so strict that while president at Princeton he had tried to prevent admission of Methodist and Episcopalian students.) Although the churches were unable to prevent the repeal of the amendment, they continued to run their temperance societies and finance treatment centres and research. In 1933, when the government delegated responsibility for alcohol legislation to individual states, those with a large Catholic minority adopted liberal legislation and went 'wet', whereas others, notably those with a large Baptist minority, stayed 'dry'. In modern America these distinctions have become meaningless, as regulations are applied with increasing laxity.[44]

In Britain, the temperance movement was also launched by Protestants and under the leadership of Cardinal Manning a Catholic temperance society, The Cross, was founded in 1859. British Protestants were never as ardent in their fight against alcohol as the Americans and resistance from moderate drinkers was sufficient to prevent total prohibition. The Free Churches advocated total abstinence and they hoped, at the very least, for abstinence on Sundays, when sermons would be devoted to alcoholism.[45] Their efforts were in vain.

Elsewhere the Protestant influence was in evidence. Magnus Huss was the son of a Lutheran pastor, but even before his time a book by Baird describing the experiences of the American temperance societies had been translated into Swedish and distributed to all parishes on the order of Charles XIV. Likewise, in Wilhelmian Germany regions with a Protestant majority – Hanover and Prussia, for example – were more active in the campaign against alcohol than their Catholic counterparts such as Bavaria and the Rhineland.

Numerous Christian communities, both Catholic and Reformist, evoke the Last Supper by celebrating a form of communion in which the priest drinks wine; for those with drink problems this posed obvious difficulties. Some Catholic and Episcopalian priests argued that this daily draught taken at the altar did not compromise their self-control; others, however, blamed it for their own drinking. For this reason, some priests and doctors have requested authorization from the papal court for former drinkers to celebrate the Eucharist with grape juice, but this has always been denied. Rome has insisted on a dogmatic interpretation of Jesus' wish that 'this be done in memory of me' and has upheld the use of wine.

The Catholic Church has always been tolerant and reserved on the subject of alcohol. In 1985, French bishops gave a solemn warning against excessive consumption which went unheard in the churches; Polish bishops did the same, with similar results. Having played such a small role in anti-alcohol campaigns during the nineteenth century, the Roman Catholic hierarchy is scarcely likely to initiate a crusade in the late twentieth century. The Roman Church has chosen to focus on certain of the mortal sins. To the neglect of greed it has emphasized lust. Books, catechisms, sermons, pastoral addresses and encyclicals perpetually condemn masturbation, pre-marital sex, adultery, abortion and artificial insemination; drunkenness is passed over in silence. In the Catholic countries of Latin culture, to which Greece may be added, there have never been attempts to prohibit or restrict alcohol consumption in any major way; the numbers of drink shops have been controlled, but no law has been passed restricting the individual's freedom to buy, stock or drink alcohol.

In explaining the difference between Protestant and Catholic attitudes to alcohol, a major factor is undoubtedly the mystical value of wine for the Catholic Church. Other considerations must be important, however, since some Reform Churches also practise consecration with wine. Furthermore, alcoholism is not simply a problem confined to wine-producing countries, and the geographical distribution of the vine does not coincide exactly with that of Catholicism. (The Anglican Church retained wine in communion and sixteenth-century English vineyards were reasonably extensive, yet Anglicans have followed Protestants in their disapproval of wine. In Germany, some wine-growing regions became Protestant. Likewise the cantons of Geneva and Neuchâtel cultivated vines and became Calvinist and Lutheran respectively.) Anti-alcoholism is therefore not linked to the absence of the vine. The evidence suggests that religion plays a greater role than socio-cultural factors. Attitudes to alcohol develop according to a general vision of the human being and his place in nature; of his relationship to the world's bounties; of his duty to God, and to himself as a divine creation. Notions of morality and sin differ between Protestant and Catholic denominations, and both adopt different positions on intemperance, lust, avarice and other sins. For some, drinking alcohol is a pleasure. Catholics can seek pardon for the mortal sin of abuse, but for most Protestants all pleasure is culpable and to be condemned. As a result, guilt is more widespread among Protestant alcoholics.

With the increasing tendency towards a uniformity of behaviour, which tends to eradicate the influences of cultural, ethnic or climatic variation between Christian countries, it is conceivable that many of the differences discussed above will become the stuff of history.

Islam

Western ignorance has led to the general view that Islam is an immutable monolith. Far from being unchanging, the religion of Muhammad during its development has known schisms and bloody ruptures comparable to those suffered by Christianity. The inspirational text of Islam, the Koran, is as equivocal on the subject of alcohol as the Bible; the Prophet Muhammad looked upon wine as the embodiment of well-being, wealth and fertility, but he recommended moderation. In Islam religious authority rests not only on the Koran, but also on early accounts of the Prophet's life, the *hadith*, and on commentaries made by subsequent Islamic scholars. All decisions taken by an *imam* or *cadi* have authority and take precedence over previous judgements.

Islam was spread in the Mediterranean world by Arabs from a dry desert land, where vines were grown only in a few oases of the Hedjez. It is said that Caliph Omar's toops drank to excess in their conquest of wine-growing regions such as Byzantine Syria, forcing Omar to forbid any recurrence of such behaviour and to outlaw drink. The Umayyad and Abbasid dynasties were probably tolerant. The stories of *The Thousand and One Nights* abound in drunken incidents and when the Arabs conquered Persia, a country which produced good wine, drinking was not forbidden. Hedonists such as Omar Khayyam left many poems and songs in praise of wine and until the fourteenth century poets such as Hafiz praised its action without being persecuted.[46] An anonymous poet living in Syria between 1222 and 1258 wrote a long poetic dialogue arguing the relative merits of alcohol and hashish. The poet could not have contemplated such a project had the imams of Damascus ruled against either form of intoxication.[47] Arab doctors from the tenth to the thirteenth century commented extensively on the therapeutic and social uses of alcohol. Rhazes (*c*.850–925), as mentioned in chapter 1, was aware of the harm done by excessive drinking, but like modern Christian doctors he did not criticize moderate consumption. In their present form, the aphorisms of Avicenna (*c*.980–1037) make no reference to alcohol, but it is possible that those suppressed by copyists in accordance with later convention dealt specifically with the subject.

Andalusian Muslims living in contact with Jews and Christians who drank did so themselves. (Had Spain remained under Arab rule, differences would undoubtedly have emerged between Muslims of East and West, as they had between Sephardic and Ashkenazi Jews.[48]) A Cordoban doctor, Aboulcassis (*c*.950–1013), the father of medieval and Renaissance surgery, described the role of wine in the daily life of his home town. Although he counselled a black wine to fortify the blood of those recovering from fractures when the bones began to heal, he advised against wine for patients who had recently suffered a fracture, and his piety was never questioned (unlike that of some of his colleagues, notably Averrhoes).

After the Moguls, from Persia and Afghanistan, had installed Islam in much of the Indian subcontinent, Muslims continued to consume both fermented and distilled drinks. Elsewhere, Ottoman sultans bore the dignified caliphal title of 'Commander of the Faithful' until the time of Mustapha Kemal and yet history records many who were drunks, as were a large number of bureaucrats in the vast Turkish empire. The division between Shiites and Sunnis did not lead to any difference in attitudes concerning wine: Persian Shiites and Sunni caliphs both drank on occasion. Amongst other sects, however, there was disagreement on the question of alcohol. Muhammad was no more explicit on certain issues than Jesus and his early followers were left to make their own interpretations of his pronouncements.

Recent centuries have seen an upsurge in intransigent conservatism: among the Wahabis of the Nedjed, today's rulers of Saudi Arabia; in Iran and Pakistan; in once-tolerant Egypt and in socialist Algeria; in the Sudan, with its sizeable Christian and animist minorities; in Tunisia, a country proud of its religious heterogeneity. Paradoxically, however, consumption of *raki* in Turkey has not diminished, beer is increasingly popular in Egypt, and in the Islamic states south of the Sahara a variety of alcoholic drinks continue to be consumed.

Muslims have long praised cosmopolitan centres such as Alexandria, Istanbul and Beirut, where they could drink at leisure. Those who have emigrated to Europe or America adopt the customs of their hosts and drink alcohol as a mark of their assimilation. Only where they remain in closed communities have they retained the abstinence of their ancestors, and this rarely exists beyond the second generation.

Religion forms the basis of state practice under sharia law and anti-alcohol propaganda takes a different form in Islamic countries. If Islam presupposes abstinence, then the state must forbid alcohol – to do otherwise would be heretical, the result of diabolic or Western influence. Today it is felt that believers in past centuries were scrupulous observers of Islamic codes – codes which have slowly been undermined by Christian influence in Muslim countries. Muslim prohibition is a form of eternal struggle with Christianity and the modern resistance to Westernization. (In a similar fashion, the Jews considered drunkenness the vice of the Gentiles.) Further religious and metaphysical reasons help explain the antipathy towards alcohol. In Islam and in Christianity, the message of the holy book has been complicated by rules and dogma whose inflexibility does not admit the power of mystical or visionary states that intervene in the relation between Man and God. Alcohol is therefore forbidden because it produces such states.

What is forbidden varies from society to society. In many instances, we might speculate that dietary prohibitions are totemic in origin. In the case of alcohol in Islamic countries, the restriction is of a religious order, invented by 'priests' and imposed on millions. There is, however, nothing to indicate that such restriction is any more than provisional; its observance is uneven and might vary in any number of ways in the future. Whatever its roots, such dogma is for the most part irrational and ephemeral, constantly threatened by Man's thirst for alcohol.

TRADE UNIONS, POLITICAL PARTIES AND ALCOHOLISM

The equivocal position of Western churches on the subject of alcoholism was mirrored by attitudes in trade unions and political parties during the period 1850–1950. Industrialization in Western Europe saw both the birth of the trade union movement and a massive increase in alcohol consumption. In the interest of productivity, sober-minded employers sought to restrict drinking among the workforce, whereas the labourers themselves, toiling in atrocious conditions, felt they were entitled to drink as they liked and considered any form of regulation as provocative. Outside the workplace, cafés and *cabarets* played an important part in workers' lives; it was here that meetings were held and wages paid. Against this background, *bourses du travail* (trade union centres) were established in major French cities at the end of the nineteenth century. These new institutions provided an opportunity for workers to educate themselves in political, economic and health issues and, since alcoholism at this period was widely regarded as a working-class phenomenon, they became the venue for lectures on the subject. In the train of this propaganda, various trade-affiliated temperance societies were created and employers accepted the principle of paying wages at the workplace.[49] On the whole, the anti-alcohol movement in France at the time was run by individuals who were out of touch with the workers, and their theories and moralizing were regarded with suspicion. Temperance societies were accused of being exploited by employers, whose only interest was in sacking alcoholic workers or using drunkenness as a pretext for not paying compensation in industrial accidents. In an effort to change the situation, Legrain helped found the *Fédération des ouvriers antialcooliques* (Federation of Anti-Alcoholic Workers), an organization run in the main by members of the abstinent Good Templars. The federation published its own paper, *La Pensée Ouvrière*.

Unions and socialists opposed the view held in wealthier sections of society that working-class poverty was the result of alcoholism, and argued on the contrary that heavy drinking was the product of low wages, difficult working conditions and poor housing. In their opinion the introduction of an eight-hour working day, an increase in wages and new housing would bring about the end of alcoholism. This was the view of men such as Vandervelde, the founder of Belgian socialism, himself a teetotaller: 'In order for socialism to emerge triumphant from the struggle with the forces which oppress and undermine the working classes, the proletariat must first pioneer a moral reformation.'[50] In France, two opposed lines of thought developed within the unions and the nascent Socialist Party, and when Zola published *L'Assommoir* some regarded it as a life-like description, whereas others saw it as an attack on a working class falsely portrayed as the slave of alcohol.

The temperance movement had little success among the French working classes, who failed to be roused by a teetotaller's version of the 'Red Flag'. There were a variety of opinions expressed within the trade union movement. Many socialists were actively hostile to the propaganda and viewed it as another diversionary tactic dreamed up by the owners to divide the workers – alcoholism would disappear with the coming revolution. Amongst anarchists and anti-militarists, some argued that military training went hand in hand with drinking, whereas others took a Malthusian line and suggested that alcohol was responsible for a population explosion. This latter line of argument led some to speak out in defence of women, whom they saw as doubly exploited, having too much work and too many children. Some workers felt that alcoholism harmed their cause, but others considered nothing more important than the fight for the eight-hour day. The most radical voices called for immediate revolution. Debate on alcohol was finally dropped from the agenda at meetings of the Socialist Party and the Confédération Général du Travail (CGT) because it caused too much disagreement. When the subject was last discussed at the congress in 1912 no clear conclusion was reached.[51]

The temperance societies had the merit of generating discussion on alcohol in factories and places where the problems were most clearly visible, but they did not succeed in influencing public opinion. There is no evidence to suggest that their activities actually resulted in any reduction in alcohol consumption among workers and debate was not resumed after the First World War.

In Germany, the social-democratic movement was equally divided, but anti-alcoholism had some limited success, largely as a result of the strict line taken by employers, who dismissed drunken workers and attempted to introduce non-alcoholic drinks into the factories. Efforts were made to pay the workers on Friday rather than Saturday, in the hope that this would reduce the amounts spent on drink at the weekends. Such measures were scarcely received with enthusiasm by the workforce and they enjoyed no more than temporary success. The unions did participate in some schemes, notably when it was demonstrated that drunkenness at work was responsible for a large number of accidents, and they were at least in part successful.[52] The German Socialist Party, however, pulled in the opposite direction and when the government tried to increase drink prices in an effort to control consumption, the socialists declared a *schnappsboycott* in 1909 and a *bierkrieg* (beer war) with street demonstrations lasted until 1910.[53] As was the case in France, the First World War put an end to the campaign and even today alcoholism is not on the agenda for public debate.

Action taken by political parties can be the result of either pressure from the membership or the need to attract support. Alcoholism is a delicate issue and Western political parties have tended not to adopt aggressive attitudes; where they have taken a combative stance, this has not endured for long. Their hesitation is explained by a balance of radical support for abstinence and more moderate opinion across the political spectrum. The more conservative parties, representing industrial and agricultural interests, have an ambivalent approach, being both opposed to alcoholism among the workers and yet representing those who profit from the alcohol trade. More liberal parties appear torn between concern for civil liberties and concern for the dangers of alcoholism. In France, no party has come out in the majority in favour of measures restricting alcohol consumption since 1870, except in times of war. Successive governments of centre-left and centre-right have introduced fiscal and marketing controls, only to see them relaxed by subsequent regimes regarding them as too restrictive. A similar situation exists in Britain, where the subject has never generated a great deal of interest in the House of Commons or the House of Lords.

The American experience has already been abundantly documented. It is sufficient at this juncture to recall that the eighteenth amendment was approved by a Congress with a Republican majority, the party with a reputation for being 'dry'; some Republicans, however, opposed the amendment, while many Democrats, including the President, Woodrow Wilson, voted in its favour. Fourteen years later, when the entire country was for abrogation, the 'wet' Democrats criticized the Republicans for their change of heart, and yet it was again a Democrat, Roosevelt, who was President when prohibition was ended.

The attitudes of the more 'revolutionary parties' are worthy of note. In their quest for revolution, such organizations tend to adopt radical social policies with an emphasis upon moral rectitude. On coming to power, Lenin banned known drunkards from the Soviet Communist Party and during the purges of 1920 and 1921 a quarter of those expelled from the party were found guilty of 'careerism, drunkenness and bourgeois life-styles'. This all seems very curious, given that the Communists had not lifted the tsar's ban on the sale of vodka, which dated from the First World War. How in such circumstances did these drinkers obtain their alcohol? The ban was not lifted until 1922, and vodka reappeared on the Soviet market just as bread was beginning to disappear.

In Hungary, alcohol was banned in 1919, under the rule of Bela Kun's Soviet-inspired regime. The move did not make his government popular and it was overthrown by supporters of Prince Horthy, who restored relative freedom to the alcohol trade.[54]

During the Spanish Civil War Republican forces occupying Barcelona were divided and various factions were left to declare their own position on moral questions. Their views were often puritanical, as illustrated by the caption to a poster produced by the Iberian Anarchist Federation in 1938:

> The dance-hall is the antechamber to the brothel: shut it.
> The tavern undermines character: shut it.
> The bar degrades the intellect: shut it.[55]

This poster again demonstrates the frequent association of lust with drunkenness. As in the prohibition years in America, the Anarchists found it easier to close down bars than to stop men drinking and their measures were not enforced during the Franco period.

In 1985, the Soviet Union recommenced its anti-alcohol campaign. Communist Party propaganda recalls a golden age when the Russian people drank only mead and blames modern consumption of wine and vodka on nefarious Western influences, an argument with a familiar ring. The Soviet government has also tried to draw the citizen's attention to the happy period of prohibition instigated under Lenin, but omits to mention, however, that it was the tsar who originally introduced the ban and that Stalin was responsible for its removal. Other familiar arguments are also employed: alcoholism is the enemy of productivity; it causes racial degeneration; it undermines the country; the alcoholic is a bad Communist. The government has introduced measures that have been tried on numerous occasions elsewhere: closing drink-shops, punishing alcohol-related absenteeism, increasing the price of vodka, and confining alcoholics in psychiatric hospitals. Experience of similar programmes elsewhere would lead us to expect an initial short-lived fall in consumption, rising once more when ways are discovered to avoid the new regulations.

Most countries have been unable to formulate any policy to control alcoholism: dominant Western religions have come to no unanimous decision on the matter, and trade unions and political parties have found themselves so divided on the question that they no longer dare discuss it. However, alcohol consumption seems to be slowly decreasing and, although the reasons for this remain uncertain, the anti-alcohol movement can derive some encouragement from this downward trend.

CONCLUSION

THIS section of the book has attempted to show the practical consequences of Magnus Huss's work on alcoholism. In many instances
new initiatives, projects and administrative decisions are still based on
schemata laid down a hundred years ago, although the mid-twentieth
century did witness some developments. The First World War had
already pushed some countries into recognition of the problem of
alcoholism, and between 1914 and 1919 reformist legislation was
introduced. The ferment of the Second World War contributed further
to new attitudes. No work better illustrates the tenor of the period than
an article published in 1950 by Paul Perrin, dealing with the social and
economic aspects of the problem.[1] His approach has all the short-
comings of which medical thought was guilty during the period 1850–
1950. The article is punctuated with aphorisms, written in Hippocratic
style, which encapsulate prevailing attitudes.

Aphorism 7. 'Alcoholism has already produced a profound racial
degeneration in some regions. It will result in complete destruction of
the French race within forty years, unless harsh measures are taken.'
When Perrin was writing, there was still no scientific proof for 'degeneration', despite all the discussions of the previous century. The forty years
of which he spoke have now almost passed without any indication that
the French race is about to disappear; on the contrary, the nation is
taller, healthier and lives longer. The reluctance of both the Fourth and
Fifth Republics to take any measures on the basis of apocalyptic
predictions expressed by some doctors now seems entirely justified.

Aphorism 8. 'The children of heavy drinkers are always degenerate
and, not infrequently, are born idiots. Large numbers of them are
destined to become alcoholics. The children of moderate drinkers are
found to have liver abnormalities and nervous disorders; at school they
make restless pupils and are incapable of paying attention.' Perrin here
takes the dogma of hereditary alcoholism as proven, but his efforts to
distinguish between different types of drinker are important in that they
represent an early attempt to draw up a typology of alcoholics.

Aphorism 9. 'Long-term heavy drinkers are incurable and, morally
speaking, resistant to re-education. Those who become violent must be

locked up to protect the public. For this to be accomplished special laws must be introduced.' In certain cases such a proposition is justified, and this was reflected in the law of 1954 governing dangerous alcoholics. (In the draft stage, however, this legislation acquired a punitive form that would give comfort to the most repressive regime.)

Although these aphorisms make reference to degeneration and mental debility with which Magnan would have been in full agreement a hundred years earlier, Perrin's contemporaries were beginning to have their doubts. His remarks concerning the mental capacities of children of alcoholics were not based on sound statistical evidence. Furthermore, it is clinically impossible to distinguish between the effects of heredity and environment; Perrin was evidently unaware that psychological disorders may be ascribed either to nature or nurture. Another fault in Perrin's work stems from the readiness with which he posits causal relationships between phenomena. The age-old association of alcohol with sex prompts him to suggest a link between alcoholism and venereal disease. The most striking link he creates, however, is between alcoholism and tuberculosis, 'because of his physical, mental and financial decline the alcoholic is predisposed to tuberculosis'. This claim is supported with evidence from Denmark: 'In 1876, the Danes were amongst the greatest consumers of alcohol in the world. In 1913, the country announced that deaths from tuberculosis had dropped by 60 per cent, mirroring falls in the country's alcohol consumption.'[2] In reality, the variation was only coincidental and there is nothing to justify Perrin's linking the two.

Perrin's work is a monument to a century of medical thought on alcoholism. His errors and naivety were shared by many others who, like him, failed to observe the rigorous scientific method established by Claude Bernard. The remedies he proposes – strychnine for nervous disorders, liver extracts to combat cirrhosis, and emetics to induce nausea – show him to be a member of the old school, as does his recognition of indirect means of fighting alcoholism such as higher wages, improved housing and, 'the surest adversary of alcoholism', instruction in household management for young girls. In 1950, the rebuilding of France eliminated the slums and yet the nation continued to drink to excess.

Perrin was innovative, in that he sought to understand why people drank. Following Jellinek and Dittmer, he made it necessary to establish different categories of alcoholic patient, which in turn suggested different forms of treatment. He replaced the all-too-commonly employed notion of 'mental degeneration' with that of 'individual disposition'. His work marks the advent of new attitudes towards alcoholism. No matter what their clinical history or social background, alcoholics suffered from an illness requiring a cure. Their treatment was no longer to be a matter of routine, but was to be dictated by their individual circumstances.

PART III

MODERN ALCOHOLOGY

WITH the development of new drugs (particularly antibiotics and improved anaesthetics) in the mid-twentieth century, enthusiasm was reawakened in medical circles. In the new world of reason and experimentation, the notion of degeneration so often used in reference to the mental and physical characteristics of alcoholism appeared artificial, tainted with moral overtones and unscientific. The concept was, in short, out of date. Doctors were to become sociologists and psychologists, they were to rediscover epidemiology and to enter into the complexities of biochemistry. The patient was seen as a whole person, an interaction of body and mind, requiring detailed investigation to reveal the most intimate mechanisms governing his behaviour.

This modern attitude is still regarded with suspicion by the more traditionalist members of the medical profession. It provides no easy answers and is characterized by dispute amongst different schools of thought, by rival classifications and by the constant reworking of terminology. The history of modern alcohology is one of conflicting opinions, leading alternatively to extremes of sterile polemic or useful therapeutic intervention. Alcohology is defined by the French 'glossary of alcohology' as 'the study of all areas of interaction between the human race and ethanol, ranging from the circumstances of its production to its consumption by the individual and the collective'.[1] The discipline has been treated by numerous authoritative studies. We will attempt here only to provide an outline of 'alcoholism' as it has come to be understood in recent decades.

9

Clinical and Biological Considerations

WHILE it would be incorrect to maintain that all parties are now agreed that alcoholism is a disease rather than a vice, it would be true to say that the majority – psychologists, doctors, the media and even governments – have arrived at a consensus view of the phenomenon. In short, alcohologists accept the notion that alcoholism has mental, spiritual and physical dimensions.[1]

ADDICTS AND OTHERS

Before the 1940s, and particularly before the work of E. M. Jellinek became well known, it was generally accepted that all alcoholics were different and that the reasons for a patient turning to drink were as varied as the wide-ranging physical effects of alcohol ingestion. Jellinek, a doctor from New England, was the first to attempt a classification of problems seen in chronic alcoholics; he founded the Research Council on Problems of Alcohol in 1937, published his first works in 1942 and was involved in the early projects of the World Health Organization (WHO). In 1952, the WHO was to accept Jellinek's definition of the alcoholic as its own: 'Alcoholics are those excessive drinkers whose dependence on alcohol has attained such a degree that it shows notable disturbance or an interference with their bodily and mental health, their personal relationships and smooth economic functioning or who show prodromal signs of such a development. They therefore need treatment.'

Jellinek undertook the first serious statistical study of the problem in the United States and established that, even when population growth was taken into account, there had been an increase of 31 per cent in the numbers of alcoholics between 1940 and 1948. This increase had occurred against the background of a fall in total consumption and, in addition, those states that had maintained a system of prohibition had significantly more alcoholics – Kansas, Oklahoma and Mississippi showing excesses of 7, 27, and 30 per cent respectively.[2] Not only did this survey demonstrate the failure of prohibition, it also showed the complexity and variability of drinking habits within populations.

Jellinek's greatest work, *The Disease Concept of Alcoholism*, was published in 1960, some hundred years after Huss's *Alcoholismus Chronicus*.[3] It defines alcoholism as 'any form of alcoholic consumption which causes harm to the individual, to society or both'. Jellinek traces the history of alcoholism as a disease concept, pointing out that in the United States the term 'alcoholism' only superseded 'inebriety' during the early twentieth century. In so doing, he concedes the inferiority of early American work on the subject in comparison with that done by British and French clinicians and German psychiatrists. He criticizes the behaviour of his compatriots during the years of prohibition: 'Americans were more interested in the problems posed by smuggling than they were in alcoholism', but he welcomes their subsequent concern – many of the more recent publications were either British or American in origin.[4] Of greatest significance was Jellinek's attempt to categorize the disease in his 'five patterns of pathological drinking'. The categories he described are not discrete entities and the drinker may display different patterns at different times:[5]

alpha: Purely psychological dependence to relieve physical or emotional pain. No loss of control.
beta: Physical complications resulting from cultural drinking patterns and poor nutrition, but no dependence.
gamma: ('Anglo-Saxon') Loss-of-control drinking, craving and withdrawal symptoms, but can abstain.
delta: (Continental) Inability to abstain, with withdrawal symptoms, but comparatively little social disruption.
epsilon: Bout drinking (dipsomania).

Jellinek did not deny the existence of other drinking habits, whether episodic – confined, for example, to public holidays – or continuous, as in wine-producing countries like France. However, he considered only those that corresponded to his classification to be truly pathological. Such a classification was an attempt to clarify what had hitherto been a hazy area and as such was sure to provoke criticism. It corresponded to North American drinking habits, but bore little relation to those of Mediterranean Europe and elsewhere. It allowed for drinkers passing from one category to the next, but not for those who, from the first, had simultaneously belonged to two categories. Finally, it did not account for one group of patients whom most doctors would call 'alcoholic', namely those who maintain blood-alcohol concentrations such that they do not experience symptoms of withdrawal.

In spite of Paul Perrin's assertion that Jellinek's classification pertained only to a 'minority' of French drinkers, many of the country's alcohol users did in fact fall into one or other of the categories described by the American.[6] However, some did not and the issue was further complicated by differing interpretations of 'alcoholism', applied by some only to those with manifest physical or mental disturbance, and by others to those showing signs of 'dependence' (a behavioural disorder characterized by enslavement to alcohol). The confusion that has arisen in this area has led many contemporary alcohologists to avoid use of the terms 'alcoholism' and 'alcoholic'.

In France, Fouquet has developed a system of classification that takes into account three factors, which he considers contributory to a *'syndrome alcoolique'*.[7] In so doing, he distinguishes between the 'psychic factor' (mental predisposition to simple character disorders or serious psychiatric illness), the 'tolerance factors' (the relationship between the amount of alcohol drunk and the effects experienced) and the 'toxic factor' (the effects of ethanol on the constitution). He goes on to describe three conditions: 'alcoholitis' (*alcoolite*), 'alcoholosis' (*alcoolose*) and 'somalcoholosis' (*somalcoolose*). The first of these accounts for about half of all alcoholics: it describes high levels of consumption, associated with raised tolerance and presentation only after years with organic complications and powerful symptoms of dependence. (Alcoholitis therefore corresponds to a development from Jellinek's category beta to delta.) Slightly less common is alcoholosis; found more amongst women, it corresponds to Jellinek's gamma-type behaviour. Somalcoholosis is a rare phenomenon found largely amongst women, who characteristically succumb to a sudden need for alcohol and become drunk very quickly, because of their low tolerance. Such a phenomenon relates to the dipsomania of Jellinek's epsilon type.

Despite their superficial similarity, the two systems of classification differed both in their creators' approach and possibly also in the type of patient under consideration. Fouquet's categories were received with scepticism and have become the subject of controversy in France and elsewhere. Furthermore, the problems of any attempt at medical classification apply here: many patients do not fit into neat categories, do not remain in a prescribed group and defy prognostic expectation.

The concept of alcohol dependence has been much criticized. Dependence has been defined as 'subjugation to ethanol, such that its withdrawal leads to psychic or somatic disturbance' in the French *Glossary of Alcohology* (*Glossaire d'alcoologie*).[8] British and American thinking on alcoholism (which holds sway in the WHO and in the American classification of mental illness) takes into consideration neither the

Modern Alcohology

variation in individual sensitivity to alcohol, nor those regular drinkers who are not dependent – a common phenomenon in wine-growing areas. The very notion of dependence has been questioned in the British medical literature,[9] and one sociologist, Shaw, considers it redundant in as far as it is of little use in treating the heavy drinker. This has met with disagreement from one group of psychiatrists and psychologists – Schick, Thorley and Stockwell – who, with certain reservations, consider the concept helpful in understanding some patients. The state of dependence is usually described by patients thought to be alcoholic – 'I just can't stop myself' – or is imputed by doctors from what is said during a consultation. (It is commonly observed in those for whom ingestion of alcohol is related to a neurotic disorder.[10]) However, as a phenomenon, it leaves many questions unanswered and does not explain why it is that some heavy drinkers showing signs both of physical and mental impairment are not dependent, why they become 'heavy drinkers' and indeed why they are considered such.

The last of these issues is easily resolved: the term 'heavy drinker' is a relative one, comparing individual consumption with a socially determined norm, which varies in different countries according to group or profession. Social factors come into play in the 'excessive drinker', but here the individual's ability to cope with ethanol is also important – thus, some consumers will become drunk after the slightest ingestion of alcohol, whereas others will present in hospital with cirrhosis after many years of heavy consumption, never having been drunk. Common usage has abbreviated terms, describing those who drink more than the norm simply as 'drinkers' – a designation uniformly disliked by alcohologists, doctors, sociologists, patients and former drinkers. The result has been to render the vocabulary of alcoholism cumbersome, poorly understood and imprecise, and has complicated the study of alcohol problems. The specialists continue to be fascinated by semantics. Our discussion of such matters will end here and we make little apology for our use of terms in current common usage, even if they do not have the same precise connotations for every reader.

In summary, habitual drinking – whether the result of social or professional circumstance – can have diverse effects: the drinker may show signs of dependence in the presence or absence of physical or mental disturbance.

Jellinek's work, in spite of its merits, is today considered unsatisfactory, in as far as it does not apply to all 'alcoholics'. It did succeed, however, in changing public, medical and religious attitudes to alcoholism, and even the messianic temperance leagues came to see the problem as a diverse one and not as a sin. In 1978, French bishops published the following declaration:

The victim of alcohol is only too often regarded as the perpetrator of a crime and is treated accordingly. Such attitudes are contrary to the notion of divine mercy and serve only to exacerbate a problem which in many cases originated in social or psychological difficulties. The alcoholic is one of those unfortunates whom Jesus came to earth to save.[11]

Modern medical science is perpetually working to establish the causes of disease with a view to appropriate treatment and eventual cure. Jellinek's work provides few answers of this kind (which may also be a reason for its recent decline in popularity), but then neither have biological scientists come forward with aetiological theories. Biochemistry and genetics are by no means categorical on the subject. Alcohol would seem to fit the biochemical model of a substance that challenges normal physiological metabolism – the body is incapable of degrading it adequately. Despite considerable progress in our understanding of such processes, the individual variation in the phenomena of tolerance, habituation and resistance to the effects of alcohol remain poorly understood. Geneticists have proposed the existence of an X-linked gene to explain this metabolic variation. Such a theory, if proven, might lead to a re-evaluation of the simplistic hypotheses of the nineteenth century: alcoholism could be considered hereditary, as criminality had been one hundred years ago. For the present, all that can be said about the variability in the assimilation of alcohol between individuals is that it may be genetically inherited. Attempts to classify ethanol with hallucinogenic and hypnotic drugs have also foundered. It resembles these drugs in that it induces tolerance (increasingly large doses are needed for it to have its desired effects and withdrawal provokes mental and physical disturbance), but important differences remain: most opiate abusers become addicts, whereas only a small proportion of drinkers do so.

In the absence of demonstrable causes of alcoholism, 'society' frequently becomes the scapegoat of those who feel the need to apportion blame for the phenomenon. Thus, for example, the 1978 episcopal commission was to declare in a peremptory statement: 'society makes alcoholics of those of its members whom it denies the opportunity of living a full life. The fight against alcoholism is a political one.' Such a declaration, which blames society for all mental suffering, is reminiscent of ideas expressed by J. J. Rousseau and of the naive notions voiced during 1968 and by the anti-psychiatry movement.

Alcoholism defies medical science in that it is not readily defined by discrete categories and does not obey the laws of a system that distinguishes between the normal and the pathological. The question of 'cure' has also been much discussed. An alcoholic whose blood-pressure falls and liver function improves when he stops drinking is not necessarily 'cured'; it is unlikely that, in keeping with the majority of the population, he will subsequently be able to consume moderate amounts of alcohol without becoming addicted.[12] Such a feat may be possible for the occasional 'trained' drinker, who drinks without a thirst from the moment he is bought a drink by a chance acquaintance in a bar. The 'cure' without total abstinence would seem to be impossible, however, for the drinker who is psychologically and physically dependent upon alcohol. Former drinkers are never referred to as 'cured drinkers', in spite of the fact that they may never again consume a drop of alcohol and have therefore 'broken the habit'; such a state of affairs may be explained by the fact that total abstinence does not represent 'normal' behaviour. Many experts in the field believe that an alcoholic is an alcoholic for life – a desperate prognosis, were not life without alcohol potentially as enjoyable as life with it.

Alcoholism thus fails to fulfil many of the criteria established by experimental medicine to satisfy the reductionist notion of a 'disease', and its existence can only be explained when other factors – psychological, sociological, cultural and political – are taken into consideration.

Doctors, unhappy with their treatment of alcoholics, may well turn to an assessment of their patient's personality. Only too often, unfortunately, do they come into contact with the latter when he is in an advanced state of intoxication and, as a result, tend to attribute any observable personality traits or pathological development to the effects of ethanol. It is conceivable, however, that such problems existed before, and indeed precipitated, the patient's recourse to alcohol. The inversion of cause and effect in this way is a possibility that has preoccupied many practitioners in recent years.[13]

The alcoholic often drinks as the result of dissatisfaction with life and so sets in motion a vicious cycle, which precludes any possibility for change. Drinking becomes his means of changing testimony, allowing him to re-create himself and his environment. Looking in the bar mirror, he sees a different self. When he lies to his doctor, he lies to himself. When he meets another alcoholic – one of the few companions he feels can truly understand him – he creates an imaginary friendship that he knows to be artificial, and yet he is able to enjoy the conscious–unconscious lie of the situation. When he hides a bottle in the chest of drawers, he does so in both the hope and the fear that he will find it again.[14] Many psychoanalytical interpretations of alcoholism have been proposed; suffice it to mention here the notion that some alcoholic patients experience impulses that are both contradictory and coherent. Thus, to have a better life, they are ready to drink themselves to death – the impulse for life borders on the impulse to die. Concealed suicidal tendencies, present in many patients before they begin to drink, are exposed by alcohol and often are manifest in the behaviour of the excessive drinker who continues to drink, despite a full appreciation of the damage he is doing himself.

Whether events prior to the onset of drinking are interpreted as some kind of archaic defect in the mental development of the patient or in terms of an 'inverted Oedipal complex' during childhood, much remains unexplained. Nevertheless, such theories, in as far as they do not place the whole blame on alcohol, may lead to fruitful psychotherapeutic intervention with alcoholics. For similar reasons, those working with alcoholics should also assess home circumstances and social milieu. Although doctors can have little influence on environmental factors and (as has already been stated) should beware of placing the blame entirely on society, their interest should extend into these areas. Alcoholics often terrorize their families, but are equally often constrained or isolated by them: spouses, for example, often contribute to the problems of their partner and to his or her relapse after a period of improvement.[15]

Contemporary understanding of the alcoholic is characterized by a complexity and variety scarcely envisaged by the simplistic attitudes of the nineteenth century. Every patient is different; every clinical picture differs from the last; great variations in individual intelligence and sensibility are recognized, as are differing reasons for drinking and different ways of doing so. Every new case of alcoholism presupposes an interaction of personality, milieu, physical constitution and the effects of the toxin itself.

Autobiographies will be discussed at a later juncture. For the present, let it suffice to quote a former alcoholic, himself a priest, whose description of drinking behaviour could be applied to many excessive drinkers: 'It was the petty fools, the decorated upstarts who drove me to drink or, as was really the case, my own inability to cope with the filth of this world. I wanted to change the world and instead foundered in alcohol. I now understand that it was by changing myself that I was able to free myself from alcohol.'[16] Fortunately, few of those who become dissatisfied with their situation in life turn to alcohol.

ALCOHOLOPATHIES

Alcoholopathy is defined as 'any pathological state related to the consumption of ethanol'.[17] It may be somatic or psychiatric in character, or it may combine visceral or nervous symptoms with a disturbance of mental state. The term refers exclusively to the health of the drinker and not to the potential casualties amongst family, work mates and road users for which the drinker might be held responsible.

The risks of alcoholopathy today should be quantified with the help of precise criteria; no longer should they be the subject of unsubstantiated hypothesis, as was the case in the nineteenth century. Given the difficulty, already demonstrated, in establishing a definition for the term 'alcoholic', the task of isolating the alcoholic population within individual countries – let alone on a world-wide scale – is by no means simple. Even studies that limit themselves to the numbers of 'individuals at risk' (those who, by their drinking habits, risk damage to their health) must be content with approximations; thus, for example, it is believed that in France such individuals number between 2 and 5 million. The only country that has been able to conduct surveys with any degree of accuracy is Finland, with its small, evenly distributed and socially homogeneous population. Since 1950, the Finns have performed a number of remarkable epidemiological studies investigating drinking habits and the relationship between excessive alcohol intake and the incidence of cancer and cardiovascular disease. Their work, using large population samples, defies criticism and has made a major contribution to our scientific understanding of alcoholism.

In France, the consumption of alcohol per head of population (over 14 years of age) has fallen from the 23 litres of pure ethanol quoted by Ledermann in 1950 to 20 litres in 1981.[18] This small decrease should not be a source of pride to the French, since it is amply accounted for by changes in the population – particularly the influx of immigrants, who for social, religious and economic reasons drink less than the native French. Furthermore, the pattern follows the global trend of small decreases in consumption, accompanied notwithstanding by continuing growth in the numbers of heavy drinkers.

The notorious imprecision of 'causes of death', as shown on death certificates, means that mortality statistics can only give a highly approximate idea of fatality attributable to alcohol. Thus the numbers of those registered as dying from 'alcoholism, alcoholic psychosis or liver cirrhosis' in France fell from 18,500 in 1960 to 17,200 in 1982 – a decrease that should not be considered significant, in view of the estimated 40,000 other alcohol-related deaths each year. This latter category includes death through chronic alcohol abuse from conditions such as chronic pancreatitis and also from accidents or suicide, which, together with death from the combined effects of ethanol and other drugs, notably opiates and hallucinogens, in overdose, may equally be the result of an acute alcoholic episode.

Not only does alcoholism result directly in death, it also increases morbidity and the risks of fatality. Pathological infections shrugged off by the normal subject can become serious in the heavy drinker. Thus, the risks of poor repair, infection, phlebitis and other complications are far greater in the alcoholic with a broken leg than in his non-drinking counterpart. Alcoholics spend at least a third more time in hospital than other patients with comparable disorders and their complications may become life-threatening, whatever the disorder. Patients with diabetes, cardiac problems, vascular disease or rheumatism run a higher risk of impotence, gangrene of the extremities, and cardiac or respiratory failure, if they are also excessive drinkers. They are also susceptible to the toxic effects of interactions between alcohol and therapeutic agents.

Numerous recent studies have highlighted the harmful results of the combination of alcohol with tobacco, which, although it neither induces dependence nor damages liver cells and nervous tissue, acts upon the mucosae aggravating the effects of ethanol. This synergy is held responsible for many malignancies in the upper airways and gastrointestinal tract – notably the oesophagus. A ban on alcohol and tobacco would reduce by one third the incidence of cancer in France.[19]

There appears to be little correlation between alcoholic mortality (the number of deaths directly or indirectly attributable to alcohol) and morbidity (the numbers of drinkers with alcohol-related disorders). The development of organic lesions, equally, seems to follow no strict pattern. In Sweden, deaths from pancreatitis and cirrhosis are declining, as too are deaths from cirrhosis in France. Psychiatric morbidity in Swedish alcoholics, however, remains unchanged, whereas in France the numbers admitted to psychiatric units rose sharply from 15,600 in 1961 to 40,000 in 1980.[20]

Alcoholism has traditionally been the reason given to explain increased morbidity amongst men. It does not, however, remain a condition exclusive to the male population, and we are now witnessing increasing incidence amongst women. In 1960, there were twelve male alcoholics for every female, a situation that had altered dramatically by 1980, when there were found to be only four times as many males as females affected by the problem. This trend was reflected in the period

1970–7, when the number of female alcoholics in psychiatric care rose from 11 to 30 per cent. Women are less able to metabolize alcohol and are accordingly more susceptible to organic malfunction and cirrhosis than their male counterparts.

Drinking problems amongst adolescents are also on the increase and remain largely unquantified.[21] In France, where children are familiar with alcohol from an early age, the problems of adolescence – endocrinological, sexual, psychological and social – may place such a strain on those with fragile personalities that they turn to drink. Fortunately such excesses are usually short-lived and disappear with the acquisition of familial or professional responsibility in society. The notion of hereditary alcoholism has already been discussed and it remains extremely difficult to establish whether social and mental maladaption in adolescents is attributable to genetic causes, to the foetal alcohol syndrome or to their early childhood environment – records of child abuse in the families of alcoholics are not easy to keep.[22]

Recent decades have seen alcohol established as the causative agent in numerous conditions. Doctors in 1950 were well acquainted with gastritis, hepatic cirrhosis and fatty degeneration of the liver, but they are now better informed about the mechanisms leading to acute alcoholic hepatitis, acute and chronic pancreatitis, and cancer of the pancreas. They know more about occlusion of the portal vein, which results in raised blood-pressure throughout the veinous system draining the digestive tract and explains the development of varices which, particularly in the lower oesophagus and stomach, have a tendency to rupture; the resultant haemorrhage frequently proves fatal. The role of tobacco and alcohol in the development of cancer in the upper airways and oesophagus has already been discussed. Less well understood, however, is the biochemistry of the liver disturbance responsible for the nervous phenomena experienced in 'porto-caval encephalopathy': these include somnolence, a spasmodic 'flopping tremor' of the hands, and disorientation in time and space, and they may develop into 'hepatic coma' and death.

The most striking discoveries have involved the circulatory system. Alcoholic cardiomyopathy is now a recognized condition characterized by increasing shortness of breath and serious cardiac insufficiency, which only improves on withdrawal from alcohol. A second disorder of the heart muscle is associated with 'alcoholic beriberi', a deficiency of vitamin B1 that mimics beriberi seen in consumers of 'polished' rice in south-east Asia. Heavy drinkers often have a raised blood-pressure when compared with the non-drinking population; this can have grave complications, which again may be averted by stopping drinking. A relationship between alcoholism and atherosclerosis has yet to be clearly established, but it would seem that alcoholism aggravates the condition (which leads to the progressive occlusion of the arteries with consequent gangrene in the limbs, cardiac infarction and strokes).[23] The popular myth that moderate consumption of whisky protects against athero-sclerosis remains unproven. Also requiring satisfactory explanation is the biochemical relationship between alcohol intake and the raised serum–cholesterol levels observed in many alcoholics. Excessive consumption of alcohol does, however, predispose to cardiac infarction and renders the consequences of such an event more severe in patients with pre-existing coronary artery disease.

Few organs remain untouched by the effects of alcohol. It disturbs digestion and possibly increases the risks of colonic cancer; it affects the glands of the digestive system, the parotids less so than the pancreas;[24] it interferes with the secretion of hormones by the endocrine system. Alcohol may also be responsible for male genital dysfunction by disrupting the sex glands, although it would seem that problems of this kind have psychological rather than hormonal origins.

In the last thirty years, neurologists have come to implicate ethanol-induced cerebral and cerebellar atrophy, and the subsequent shrinking and disappearance of certain areas of brain tissue, as causative in progressive intellectual deterioration, leading to the state of major alcoholic dementia.[25] Anatomical and biochemical evidence has also accumulated to explain neuro-psychiatric complications and epilepsy in alcoholics. Admissions to psychiatric institutions are less frequent than in the 1890s (thus refuting Legrain's anxious predictions), but are associated with greater severity of disorder. Nevertheless, 25 per cent of the patients in mental establishments in Brittany, Normandy, Alsace or Paris show alcohol-related symptomatology – long-term confusion, visual and auditory hallucinations – and are often progressing towards dementia.[26] Many other alcoholics who experience temporary psychiatric disturbance are not admitted to hospital and therefore do not figure in the statistics. These individuals are susceptible to acute delirium, to recurrent bouts of often suicidal depression, and trauma or coexistent infection remains a serious condition.[27]

Mention should also be made of the violent acts so often seen in alcoholics, which frequently lead to domestic disturbance. In France, a law designed to deal with the 'dangerous alcoholic' was passed in 1954 and has been criticized by some as a retrograde, primitive measure.

Invoking former legislation of 1838, its aim was preventative: to protect society without major infringement of individual freedom by allowing medical intervention in crisis situations. Regional committees were established to study individual cases, the social services were to provide information about the domestic situation and make home-visits, and police intervention and internment were sanctioned, if considered necessary. The involvement of numerous agencies in the implementation of this legislation means that its efficacy depends largely on the goodwill and co-operation of all involved and is consequently extremely variable. It remains nevertheless in existence and represents an attempt to palliate the potentially tragic consequences of alcoholism by reconciliation of two opposing interests – the freedom of the individual to drink himself to death and the need for society to be protected from the dangerous behaviour of the alcoholic.

Few people – in France at any rate – abstain completely from alcohol and it would be useful if some sort of threshold could be established beyond which consumption could be said to increase the risk of serious complications. For this to be possible, a knowledge of the relationship between dose and effect is required.[28] This discussion will limit itself to such phenomena in the context of long-term alcoholic consumption.

Paradoxically, the relationship is easier to establish for populations than it is for individuals and would in the former case be expressed in terms of a statement of statistical probability relating to groups presumed to have similar drinking habits. If one group drinking a given amount of pure ethanol each year appears more susceptible to oesophageal or pancreatic cancer and hepatic cirrhosis than another, more abstemious population, then it should be possible to ascertain the level of consumption at which the risk of complications of this nature begins to increase.

For the individual, there is probably no such 'danger threshold', as there are so many variables at play that a 'normal dose–effect relationship', if it exists at all, is impossible to establish. For example, in cirrhosis alcohol consumption is not the sole aetiological variable – a feature underlined by the fact that 10 per cent of cirrhotics have been shown to be non-drinkers. Although daily alcohol intake is one important determinant, many others – amongst them nutritional status, dietary habits, previous infective states and ability to metabolize ethanol – must also be taken into consideration, if the risk of developing the condition is to be calculated.

It would be interesting to take the investigation one step further and attempt to establish a link between specific drinks and known complications – to be able to state categorically, for example, that wine was associated with cirrhosis or that whisky predisposed to oesophageal cancer. One group of French researchers has attempted studies of this kind, which are so often thwarted by the non-specific drinking habits of their subjects, as it is rare to find drinkers who adhere only to one form of alcohol in preference to all others.[29] This heterogeneity of alcoholic consumption explains the difficulty encountered, for example, in establishing the relative 'cirrhogeneity' of wines produced from different kinds of grape. One alternative might be to use animal experiments similar to those conducted by Magnan a century ago, but here again problems are encountered, namely those of transposing results from one species to another. Meaningful results in this area of study could herald a new approach to alcohol research, in that they might bring us to question the view that the toxicity of alcoholic drink is attributable solely to the ethanol it contains.

ACCIDENTS AND ALCOHOL

Legislation introduced in recent years to control the practice of drinking and driving has drawn public attention to the numbers of deaths and injuries that occur on the roads. The problem predates the mechanization of overland transport (a fact often overlooked in the twentieth century).[30] In France, it was only after the recovery of the car industry following the Second World War that any interest in accident statistics was shown. However, despite concerted efforts to improve conditions on the roads, France continues to have the highest mortality rates of any of the industrialized countries, irrespective of whether such rates are measured per head of the population (two and a half times greater than Great Britain), per vehicle (twice that of Japan) or per kilometre travelled. Improvements in infrastructure, new motorways, safer cars, harsher penalties for road traffic offences, a more stringent driving test have all failed to prevent the deaths of 12,000–13,000 road users each year. Although alcohol is not the sole cause of road accidents in France, more drivers involved in accidents in that country have blood–alcohol levels in excess of 1 g/l than in Great Britain, Canada or the United States.[31]

Alcohol affects performance well before a state of drunkenness is reached. Relatively small amounts increase the driver's temerity and, without him realizing it, reduce visual acuity, vigilance and the precision with which actions are performed. The tendency to commit errors of judgement both of speed and distance will accordingly be far greater. Statistics published by the police and the *Organisme national de sécurité routière* (National Organization for Road Safety) show that the risk of fatal accident, when compared with drivers having less than 0.4 g/l of alcohol in their blood, is increased eight-fold between 0.8 and 1.2 g/l, forty-fold for the range 1.2–2.0 g/l and 100-fold, if levels exceed 2 g/l. Furthermore, almost 45 per cent of drivers involved in a fatal accident have blood–alcohol levels greater than 0.8 g/l, the legal limit in France. This represents a total of between 5,000 and 6,000 deaths associated with illegal driving every year.[32] Drivers are not the sole contributors to this statistic, which applies to other road users – passengers, cyclists and pedestrians – who also run the risk either of provoking or becoming the victim of accidents.

Alcohol restricts our ability to perform tasks in all walks of life and not just on the roads. In 1982–3, the French High Committee on Alcoholism (*Haut Comité de l'Alcoolisme*) conducted a survey of 4,800 patients treated in hospital after an accident, irrespective of the circumstances of its occurrence.[33] Alcohol levels in patients under the age of 30 exceeded 2 g/l in 34 per cent of men and 32 per cent of women, whereas in those over 30 years of age the same level was exceeded by 57 per cent of men and 49 per cent of women. These results would seem to indicate that 'accidents' are rarely attributable to chance alone and are possibly better explained within the context of the acute effects of alcohol ingestion. Patients and their relatives rarely admit that the element of 'chance' might be better expressed as a given behaviour rendered risky by alcohol. The survey also found that blood–alcohol levels varied in accordance with the activity pursued at the time of the accident.

Accidents at work have serious judicial and financial consequences, notably in the area of compensation. It is certain that alcohol plays an important role in the evolution of occupational mishap; unfortunately, however, the reticence displayed by victims, colleagues and employers when questioned about alcohol in the workplace means that the importance of such a role cannot be evaluated.

Patients are often anxious to know exactly how much alcohol they can consume before they will experience sensory impairment or before their blood levels will exceed the legal limit for drivers. Doctors cannot provide precise answers to requests of this kind, since the effects of alcohol on the psycho-motor system vary enormously between in- dividuals (depending, amongst other things, on their size and ability to metabolize ethanol and on the time that has elapsed since their last meal). It would therefore be dangerous for the medical profession to 'prescribe' given amounts of specific forms of alcohol, since this would imply a scientific basis for such a practice where none exists. The picture is also further complicated by the phenomenon of 'tolerance', whereby increasing quantities of alcohol are required to reproduce symptoms of euphoria or psycho-sensory disturbance; the change in behaviour of the initiate on drinking a given amount of alcohol will be more remarkable than that observed in the inveterate alcoholic.

The notion of a 'danger threshold' for alcohol consumption is beguiling and harks back to physiological principles developed by Magendie. It implies the existence of a critical dose that, if exceeded, would result in the emergence of toxic side-effects. Such a model of an 'all or nothing' response does not hold true for the effects of alcohol; not only are there too many variables to be taken into consideration, but recent clinical and experimental work also suggests that these phenomena are only understandable if each molecule of alcohol ingested is considered toxic in its own right. The establishment of a fixed legal limit of 0.80 g/l for drivers is thus not based on scientific truth, but is required as a criterion whereby the law can be applied. As an arbitrary figure, it may well be that the limit is set too high or indeed too low; unfortunately, however, the very fact that it represents a division between legal and illegal reinforces the erroneous 'threshold theory' within society.

This discussion has confined itself to acute alcoholic episodes, which are easier to document than the effects of chronic alcohol ingestion, which develop more insidiously. Only gradually does the machine operator become a danger to himself and others; only gradually does his hand lose its steadiness and his eye its acuity; only gradually do his reaction times and colour vision deteriorate. The number of accidents caused by the effects of chronic alcoholism will for this reason never be known. They will therefore only ever be averted by early diagnosis of the condition.

DIAGNOSIS

Doctors have been familiar with the signs of chronic alcoholism since the nineteenth century. Although individual practitioners may attach greater or less significance to such phenomena (which include trembling hands, slurred speech and bloodshot eyes), most will recognize their import even in the course of unrelated consultations or when heavy drinking is denied. In this way, chronic alcohol intoxication will frequently be apparent to the trained clinical observer before the patient becomes troubled by disagreeable symptoms.

During the 1960s, a system of classification of the signs of chronic alcohol abuse was developed by Le Gô and Pertusier in their work with French railway workers. The system, which now bears Le Gô's name, placed such observations on a pseudo-objective basis and involved the scoring of phenomena such as insomnia, nightmares, digestive upsets and abnormalities of movement and gait reported by patients and signs such as physical appearance, liver disturbance and raised blood-pressure noted by the examining doctor. Specific signs are scored on a range from 0 to 5, according to severity, and are entered into a grid with a potential maximum cumulative score of 30. Individual totals thus represent a combination of the patient's view of the problem and a more objective chemical evaluation, which may be useful in areas such as the assessment of suitability for employment and as an indicator to the need for counselling and treatment. Le Gô's grid has indeed proved of use to alcoholics over the years – one of its main advantages being that it indicates the degree of improvement or deterioration during follow-up – and its conception predated the now-common use of scoring systems in the assessment of physical and mental states. Specific criticism of Le Gô's ratings, however, has been voiced and pertains to his omission of consideration of social milieu: no reference is made to the patient's family, social or occupational situation – factors highly relevant to assessment of alcoholism, in that they highlight the psychological maladaptation that so often predisposes to the condition.

Biological tests developed in recent years provide a more accurate and scientific approach to the problem. Not only are they efficient in the follow-up of patients under treatment, but they also uncover those endangered by a high alcohol intake that they refuse to acknowledge. Considerable research in this area will undoubtedly lead to the development of new investigations and this account will limit itself to the more common tests performed without entering into detail about the breakdown of ethanol within the body. The levels of one enzyme, gamma glutamyl transferase (γ GT), in particular, are raised in heavy drinkers, and although such an elevation is not specific to alcoholics, it becomes almost diagnostic, if levels fall within five days of the last ingestion of alcohol. A second investigation involves the measurement of the average volume of red blood cells (the 'mean corpuscular volume' or MCV). If this parameter is significantly increased in a subject, there is a 50 per cent probability that he is consuming dangerously high quantities of alcohol. However, since, as with a raised γ GT, such a finding is not exclusive to the heavy drinker, further, less routine investigations should be performed as a means of verification. Thus levels of immunoglobin A

(IgA) and of the iron transport protein, transferrin (Tf), are measured and if the ratio of the former to the latter is greater than 2 : 1 and returns to normal on abstinence from alcohol, this is highly suggestive of a degree of hepatic cirrhosis, which may as yet be asymptomatic. Other tests are also sometimes performed to assess blood levels of glucose, uric acid and triglycerides (including cholesterol); these, however, are less sensitive to changes provoked by alcohol.

Other investigations will undoubtedly emerge from research findings – for example, from the fact that we now know that ethanol is destroyed by the enzyme aldehyde dehydrogenase, the level and activity of which would appear to be reduced in excessive drinkers. Many south-east Asians are unable to tolerate alcohol because they have only low levels of the enzyme: they become drunk rapidly and are less susceptible to chronic alcoholic habits.

Biological testing methods are used by health insurance companies, who perform some 400,000 check-ups each year in France and who, as a result, are in a position to appreciate the extent of alcohol intoxication amongst the French.[34] Also of value are the findings of the *Haut Comité de l'Alcoolisme* survey already discussed. When blood tests were performed on their sample of accident victims, the committee discovered results suggestive of chronic alcohol ingestion in 27 per cent of men and 31 per cent of women. Although these figures do not prove conclusively either that chronic alcoholics are involved in a higher proportion of accidents or that about 30 per cent of the French population drinks too much, they are interesting in that they reveal the widespread incidence of alcohol abuse and the increased risks of avoidable poor health and accidents amongst drinkers.

10
Help for the Alcoholic

A SPECIAL DISEASE

ALCOHOLICS are not 'ill' in the same way as those suffering, for example, from an infectious disease and they must be considered as a special patient group. In their various guises they are not easy people to deal with either socially or in the therapeutic situation, and even individuals who present a docile, smiling exterior are often unpredictable and lacking in self-discipline. Their behaviour frequently scandalizes the medical profession and leads to the failure of treatment.[1]

For their part, doctors enjoy definitive results in their work and show a tendency to treat the consequences of alcoholism in preference to the underlying disorder; thus a surgeon will be satisfied with the repair of accidental injury and the physician will content himself with symptomatic improvement in alcohol-related conditions such as hepatic cirrhosis or gastrointestinal haemorrhage. Similarly, the casualty officer faced with the drunk brought into hospital because his condition exposes him to life-threatening danger on the streets will be as unhappy about confining his patient to police custody, where he might inhale vomit and asphyxiate, as he will be about admitting him to a general ward, where he will make demands on the nursing staff and disturb other patients who are more seriously ill. The heavy drinker with his frequent relapses and offensive behaviour not only becomes alienated from family and friends, but also from the 'caring professions', who rarely provide the understanding and support required. Fortunately, however, attitudes are changing and the number of benevolent institutions for alcoholics – in France at least – is increasing.

Difficulties encountered in helping alcoholics are compounded by their reluctance to seek assistance. Other than at times of emergency (delirium tremens, problems with the law, accidents), they rarely arrive in the doctor's surgery because they have 'a drinking problem'; when they do, it is more often than not with reluctance after persistent cajoling from a spouse, a colleague or a member of the occupational health department at work. On other occasions, the doctor is consulted for failing vision, bouts of vomiting or muscle cramps, which the drinker will refuse to associate with his high alcohol intake; he denies that he has a drinking problem and becomes frustrated at the inefficacy of the drugs prescribed.

Doctors, too, are at fault in so far as they frequently divide disease into neat physical or mental entities, a tendency that renders them ill equipped to deal with alcoholism. The cause of those favouring a somatic approach has been built on changes observed in the human brain, in enzyme levels, deficiencies in cerebral hormones that normally regulate biological function and other physical disturbances. They refuse to countenance psychological approaches and believe that their case has been strengthened in recent years with the realization that many processes in alcoholic pathology – amongst them cirrhosis, dropsy and polyneuropathy – are amenable to therapeutic intervention, when they were hitherto considered irreversible and carried a gloomy prognosis. Such scientism – the notion that a metabolic disorder can be treated adequately by drug therapy alone – is inappropriate in the case of alcoholism; neuroscience is in its infancy and the notion that human psychology can be reduced to mere neuronal phenomena remains.

The medical profession has come to realize not only that the alcoholic is not a morally culpable individual, but also that he is more than simply a sufferer from some kind of disease. In addition to medical investigation, he needs psychological and social assistance – the support, esteem and encouragement of family, friends, colleagues and fellow alcoholics. There can be no therapeutic monopoly in cases of alcoholism, and all disciplines and influences must be harnessed to help those at risk. Such a philosophy has been slow to emerge, but is now generally accepted in the 1980s.

DRUG THERAPY

Since 1950 numerous advances have been made in the general treatment of alcohol-related disease. These include the development of operations such as porto-caval anastemosis to palliate the effects of gastrointestinal haemorrhage, and vitamin therapies (supplements of vitamins B_1, B_5, miotinic acid and folic acid) to prevent cardiac and nervous disorders. Such measures are not without their own complications, and operations on the digestive tract, which themselves carry risks of porto-caval encephalopathy, will undoubtedly be performed less in years to come, as other therapies improve and become more widespread.

The development of psychotropic drugs in the 1960s also proved useful in the treatment of mental disturbances and tranquillizers, neuroleptic or hypnotic drugs are frequently prescribed to drinkers with psychiatric symptoms. Prescription of antidepressant drugs, however, is problematic, in that it must first be established whether depression is primary or secondary to the ingestion of alcohol. (In primary depression the alcoholic drinks because he is depressed, whereas in secondary depression the inverse is true.) Treatment for the two conditions is different and the prognosis is more favourable in cases of secondary depression.

Many of the principles of the therapeutics of alcoholism are beyond the scope of this work and we will here confine ourselves to an outline of therapies – largely aversive in nature – that have found favour in recent years.

Apomorphine was used in this context, and drinkers were encouraged to drink a quantity of their favourite liquor a few minutes after injection of the drug. The bouts of vomiting induced after this procedure, often repeated on a daily basis, were intended to engender a profound distaste for ethanol. (Unfortunately subjects do not always vomit and even when they do, in some cases they experience no repulsion.) A similar rationale prompted the introduction of disulfiram (otherwise known as 'antabuse') by the Danes Hald and Jacobsen in 1948, and of metronidazole (or 'flagyl') on a more limited scale in France. Disulfiram can be taken daily by mouth or be slowly absorbed from an abdominal implant and, in addition to giving alcohol an unpleasant taste, produces systemic symptoms – hot flushes, nausea and palpitations – in those who succumb to their cravings for drink. Such symptoms are potentially dangerous and for this reason disulfiram should be prescribed only to those who are firmly resolved to give up (particularly since the drug itself does nothing to suppress the desire for alcohol).

In 1965, a different approach was tried by Champeau, who injected alcoholic patients with magnesium sulphate. This produced generalized feelings of warmth and well-being and, more importantly, provoked an intense thirst, which the subjects were then encouraged to satisfy by drinking water. This procedure was intended to help drinkers rediscover the thirst-quenching qualities of water, which, it was hoped, they would come to drink habitually.[2]

Although such methods today might appear naive and to some extent cruel, they have proved successful in certain cases where alcoholics complied with treatment and were adequately supported and encouraged in their effort to 'kick the habit'.

INSTITUTIONAL CARE

During the early nineteenth century, the question of specialized institutions for the treatment of alcoholics had been discussed in the United

States, but, probably for financial rather than medical reasons, such provisions received little enthusiastic support. This had also been the case in Britain, where, once disowned by family and friends, rich and poor drinkers alike were treated as mental patients and often locked up in asylums. In France, violent or severely disordered alcoholics were similarly confined (asylums had been built in every *département* in accordance with the law of 1838), and the elderly and less disruptive were frequently placed in hospices. Not until the 1950s did Western society come to offer a more diverse range of therapies for the unfortunate drinker.

Early diagnosis in the modern era has meant that fewer alcoholics arrive at a stage of intellectual impairment necessitating admission to an institution, and doctors and patients increasingly find such measures distasteful. As a result, most heavy drinkers are treated by general practitioners or psychiatrists, physicians and surgeons on a hospital out-patient basis. In France, the 1970s saw the creation of *consultations d'hygiène alimentaires* (Alimentary Care Clincs), which were designed specifically for those with alcohol problems. The designation of such a facility, which omits mention of alcohol entirely, might be considered hypocritical or discreet, depending on one's point of view; it reflects, however, patients' dislike of the label 'alcoholic' and the need for their condition to be treated on occasion without the knowledge of family, friends or colleagues. (Similar delicacy, which was formerly employed in the treatment of tuberculosis, is still exercised in mental care and with some cancer patients, and it will undoubtedly be required in dealing with those suffering from AIDS.) In 1975, the clinics became known as *Centres d'hygiène alimentaire* or CHAs (Centres for Alimentary Care). A ministerial decree revealed their true function in 1983, when they received the new title, *Centres d'hygiène alimentaire et d'alcoologie* or CHAAs (Centres for Alimentary Care and Alcohology). The flexible management of the latter organizations makes them adaptable to local requirements: in some areas, they are run by locally constituted bodies such as the regional Committees for the Prevention of Alcoholism, whereas in others responsibility is placed in the hands of local author-ities and hospitals. Treatment is multidisciplinary and patients, who are accepted with or without referral from other agencies, are seen not only by doctors, but also by nurses and social workers. The centres, which have multiplied in number from 15 CHAs nationwide in 1976 to more than 300 CHAAs today, provide a number of services in association with general practitioners, hospitals, social services and voluntary organizations. They function also as training establishments for those working with alcoholics, they provide information and in certain cases, where funds and personnel are available, they promote epidemiological and clinical research.

Some patients require admission to hospital, whether for treatment of severe alcohol-related disorders or because medical staff need to follow the process of detoxification. In France, the majority are treated in general hospitals by specialists in gastroenterology and neurology, although psychiatrists, who since the 1970s are to be found increasingly in medical institutions other than asylums, are also involved. Some hospitals enjoy the luxury of a 'department of alcohology', but, as long as the essentials of the treatment of alcoholics are kept in mind by medical staff, such a specialty is by no means indispensable. The basic principle of such care is that alcoholism itself must be tackled and not just attendant disorders such as cancer or cirrhosis; furthermore, there can be no excuse for failure to enlist the help of specialist organizations like the CHAAs.

A minority of alcoholics, however, must be confined to the care of psychiatric institutions, euphemistically known as *Centres hospitaliers spécialisés* or CHS (special hospitals) in France. Long-term confinement is far less common than in former times and patients are allowed home as soon as they are considered able to lead a normal family, social or even professional existence. This does not mean that they are left to fend for themselves on leaving hospital, and their progress is generally followed by the same team of doctors and social workers who looked after them on the wards. Since the 1960s, the staff of the CHS has been responsible not only for hospital in-patients, but also for the mental care of those living within its locality. The practical working of this 'sectorization' of community care has been beset by organizational and financial difficulties, which legislation passed in 1985 was designed to resolve by financing the operation from health insurance payments.

Similar problems were encountered in the implementation of an earlier law dating from 1954, which stipulated that 'all dangerous alcoholics must be placed in the care of the health authorities'. The civil tribunal administering this measure was empowered, having taken medical advice, to place alcoholics for periods of six months at a time in specialized rehabilitation centres designed to help in the detoxification and rehabilitation process and to isolate those who represent a 'danger to others or to themselves'. In reality, few specialist centres were created and all parties involved with the legislation – doctors, magistrates, social workers and the police – were less than happy with its coercive implications. The 'medical commissions' set up to advise civil tribunals with respect to the 1954 Act gained authority by developing their activities beyond those prescribed, and they were able to help and advise individuals appearing before them according to their relative needs. Although legislation had failed to realize its avowed intentions, it led indirectly to an improvement in the care of alcoholics.[3]

After the process of withdrawal and after he has received treatment, it is by no means certain that the former drinker will renounce alcohol for good. When he returns to everyday life, the reception he is given will be extremely variable, he will suffer jokes at his own expense and he will constantly be tempted into drinking by others. All too often the 'cured' alcoholic relapses and is readmitted to hospital at a later date, and it is for this reason that careful, long-term follow-up of these difficult patients is necessary. Many projects have tried to help alcoholics through the process of social reintegration and to provide intermediary assistance. Whether such projects take the form of 'half-way houses', rest homes, workshops or centres providing medical and psychological support, they are frequently poorly funded, and, given their 'clientele', often have staffing difficulties. Even if they are successful in achieving physical and social rehabilitation and can prepare patients for a return to 'normal life', it is often that very return that provokes the first relapses. According to the French Ministry of Health in 1984, there were only 64 projects of this kind in France.

PSYCHOLOGICAL SUPPORT

Doctors cannot satisfy the every need of their alcoholic patients; even with the maximum of medical and psychological insight, and the benefit of long-standing acquaintance, they cannot hope to fulfil all expectations. Support and understanding for the alcoholic are to be found within organizations created to help drinkers, which were first founded during the nineteenth century.[4]

For many years, relations between the medical profession and self-help groups for alcoholics were poor. Doctors resented the intrusion of untrained individuals who were frequently more successful in their work with alcoholics, and the groups feared identification with medical authority and learning. The climate has changed in recent years, as both parties have come to realize that their activities are directed towards different areas and that they can frequently complement one another. Greater co-operation and co-ordination in treating alcoholics has been the result.

Mention has already been made of the Blue Cross (formed in Geneva in 1877 and established in France six years later), a group that has cast aside its Protestant origins, but continues to enlist 'God's help' in its work, organizing rehabilitation centres and publishing its own magazine. The Gold Cross (*croix d'or*) was the Catholic equivalent; founded in 1910, it is now a lay society with detoxification and rehabilitation centres. Other lay organizations include *Vie Libre* (Free Life), formed in 1953, and Alcoholics Anonymous (AA), founded in the United States in 1935 and operating in France since 1960. *Vie Libre* caters largely for the working population, making use of the public education network and running hostels where former drinkers are helped to reintegrate into professional life. Alcoholics Anonymous has over one million members world-wide and uses reformed alcoholics to help those prepared to acknowledge that they have a drinking problem; treatment in this context involves a twelve-stage programme. (A sister organization, AL Anon, works with the families and friends of alcoholics.) Further work is done by other groups such as *Joie et Santé* (Happiness and Health); professional bodies such as the French Interprofessional Organization for the Prevention of Alcoholism and Other Toxicomanias, which has branches in many areas of working life; and to some extent by religious sects requiring abstinence, such as the Seventh Day Adventists.[5]

The wide variety of organizations whose doors are open to alcoholics means that those with drink problems have a good chance of finding adequate and appropriate support. Attitudes and ideologies vary considerably across the spectrum. Until recently, many groups wavered between moderation and total abstinence; the latter is now favoured by most. Some organizations encourage group participation by members of drinkers' families, others insist on separation. Some groups cultivate an easy familiarity, others respect anonymity and a few require strict allegiance. Whatever the principles of practice, one aspect of such therapy is indispensable: the alcoholic must be in contact with others who have experienced and overcome the trials of withdrawal themselves. Where relations with doctors are often stormy, those with fellow sufferers involve less conflict and denial, leading to acceptance and co-operation. Through group discussion, the drinker will come to realize that he is no longer alone and that he belongs to a brotherhood which, despite a common interest in alcohol, differs fundamentally from the company of alcoholics he may formerly have frequented.

The use of dialogue is thus central to therapy and it is perhaps no coincidence that the first self-help groups for alcoholics were founded by Protestants. Since the Reformation many Protestant sects have favoured the practice of public confession, which contrasts with the confidentiality of its Catholic counterpart. An admission of dependence on alcohol and attendant social difficulties and failings is a first step towards freedom from addiction; it improves self-esteem and provides relief through the mere process of communication. Furthermore, during discussion, particularly at times of weakened resolve, the former drinker can draw upon his interlocutors for the strength he requires to remain abstinent. Only during the last forty years has the importance of dialogue found recognition; despite all their good intentions, the likes of Magnan, Legrain and Perrin can only have contributed to the misery of alcoholics by leaving them alone with their problem and abandoning them in the hands of fate. Modern groups differ from those in existence a hundred years ago in that they no longer represent a moral or political force, as they did in Scandinavia, Britain and America; they now devote themselves almost exclusively to alcoholics, leaving the rest of society in peace and making no attempt to put non-alcoholics on the right path.

Some doctors now also use the technique of public confession when dealing with alcoholic patients and their families.[6] Others advocate an alternative mode of introspection and recommend that patients should write their autobiography, an activity which again involves the process of confession, but which is just as open to a 'bending' of the truth. Alcoholic writers have also written first-person accounts of their experiences; with the intention of helping fellow-sufferers, they describe the development of their subjugation to alcohol and how they were able to fight against and free themselves from drink. Jack London's *John Barleycorn* was amongst the earliest and most successful of such works.[7] As sailor-hero, London recounts his travels in the Pacific, his drinking sessions in the ports of America and South-East Asia, his attempts to create a happy socialist world in California, where alcohol would be superfluous. Sadly London was driven to suicide in 1916 at the age of 40.

John Barleycorn was immensely popular in the United States and was used for propaganda purposes by both prohibitionists and those in favour of women's suffrage. London himself was convinced that the female vote alone would be sufficient to bring about prohibition: 'when women get the ballot, they will vote for prohibition,' I said. 'It is the wives, and sisters, and mothers, and the above, who will drive the nails into the coffin of John Barleycorn.'[8] In the work, one phrase in particular – the denial, 'I, who am not an alcoholic...' – is repeated on several occasions and surprises the reader, who is by now familiar with the narrator's bouts of drinking. The theme of obligation is also prominent: obligations to friends or chance acquaintances met in bars, obligations to editors, all serve to set the cycle of drinking in motion after weeks of sobriety. London reiterates that he does not drink for pleasure: how can one enjoy being the slave, the victim of an uncontrollable force? In spite of his denial, which once again demonstrates the ambiguities of the term, there is little doubt today that he lived and died an alcoholic.

There have been numerous imitations of *John Barleycorn* since its publication in 1913. Variable in quality, they are characterized by a touching sincerity and pervaded with endless anxieties: 'Will I kick the habit?' 'Will I relapse?' There is the recurrent emphasis on 'falling' (evocative of the stumbling drunkard, the reformed drinker who relapses, or even of the fall of Man), and the tone is frequently that of a preacher, albeit one who preaches by example. Man is drunk on sorrow, Lucifer the angel of light is thrown into darkness (Night Anxiety) and the fires of hell burn for ever (the volcano). Although it is possible that autobiography helped writers to remain abstinent, the completion of some works was brutally curtailed by the untimely demise of their creators, related not infrequently to alcoholic intoxication. These books frequently provide a terrifying premonition of such a conclusion, reminiscent of Faulkner's *As I Lay Dying*.

Confessions of this genre clearly reach a far larger audience than those delivered within the context of the self-help group.[9] Their influence and that of other figures in public life, who write about their experiences at least in part as a means of narcissistic gratification, remain impossible to gauge. We will never know how many drinkers who, on reading such accounts, are prompted to exclaim: 'If he can do it, then so can I.'

Alcoholism is a condition for life; even when 'cured', sufferers require emotional support and medical follow-up. Traps await the unwary and the conscientious individual who drinks only grape juice or 'non-alcoholic' beer may relapse as a result of the small quantities of ethanol they contain; he may also poison himself with artificial flavourings such as glycyrhizine, if he retains his drinker's thirst and consumes copious quantities of soft drinks. The sheer complexity of the needs of alcoholic patients should alert those who consider the problem a simple one, reversible by some magic antidote, to the dangers of such an approach. Alcoholic care should also serve as a paradigm in the treatment of other toxicomanias: the need for intoxication is as powerful as the effects of the drug itself and it is far more difficult to treat.

11

Prevention

THROUGHOUT the nineteenth century many had decried the harm done
by alcohol. Their efforts, however, often met with the scepticism of a
public suspicious of their motives. The situation has not greatly altered
and, if anything, secular resistance to the problem of alcoholism has
increased, as have profits to be made from the trade, and the number of
consumers at risk.

THE CASE FOR PREVENTION

Prevention is better than cure. If it were possible to prevent people
falling under the spell of alcohol, then much misery could be avoided.
This has been the praiseworthy objective of the anti-alcohol movement
for the last two hundred years. The justifications for preventing alcoholism are numerous and such a course of action would reduce considerably the incidence of physical disorders (such as cirrhosis, polyneuritis
and cerebral atrophy) and domestic strife (violence directed at women
and children and divorce). Drink has long been blamed for crime and it
has been argued that reduced alcohol consumption would bring about a
fall in delinquency. Today's magistrates, criminologists and statisticians
are unconvinced about the truth of such statements. It may be true that
many alcoholics find their way into prison, but they are not representative of the general population or even of prisoners as a whole. Latter-day
researchers maintain that the criminals in question may well have had
violent tendencies prior to committing the crime for which they were
convicted. Quarrelsome, anti-social behaviour can be observed in people
who never drink and alcohol may be the factor which provokes acts of
violence which lead to their imprisonment. Furthermore, prisoners are
those criminals who have been caught, and since alcoholism makes
people operate less efficiently, they may act less cautiously and thus be
more likely to end up in prison. It therefore comes as no surprise to find
a large proportion of heavy drinkers among those incarcerated – those
who do not drink are likely to remain at large and never figure in
criminal statistics. The influence of such factors is now taken far more

into consideration in studies such as that commissioned by the Council of Europe in 1984 to determine the relationship between crime and alcoholism. The advent of a more critical approach has undermined the traditional equation of alcoholism with delinquency, an argument which will doubtless continue to be cited in justification of coercive measures taken against alcoholism.

The incidence of drink-related accidents provides strong grounds for preventative steps. Western countries have dealt with this particular problem in different ways. The United States and Canada have had notable success in reducing drunken driving – a success matched by their corresponding failure to prevent accidents linked to alcohol at work, which the French and Germans have dealt with far more effectively.

The sheer cost of alcoholism provided the prevention lobby with further ammunition. This issue only emerged after the Second World War, when the health services of European countries transferred financial responsibility for the growing cost of medical care to the community. Calculation of the medical cost of alcoholism, however, is not a procedure exempt from moral considerations, as it raises the question of responsibility for self-inflicted disease. Once it has been established, however, that health is a basic right for all members of the community, and it is agreed that the healthy should contribute to the treatment of the sick, there can be no grounds for discrimination against those considered to have brought their condition upon themselves, or for distinguishing between diseases that qualify for treatment and those that do not.

In terms of hospital management, costing is a justifiable exercise, but it is by no means a clear-cut calculation. Although it is possible to count all those hospitalized with cirrhosis, pancreatitis or other conditions associated with alcohol abuse, the exact proportion of patients who are in hospital as a direct result of drinking cannot be gauged accurately, since none of these illnesses are caused exclusively by ethanol. Similarly, the number of road accidents linked to excessive drinking can be recorded with accuracy, but if a drunken driver skids on an icy road, it is impossible to assess the extent to which alcohol has contributed to his injuries. After an accident it is cheaper to deal with a corpse than an injured person, but such a calculation takes no account of the expense of emotional damage to the family of the deceased. Estimates of the cost of alcoholism in France range from 80,000 to 100,000 million francs, almost half the country's total expenditure on health care. (These figures are doubtless influenced by anti-alcohol propaganda and probably overestimate the problem.[1]) Naturally, any comparisons made between different countries on the basis of cost can only result in rough approximations. Be that as it may, cutting the cost of a disease is a laudable exercise, but it must always remain secondary to the main objective of prevention – that is, the elimination of all health and social problems linked to alcohol abuse.

INFORMATION AND EDUCATION

In France, public health education did not become a major concern until the last decades of the nineteenth century. Initially it took the form of poster campaigns in hospitals, chemists, railway stations and barracks. Its first target was tuberculosis; 'spitting endangers life' and similar slogans abounded. Elsewhere, young men on national service were given lectures on the dangers of venereal disease. Curiously, however, early campaigns against alcoholism were initiated in schools: posters in classrooms depicted swollen, yellow livers for the enlightenment of children who knew neither what the liver was, nor where it might be found. By the time they came to do their national service, these early lessons had been long forgotten. The mid-twentieth century saw a change in style. It has already been noted that nineteenth-century doctors were more active in the anti-alcohol movement than their twentieth-century counterparts. During the inter-war period, doctors viewed alcoholism as an inevitable occurrence and considered that alcoholics themselves were responsible for finding the strength to overcome their addiction. In the 1950s this attitude changed and the number of doctors concerned with alcoholism grew. These new partisans formed the *Société d'alcoologie*; a body which organized conferences and international symposia and published its own journal. This revival of interest has led to the official recognition of alcohology, and since 1976 in France it has been an obligatory part of medical studies.[2] With the arrival of alcohology as a distinct sub-branch of medicine, doctors became more scientific in their attitudes to alcoholism and were prepared to adopt a more subtle approach to its psychological aspects.

Attitudes were also changing in other walks of life. In 1954, Pierre Mendès France established the *Haut Comité d'étude et d'information sur l'alcoolisme* (High Committee for Study and Information about Alcoholism). Mendès France was a politician who worked passionately for numerous popular causes and, like Roussel in the 1870s, he was disturbed by the damage caused by alcohol among peasants and workers which, as *député* for the Eure, he was well placed to judge. A man who led by example, Mendès France ostentatiously drank milk in public;

for the majority, however, his austerity had little attraction and his presidency was short-lived. The High Committee, however, survived and flourished: it promoted research into alcoholism, advised governments on possible legislative or regulatory actions, and encouraged any initiatives in the field. Its extensive archives are open to all who wish to consult them. In the thirty years since its inception, the body has become central to the struggle against alcoholism in France and has been the originator of almost all administrative measures taken by successive governments.

Le Comité national de défense contre l'alcoolisme (The National Committee for Defence against Alcoholism) was also formed in the 1950s, when numerous local temperance societies came together to form a federation. In addition to providing help for problem drinkers, the body plays an important educational role, sponsoring or organizing local groups involved in health education in factories and schools throughout France. Its permanent salaried staff of more than 500, excluding voluntary workers, produces a review, bulletins, brochures and posters directed at all groups in French society. At the local level, it is the National Committee that has the greatest influence. Its activities are supplemented by the High Committee in other areas and, together, the two groups provide an information and support network for all citizens. Other health professions have also played an important role in diffusing information on alcohol research. Much of the effort has been directed towards educating children and adolescents into good drinking habits. Using methods similar to those employed in French schools at the turn of the century, the Ministry of Education and the National Committee for Defence against Alcoholism have organized study days for both children and teachers, in which together they look at problems relating to alcoholism. As a group, schoolchildren have shown more interest in the subject than might have been expected and health clubs established in secondary schools have proved an unforeseen success. Surveys conducted in schools in the west of France have shown that in the minds of children alcoholism conjures up images of violence, irrational behaviour, ruined health and car crashes. For these youngsters, it represented the exact antithesis of everything positive about sport. Further research with the same children after they had received health education lessons demonstrated that this had served to reinforce their negative view of excessive drinking.[3] The High Committee on Alcoholism has also produced a package of teaching materials for use with children of all ages.[4] Groups that were originally established specifically to reform alcoholics also make an educational contribution, particularly in helping the families of alcoholics come to terms with the problem. *Le Comité français d'éducation pour la santé* (the French Committee for Health Education) and its branches in the various *départements* periodically chooses alcohol as a target for its activities.

Government departments responsible for social security and national insurance also participate in campaigns against alcohol; since 1968 many televised public information films have looked at the problem of alcoholism. During the last twenty years the media in general have advocated moderation in drinking matters, linking health with sobriety. The success of such a programme, however, requires a certain skill, and must be based on good market research, if the problem is not to be over-dramaticized (thereby offending both the public and powerful alcohol producers).

Table 11.1 Total consumption of pure alcohol in France (includes beer, cider, wine and spirits)

Years	Total consumption in 10 hl of pure alcohol[1]	Average consumption in litres: adults aged 20 and above	Average consumption in litres: aged 15 and above[2]
1970	8489	25.0	22.2
1971	8682	25.2	22.5
1972	8774	25.2	22.5
1973	8921	25.3	22.6
1974	8766	24.6	22.0
1975	8832	24.6	22.0
1976	8875	24.7	22.0
1977	8790	24.2	21.7
1978	8520	23.2	20.8
1979	8418	22.8	20.4
1980	8780	23.2	20.8
1981	8398	22.3	20.0
1982	8380	22.1	19.9
1983	8250	21.2	19.1

1 Wine represents 50% to 70% of the alcohol consumed by the French.
2 As most countries in the EEC calculate alcohol consumption in those aged 15 and above, we think it useful to take this statistic into account.

Source: I.N.S.E.E.

A further attempt to inform the consumer by indication of alcoholic content on all containers has also been made. The *Académie de Médecine* and the *Conseil supérieur d'hygiène publique* (High Council for Public Health) believe that clear labelling will make the public more responsible in their drinking habits. Once people are aware of the alcoholic content of drinks, it is hoped that they will drink less. Since stronger wines are generally regarded as better wines, such a strategy may be of dubious benefit; wines containing 10 per cent alcohol by volume, which were common fifty years ago, are no longer available and French consumers now demand wines of at least 11 per cent. Such a trend, observed albeit only in the case of wine, has led to the suggestion that detailed labelling will result in increased levels of alcohol consumption.

The struggle against alcoholism must be taken up afresh by each new generation and its scope should be wide enough to include everybody. Where children are concerned, it is impossible to say what the long-term effect of specific teaching will be. Whatever the case, such educational programmes, tailored to the prevailing social and cultural climate, must continue. The form they take will ultimately be decided by the country concerned. In Bulgaria, for example, children are taught that alcoholism is a weapon used to oppress workers and subjugate colonies.[5] It is impossible to judge whether this message is more effective than any other, since Bulgaria releases no statistics dealing with alcoholism.

PREVENTION AND THE LAW

The decision to outlaw certain forms of behaviour may have a preventative function, but in the case of drink it is difficult to imagine effective legal controls, short of total prohibition. This is because susceptibility to alcohol is so varied and a law that forbids individuals to drink more than their own personal limits is inconceivable. Other legal alternatives, such as restrictions placed on the availability of drink, affect alcohol consumption indirectly. There is no evidence to suggest that controlling the number of drink outlets reduces levels of alcohol consumption; the two are not necessarily linked. (In Tunisia, a Muslim country, the number of outlets fell from 665 in 1956 to 337 in 1972, but overall consumption levels have been steadily on the increase.[6]) Any licensing system doubtless has its drawbacks and constantly requires revision in order to keep pace with changing consumer practices, but it does give the authorities some measure of control. In 1976, Scottish licensing laws became less strict and although public drunkenness decreased more significantly than in England or Wales, no effect on alcohol-related morbidity or mortality was observed.[7]

Licences to sell drink exist in many countries and in France fall into four categories, depending on the type of drinks sold and whether they are consumed on the premises. (In 1982 some 184,000 licences were in existence, a figure that should have remained constant, as new licences are only issued when an old one is surrendered. In fact, the number of licences has fallen by 70,000 since 1960.) As discussed in chapter 5, the French code governing the sale of alcohol not only controls the number of drink outlets, but it also limits the areas in which they can be established. Governmental dispensation to circumvent restrictions is rarely granted, and then only with the agreement of the High Committee on Alcoholism, which seldom lends support to such cases. None the less, social change is making the codes increasingly difficult to enforce – modern business life requires more temporary licences for fairs, exhibitions and congresses, and developments in international travel have also made alcohol more available.[8] The important role of the café in French social life was acknowledged in 1985, when the total ban on bars within the limits of housing estates was lifted. This restriction had been in force since the 1920s, when new cheap housing for the working classes was constructed under the Loucheur law, and it was reinforced after the Second World War in similar schemes to meet popular housing requirements. The architects of these utopias envisaged their inhabitants to be the 'poor', the group which the rest of society has always viewed as inveterate drinkers. These housing developments, constructed far from urban centres, were to become human wastelands.

Legal measures to restrict the numbers of those able to buy alcohol are also possible. French law forbids sales to children under the age of 14, although in larger supermarkets they are effectively able to buy anything they want. In 1984, the US federal government introduced a law that distinguished between the age of legal consent, 18, and the age at which alcohol can be purchased, 21 (although some states refused to implement the restrictions). Another method of restricting sales is to increase prices. Many governments, however, have increased the tax levied on alcohol not for health reasons, but for financial gain. (It is generally considered that price increases only have a temporary effect on sales, but in times of economic crisis their effects may be more pronounced.[9])

In matters of restrictive regulation it is difficult to judge whether decisions should be taken by central government or local authorities. Drinking habits vary from place to place, even in a relatively homogeneous country like France, where local authorities would seem better placed to judge what forms of regulation might prove most effective.[10] Unfortunately, regional responsibility tends to promote illicit trade and can result in some absurd situations. One small Methodist town in Ontario, for example, which subsequently became a suburb of Toronto, banned all saloons; now, in order to buy liquor, its inhabitants need only travel several blocks to a district where the rules are different.

Equally ludicrous is the situation that exists in a part of Mississippi where the sale of beer, but not whisky, is forbidden.

All forms of regulation aim to restrict access to drink and their effects are variable. Laws that are punitive, however, are a different matter. Throughout the world, public drunkenness is a punishable offence, although penalties vary in relation to the tolerance of the society concerned. The last thirty years have witnessed the emergence of drunken driving as a focus for concern and many countries now regard it as a criminal activity. In France, legislation was introduced in stages. As early as 1954, a law was passed making those driving 'under the influence of alcohol' responsible for the cost of any damage they caused. In 1970, the subject was placed on a more scientific footing with the introduction of blood–alcohol guidelines; drivers with blood–alcohol levels exceeding 0.8 g/l became liable to fines, whereas those with levels exceeding 1.2 g/l were dealt with more harshly. Subsequent laws have given police the power to immobilize vehicles, confiscate driving licences and 'breathalyse' motorists at random. Penalties for those motorists with blood–alcohol levels above 0.8 g/l have also been increased.[11]

In France such laws have not proved easy to apply. Accurate measurement of blood–alcohol levels depends on the sensitivity of the equipment used and the authorities have been slow to provide the police with alcohol meters that are both reliable and portable. Blood–alcohol levels are also subject to rapid changes, so that if a reading is taken too long after the initial dosage, then the suspect may escape punishment. Furthermore, individuals eliminate alcohol from their blood and lungs at different rates; equality in the eyes of the law is a basic axiom of the constitution that does not hold for biochemical metabolism. None the less, the French have grown accustomed to the idea that they may be breathalysed at any time and that they may be required to submit to a blood test. The desired psychological effect of such measures has thus been partially achieved, although it is still too early to state with assurance that these changes in the law have been responsible for the regular, but slow, decrease in fatalities on the road. In general, judges deal leniently with drink–driving offences, opting in favour of a light sentence or fine; all too often the possibility of a family losing its livelihood has meant that driving bans are rarely applied. Both in parliament and the courts, it is frequently forgotten that a driving licence in the hands of a drunk is a licence to kill. Similar measures have been taken in most European countries. Most severe are the Scandinavians; in Finland, failure to switch on car headlights at dusk warrants a blood test which, if positive, results in confiscation of the driving licence and possible imprisonment. Even if member states were to adopt 0.8 g/l as the critical blood–alcohol level, it is unlikely that regulations will be standardized within the EEC in the near future.

Legal codes governing accidents at work apply indirectly to alcoholism, in that insurance companies refuse to pay compensation in cases where the worker was evidently responsible. Restrictive laws in the workplace seem to have less effect on behaviour than the overall attitudes of employers and staff.[12] In France, there tend to be few reported accidents at work related to drink; in all probability, the interested parties – worker and employer – collude to deny the role of alcohol in any accident. This is an area where the law is relatively powerless; it obliges employers to provide drinking water for workers and prohibits alcohol in certain types of establishment. Such measures are preventative in aim, but are poorly respected.

Legislation alone will not rid a country of alcoholism, but it may make a contribution to this end. Laws must be constantly revised to close loopholes exploited by drinkers and manufacturers alike, and governments should appoint advisory working committees. In the struggle against alcoholism legal measures are indispensable, but their effects are difficult to predict. The drink–driving laws, for example, have resulted in a decrease in major road accidents, but they have had no effect on overall levels of alcohol consumption; legislation has the power to influence drinking habits, but not the amount drunk. Nevertheless, although the exact relationship between consumption and alcoholism is by no means clear, the two are linked and measures that reduce the former may also reduce the latter.

STATE VERSUS NATION

When levels of consumption are high, the state benefits enormously from the alcohol trade. Much of state revenue is derived from taxes on commercial activities. Alcohol, however, is not a simple commodity, but a poison, and ultimately the state does not gain from increased sales. From the moment the state accepts financial responsibility for the medical care of alcoholics, it stands to lose. To the more obvious costs of hospitalization, economists add the hidden expenses of production, transportation and the labour of all in the drink industry. Although it is impossible to produce a perfectly ordered balance-sheet of the costs of alcohol, it seems certain that the nation as a whole is a net loser, despite the revenue accruing to the state in the form of taxes. The nation is also poorer, because of the needless loss of human potential from alcohol abuse.[13] Given that much of the profit derived from alcohol goes to private individuals, the nation could be said to subsidize them by keeping drinkers alive. When the state takes responsibility for alcohol sales, as it did in Finland (a country that also had a spell of prohibition between 1919 and 1932), it finds itself obliged to encourage consumption in order to increase its revenues.[14] In Poland, a monopoly on alcohol accounts for 14 per cent of state income; however, only 6.7 per cent of the budget is used to fund the health service.[15]

In France a partial monopoly exists; the state alone can buy and sell ethanol at concentrations greater than 70 per cent. This is produced from wine surpluses or sugar beet, and is sold to pharmaceutical and cosmetics laboratories, manufacturers of fortified drinks and the chemical industry. The system is absurd: in order to maintain the income of wine-growers, the state, by subsidizing excess production, encourages them to grow more than is required. Much of what is then produced finds its way onto the market as liquor, which is even more toxic than wine. To make matters worse, the state is a bad businessman and, in spite of its monopoly, still manages to lose almost 100 million francs a year.

Similar incoherence marks pricing policies. Although the state periodically increases prices of alcoholic drinks and the various taxes imposed upon them, it does so at a rate that does not keep pace with inflation. As a result, wine is cheaper today than it was a hundred years ago. In France, wine is actually cheaper than the real cost of its production, and the wine industry in effect is state subsidized (as is the production of tobacco). Unfortunately the margins for manoeuvre are limited. A dramatic increase in prices would have considerable effects on the market, but the consequences would be uncertain: a tough line on spirits simply encourages illicit distillation. Changes in agricultural practices require time as well as new outlooks and adequate funding. Within the Common Market, tariff regulations are slowly being introduced, but their exact co-ordination among member states remains unfinalized. Accordingly, the French state is hesitant to introduce reform and financial considerations triumph over the nation's health. This failure to implement an anti-alcohol policy is exacerbated by the absence of any policy on drink. A glass of mineral water, a natural product that requires neither land nor costly expenditure on equipment and fertilizers, costs more than a glass of wine. Small wonder, then, that people continue to drink the latter. A policy of promoting soft drinks has long been advocated; those opposing such a programme argue, however, that all fruit juices inevitably contain a small quantity of ethanol (just under 1 per cent, to be exact) and their production is costly because of the requirements of quality control. All this may well be true, but it is also the case that no effort is made to stimulate research into ways of overcoming such obstacles.

Finally, there are inconsistencies in law: the administrative and judicial authorities are ambivalent in their attitudes to drunkenness and chronic intoxication. On occasions inebriation is viewed as a mitigating circumstance, whereas on others it is seen to compound the crime. Such differences do little to encourage alcoholics to seek a cure, nor do they promote moderate drinking. In its role as protector of individual freedom and national health, the state has failed to adopt clear policies or take the right decisions.

PROPAGANDA FOR ALCOHOL

Although those who speak out on behalf of alcohol certainly make no defence of alcoholism, they make use of every opportunity to increase consumption. The simplest of their methods is to minimize the dangers of excessive drinking by claiming that statistics are falsified or that equipment for measuring alcohol levels is inaccurate. Advocates of drink are to be found in all classes and professions. In alcohol-producing areas, they have argued for the fundamental economic role of the trade and the vital cultural values embodied in drinking. Distillers maintain a permanent legal barrage for legislative changes in their favour. In France, as elsewhere, the pro-alcohol lobby has vast funds at its disposal and uses them liberally to promote its cause and support friends and spokesmen in parliament. As in the days of Péguy, political opponents forget their ideological differences and unite in favour of alcohol. Propagandists have even found a voice in international organizations; the EEC has issued statements critical of 'underconsumption' of wine in Britain and Germany (even though wine-drinking is on the increase in these countries), and the WHO, doubtless reflecting the lack of zeal felt by its members in this direction, keeps its remarks on alcohol within the bounds of discretion.[16]

Alcohol producers feign innocence before the medical facts. Excessive drinking, they claim, is no more their responsibility than obesity is that of the food industry. Making a show of their own virtue, they contribute modestly to research on alcohol abuse, patronize the arts and sponsor sporting events. When criticized, they defend themselves with alacrity, pleading their good faith and vilifying their detractors.[17] Their allies are to be found everywhere, even in the health professions.[18]

The romanticism that surrounds wine also plays a propagandist role in its favour.[19] The myth of Dionysus is as strong now as it has ever been, masking the financial interests behind all the alcohol industry's efforts to ingratiate itself with the general public.[20] The question of advertising requires investigation in this light. Under the Vichy regime, production and distribution of alcoholic drinks were strictly controlled and advertising was almost totally outlawed. During the Fourth Republic, these restrictions were lifted and in 1951 authorization was granted to advertise wine-based drinks. The regulations that now exist were formulated in 1960: in the case of beer, wine and cider, there are no restrictions, as is the case for liqueurs, anisettes, cognacs and eaux-de-vie; wine-based drinks must indicate their ingredients and the name of the manufacturer, but whisky, gin and vodka are classed separately and for them advertising is forbidden. This last restriction indicates that the regulations were not formulated on health grounds – cognac is every bit as alcoholic as gin.

When public broadcasting networks were first established in France their codes of practice included a ban on advertising alcoholic drinks, with which independent companies also complied. In 1985, however, the French government granted Channel Five permission to carry advertisements for drinks containing less than 9 per cent alcohol. Whether such favouritism will go unchallenged by other networks remains to be seen.

Alcohol producers and the advertising industry would be satisfied with a self-regulated code of conduct. They argue that advertising is normal practice in the business world, that it serves only to promote one brand over another and does not increase overall consumption. Like producers, publicity people deny responsibility for the consequences of their work; their job is to sell a 'product', what the public does with it is its own affair.

In a public opinion poll sponsored by the High Committee on Alcoholism, 21 per cent of those questioned felt that all forms of alcohol advertising should be banned, 58 per cent stated that advertisements inciting people to drink more should be outlawed, and only 18 per cent felt that no special provisions were required. When asked why it was that they thought the state seemed so powerless to control alcohol advertising effectively, 71 per cent of respondents suggested that it was the result of financial benefits derived from the industry.

In response to public opinion and to pressure from the EEC, the French government has recently passed radical new laws concerning the advertisement of alcoholic liquor. Such advertising is now prohibited at all sporting, cultural and artistic events, even if these have been sponsored by an alcohol producer. Furthermore, television and cinema publicity is allowed only for drinks containing less than 1 per cent alcohol. This legislation is too recent for its influence on the sales and consumption of alcohol to be ascertained at present.

12

Modern Alcoholism

THIS is a historical work, which cannot hope to treat modern alcohology in any great detail. None the less, certain tendencies now evident in the study of alcoholism merit attention. The vocabulary used to describe alcoholics has changed. No longer are they viewed simply as 'drunks' and treated with disdain. Today they receive the same sympathy that doctors extend to their other patients. The general public, too, is more aware of the dangers of excessive drinking. Surveys conducted in France revealed that 94 per cent of those questioned viewed alcoholic drink as the major cause of road accidents; 80 per cent considered that it played a major role in crime; and 62 per cent regarded it as a significant health risk. Although these figures may overestimate the effects of alcohol, they demonstrate that the message of the anti-alcohol campaigners has been well received in recent decades.[1] The public continue, however, to make moral judgements: alcoholics come a close second to criminals in surveys investigating the least desirable attributes of potential next-door neighbours – well ahead of 'Arabs', 'blacks' and unmarried mothers.

Looking to the future, the only certainty is that there will be change, both in drinking patterns and in methods of prevention and treatment.[2] None the less, it is striking that, in a world of progress, beliefs and ideas that have long been shown to be fallacious survive and continue to exert their influence. In France, this is exemplified by trade union organizers when they are approached on the subject of alcoholism. According to figures from the International Labour Office (ILO), 70 per cent of the world's alcoholics hold down steady jobs.[3] This figure poses a threat to important union tenets, which hold wage-earner to be synonymous with 'blue-collar worker', and is thus interpreted as a slur on the working classes. This reasoning properly belongs to the nineteenth century. Today, it is generally accepted that alcoholism is as common in the 'white-collar' sector as it is amongst manual workers. The unions, however, persist in regarding mention of the subject as an affront to the working classes, rather than treating the problem as a source of concern to the whole of society.

In response to an opinion poll conducted in 1984, similarly outmoded thinking led 150 Swedish doctors to issue a statement calling for a return to individual drink-rationing, coupled with restrictions on the sale of alcohol to those under 25 years of age, married women and known alcohol abusers.[4] Even Huss's pastor father would not have countenanced such severe measures, and it is hard to see what criteria prompted these doctors to focus on the under-25s and married women. Furthermore, they failed to define what they understood by the term 'abuser'.

In the past, the Soviet government has been guarded on the subject of alcoholism and has attempted to limit speculation as to its prevalence and the problems it causes. In recent years, the moral climate has changed and the drinker is now seen as a poor citizen and a bad Communist. His behaviour upsets the production goals of the Soviet economy and he is therefore a traitor worthy of punishment. Reformed alcoholics who relapse risk internment until they can regain control of their habit. In addition, measures better suited to the moral climate of the nineteenth century have been taken: taxes on vodka have been increased and production has fallen; the number of outlets has been reduced and stiffer penalties for public drunkenness have been imposed; alcohol at the workplace is now strictly controlled and individual rationing has been introduced. These authoritarian measures recall similar restrictive policies proposed by Western governments in the course of the last hundred years and their effect will probably be equally short-lived.[5]

Modern alcoholic drinks differ from their predecessors; new farming techniques, fertilizers and mechanization have increased agricultural output and this has resulted in greater alcohol production. Fermented drinks on sale to the public are stronger. In France, fifty years ago, the usual alcohol content of wine was about 10 per cent, whereas today it approaches 13 per cent. A similar pattern can be observed with beer, the strength of which may now exceed 9 per cent. In defence of this trend, it is maintained that stronger wines are easier to store and transport.

Systems of marketing have also changed. In most Western countries, the number of bars has declined steadily, but alcohol is increasingly available from other sources and is now frequently consumed in the home. Fashions, too, have changed. In France, wine consumption is being replaced by spirits and soft drinks, and the cultural influence of America has meant that whisky is preferred to cognac, armagnac and anise. Modern times have witnessed more unified drinking habits (even if regional differences persist in some parts of the world).[6] In many areas, the local brew is no longer the most popular drink. It might be an exaggeration to suggest that the disappearance of local drinking habits mirrors the decline of distinct regional cultures; nevertheless, the two are linked and travel inevitably brings about a homogenization of behaviour and habits. Fashion can also bring about a decrease in consumption. This seems to be the case in the USA, where concern over a general increase in accidents linked to alcohol (notably airline disasters) has meant that it is now common at receptions to be offered a soft drink before any form of alcohol.

Within individual countries, imitation from one generation to the next is no longer the rule. In France, those aged between 16 and 20 years drink less on a daily basis and tend to restrict their drinking to Saturday nights.[7] It is a strange twist of fate that this form of drinking, which the French have long regarded as a Scandinavian characteristic, should appear at a time when Scandinavians are moving towards a more French pattern of drinking, with greater daily consumption of wine.

Alcoholism amongst women continues to rise and it is impossible to say whether this will continue in future. Sexual equality will have some influence here, but female drinking is still largely restricted to the home and female alcoholism is often regarded as more reprehensible than it is amongst men. Such factors mean that the true extent of the problem remains hidden and make epidemiological studies difficult to conduct.

International trade and communications have contributed to the increasing uniformity observed in drinking patterns on a global scale (see table 12.1).[8] The Scandinavians now have access to wines from all over the world, whereas their predecessors had to content themselves with beer and aquavit. Generally, a rise in standard of living manifests itself in increased alcohol consumption with a more regular pattern of drinking, which has replaced Saturday night bingeing. The declining influence of religion in everyday life has had a similar effect.

In the developing world, generalizations about the problem are more difficult to make, because of the diversity of situations encountered. There has, however, been an enormous increase in overall consumption in comparison with industrialized countries, where levels have remained stable or have fallen.[9] This phenomenon probably has its origins in the colonial era; with the arrival of independence, many countries developed their own national brewing industries with the aid of foreign capital (see figures 12.1 and 12.2). These industries make a significant contribution to both the rural and urban economy in the world's poorer countries; furthermore, they are often in the hands of multinational companies, which means that in return for desperately needed jobs the authorities must accept that more alcohol will be sold to their citizens. The overcrowded cities of the Third World offer greatest scope for increases

Table 12.1 Annual pure alcohol consumption per inhabitant (in litres) in different countries (fermented and distilled drinks)

Rank	Country	Year	Consumption
1	Luxemburg	1984	ca. 18
2	France	1984	13.5
3	Portugal	1984	12.8
4	Italy	1984	12.1
5	Hungary	1984	11.7
6	Spain	1984	11.2
7	Switzerland	1984	11.1
8	West Germany	1984	10.7
9	Belgium	1984	10.6
10	East Germany	1983	10.4
11	Denmark	1984	10.2
12	Austria	1984	10
13	Czechoslovakia	1984	9.5
14	Argentina	1984	9.5
15	Australia	1984–85	9.3
16	New Zealand	1984	9.1
17	Bulgaria	1984	8.7
18	Holland	1984	8.6
19	Canada	1983–84	8.5
20	Yugoslavia	1983	ca. 8.4
21	USA	1984	8
22	Rumania	1983	7.7
23	Great Britain	1984	6.9
24	Greece	1984	6.8
25	Ireland	1984	6.7
26	Poland	1984	6.5
27	Finland	1984	6.3
28	USSR	1984	6
29	Cyprus	1984	5.7
30	Japan	1984	5.7
31	Sweden	1984	5.2
32	Chile	1984	5.0
33	Uruguay	1983	4.6

Source: Produced for the distillers, Dranken, Schiedam (Holland) 1985.

in alcohol consumption and in many countries beer consumption has increased faster than corresponding rises in population. Hard statistics, however, are difficult to come by, but the results of studies conducted in Zambia and Trinidad give considerable cause for concern.[10]

Official sources make no account of hidden alcohol production, which must constitute a sizeable proportion of world output. All indications are that this is on the increase. The incidence of clandestine production varies according to circumstance. In the world's industrial countries, the risks run by producers become acceptable when alcohol becomes too expensive. In Sweden today, it is estimated that there are

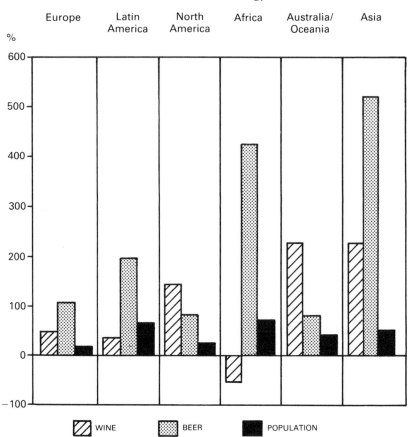

Figure 12.1 Comparison of beer and wine production growth in six regions of the world between 1960 and 1980 (figures indicate percentage increase)

Source: Finnish Foundation for Studies on Alcohol and Bureau régional OMS de l'Europe (1977), *International statistics on alcoholic beverages; production, trade and consumption, 1950–1972*, Helsinki, vol. 27. FAO (1981), *Annuaire de la production 1980*, Rome.

100,000 illegal stills in operation, and in Norway clandestine production may amount to as much as 35 per cent of the legal trade. In Western Europe and North America, illicit trade no longer represents a serious problem. This is not the case in the developing world, where customs agreements are rare and taxes vary enormously, resulting in massive fraud, which the authorities are often powerless to prevent.

In the Islamic world, illicit production of alcohol is a particularly risky enterprise because, in addition to contravention of fiscal regulations, it also represents a breach of religious codes.[11] Many Muslim countries,

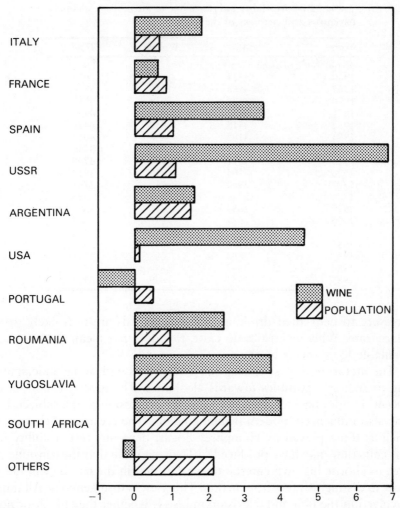

Figure 12.2 Average annual percentage increase in wine production in relation to population growth in ten large wine-producing countries between 1960 and 1980

Source: Finnish Foundation for Studies on Alcohol and Bureau régional OMS de l'Europe (1977), *International statistics on alcoholic beverages; production, trade and consumption, 1950–1972*, Helsinki, vol. 27. FAO (1981), *Annuaire de la production 1980*, Rome.

however, have their own wine and beer industries, but because alcohol is such a sensitive issue, levels and patterns of drinking are largely unknown. Alcohol-related disease does not serve as a guide to levels of consumption – the non-alcoholic causes of cirrhosis, for example, are greater in Africa and Asia, and patients in Islamic countries are under

Table 12.2   Mortality in France due to alcoholism, alcoholic psychosis and cirrhosis of the liver, by sex

Years	Men	Women	Total
Alcoholism and alcoholic psychosis			
1960	3924	1150	5074
1965	4568	1248	5816
1970	3125	938	4063
1971	3433	919	4352
1972	3518	958	4476
1973	3182	836	4018
1974	2970	740	3710
1975	3371	877	4248
1976	3103	810	3913
1977	2984	717	3701
1978	2796	758	3554
1979	2684	687	3371
1980	2688	679	3367
1981	2731	692	3423
1982	2690	649	3339
1983	2868	683	3551
1984	2667	654	3321
1985	2563	649	3212

pressure to deny their drinking. Medical records are thus likely to be inaccurate. Where statistics do exist, this does not mean that they are available for scrutiny by the rest of the world.

The literature of past epochs has provided us with some understanding of society's attitudes towards alcoholics. The media revolution of recent decades has not only given greater expression to the subject, but has also influenced modern drinking habits. The creators of characters such as those played by Humphrey Bogart deny any responsibility for the cults they may have produced.[12] They maintain that the consumer is free to choose his own entertainment and that in the end he will know how to distinguish fact from fiction. This view is disingenuous. All those involved in the film and television industry, whether they like it or not, play an educative role in society and must respect certain fundamental rules. Most Western countries have guidelines governing sex and violence in the media, but the public is less well protected from tobacco and alcohol. In America, Prohibition complicated the issue.[13] Prior to 1919 and during the initial phases of Prohibition, a popular film genre was the 'temperance melodrama'. These propagandist films portrayed the distress and anguish that resulted from drink. They were followed, however, by films portraying the alcoholic as free and independent, a man who knew exactly what was good for him. This new image was clearly powerful, provoking one movie mogul from Metro Goldwyn

Table 12.2 Continued

Years	Men	Women	Total
Cirrhosis of the liver			
1960	9007	4394	13401
1965	11527	5222	16749
1970	11814	5140	16954
1971	12398	5450	17848
1972	12389	5312	17701
1973	12564	5408	17972
1974	12236	4990	17226
1975	12477	5277	17754
1976	12322	5096	17418
1977	11923	4805	16728
1978	11572	4826	16398
1979	11182	4525	15707
1980	10554	4380	14934
1981	10312	4275	14587
1982	9869	3997	13866
1983	9612	4000	13612
1984	9261	3700	12961
1985	8604	3480	12084

Source: INSERM (definitive results).

Mayer to remark, after the repeal of the eighteenth amendment, that during Prohibition, 'films showed alcohol to play a major role in American life and changed peoples' views on the subject'.

The years after Prohibition saw the theme of individual liberty decline in popularity, but alcoholism continued to be a source of drama. New productions portrayed the alcoholic as weak or depraved, who, having neglected all social duties, was destined either to meet a sorry end or redeem himself by some desperate act of heroism. Since the Second World War, there were further transformations in the image of the drinker, which were transposed to the television screen. 'Action' films portray two sorts of drinker, the 'goody' and the 'baddy'. For the 'goodies', typified by the private detective who drinks solidly without impairment of judgement, alcohol signals strength and power and can be consumed with impunity. For the 'baddies', however, drinking is a sign of weakness – they meet with failure because they drink. The post-war period also saw the appearance of family dramas in which the alcoholic is not held responsible for drinking. In such films the alcoholic's past is explored to reveal the Freudian roots of his problem in infancy.

Similar themes occur in French cinema.[14] In general, male alcoholics are portrayed as disruptive working-class individuals. Female drinkers are far less common and are treated with greater sympathy. Some productions have been positively clinical in character: J.-P. Melville's adaptation of Zola's *L'Assommoir*, for example, vividly recreates the state of alcoholic zoopsy (wherein the drinker experiences terrifying animal nightmares).[15] Only rarely does the alcoholic meet a happy end; abstinence never lasts and detoxification cures are unsuccessful. In more recent films the drinker is to be pitied.[16]

Developments in alcohology reflect general progress made in medicine as a whole. The nature of alcoholic disease and its treatment has changed over the last century. In the past, alcoholics frequently died

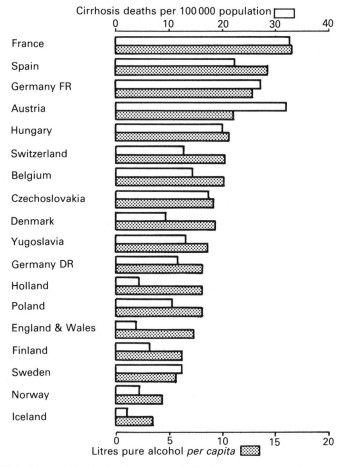

Figure 12.3 Liver cirrhosis death rates and alcohol consumption in various countries in the mid-1970s

Source: Office of Health Economics (1981) *Alcohol – Reducing the Harm*. London. OHE. Reproduced with permission of the publisher.

because they were malnourished or as the result of infections such as pneumonia or tuberculosis. Today, diet has improved and many of the conditions associated with alcoholism – delirium tremens, cirrhosis and vitamin deficiencies – are treatable. Alcoholics, in common with the rest of the population, now live longer. This explains why the contemporary period witnesses a higher incidence of liver cirrhosis than in the past, when drinkers would have died of other causes before the condition developed (see table 12.2).[17]

For reasons that remain unknown, there are fewer cases of delirium tremens and alcoholic polyneuropathy observed today. Other previously unrecognized conditions, such as grave and irreversible damage to cardiac muscle, diseases of the pancreas, and secretory problems resulting in diarrhoea and cachexia have become more prominent. Doctors are increasingly able to distinguish between those conditions that are the direct result of excessive alcohol consumption and those that may be exacerbated by alcohol. Discrimination is important here because in the past doctors have attributed illnesses due to other causes solely to alcoholism. Developments in therapeutics, biology, biochemistry and statistical epidemiology have made alcohology a far more exacting discipline. Paradoxically, biological certainties have become increasingly rare with the realization of the complexity of the metabolism of ethanol within the human body. Concern has led most Western countries to increase not only the scope of treatment provided for alcoholics, but also to redouble their research efforts in the realms of psychology, biochemistry and genetics.

CONCLUSION

AN ACCEPTABLE POISON?

THIS history, brief and simplified though it may be, endeavours to demonstrate that the word alcoholism conveys a reality which is altogether more complex than is generally held. No matter how the question is approached, whether from a moral, social or medical perspective, we discover that it has evolved through time, an evolution which continues today.

Ethanol is a poison and, sooner or later, those who abuse it will find this out to their own cost when, under its influence, they transgress accepted codes of law and behaviour. Such transgressions vary in importance from one culture to another and according to the epoch. Alcoholism, like smoking, has been greeted with varying degrees of disapproval. Countries in the West now recognize that prohibition is intolerable and impossible to enforce, but they also know that total licence threatens their very existence. Accordingly, they try to regulate alcohol, to tax and ration it, with varying degrees of provisional success. In this way countries try to achieve a compromise between acceptable and dangerous levels of consumption. Unconsciously, the bias of ever-changing legislation ensures that a certain degree of tolerance prevails.

It would be dangerous to paint too black a picture and to orientate all health, tax and agricultural policy towards the fight against alcoholism. The phenomenon is often rather dubiously held responsible for the decline in moral standards, lack of respect for the old, for the decline of workmanship in modern times. Arguments of this sort have been with us for thousands of years and in spite of them, society has survived. In France, in fact, less alcohol is consumed than a hundred years ago; furthermore, as a threat, it cannot be likened to plague or cholera. It would be equally dangerous to minimize the damage caused by drink, which is far greater than that occasioned by atmospheric pollutants, which are also the object of abolitionist campaigns (the supporters of which, in their excesses, resemble the anti-alcohol campaigners of the last century).

We have already discussed measures that might be adopted to combat alcoholism: the restriction of access to alcohol, the imposition of in-creased taxes on its sale, the promotion of health education, the introduction of stiffer penalties and so on. Their effect, however, will always be limited by the unknowns that still surround alcohol today – our understanding of alcohol and alcoholism is far from complete. On a population basis, little is known of the relationship between alcohol consumption and its effect on general physical, mental, economic and social well-being. The relationship is probably direct, but its precise nature eludes us. At the individual level, we cannot predict which drinkers will find themselves unable to relinquish their habit and the heaviest drinkers are not necessarily those who sustain the severest forms of alcoholic damage.

Society has made a further compromise by conferring legal status on alcohol and tobacco, but it continues to outlaw other drugs such as hashish, cocaine and the opiates. Authorized or not, all these products have the power to reduce people to addiction and its attendant problems. This legality is granted only through laziness, since production cannot be halted and man's need for ethanol would seem to be insatiable. We would never dream of placing the wine-producer alongside the heroin trafficker, whose business we endeavour to stamp out. Overall, however, heroin does far less damage than alcohol and our attitudes are therefore inconsistent.

Faced with such apparent contradictions, there is no reason to suppose that the history of alcoholism is nearing its end. The terms in which alcohol is discussed will continue to be subject to change and revision, as will our attitudes to the suffering it provokes.

FINAL NOTE

THE conclusion to this work should not conjure up a vision of impending doom; one in which mankind is bound irredeemably to the misery of alcoholism, as was Prometheus to the vulture. If we concede that man will always be in need of poisons to alleviate the pressures of his existence, we can also accept that his relationship with alcohol need not be doomed entirely from the outset.

We will begin with the grounds for pessimism. It is certain that the consumption of alcohol, and therefore also the prevalence of alcohol-related disease, will continue to rise in the developing countries. Not only is domestic production on the increase, but so also is industrial production on a local scale, especially that of beer. Such trends are to be seen throughout the world, regardless of political philosophy or religious creed; even the poorest nations are spending more on alcohol. In addition, the dictates of world economics are such that, with the decrease in alcohol consumption amongst wealthier nations, producers will look for markets elsewhere and will seek to exploit poorer countries, either by exporting to them or by installing plant within their territory. Falls in consumption in some areas will thus create increases elsewhere.

Fortunately, there are also grounds for optimism – at least in more developed countries, assuming that governments, teachers and doctors are aware of the problems posed by alcohol. Since total prohibition is impracticable, political energies should be directed at curbing production: by reducing the numbers of vineyards and controlling the numbers of breweries and distilleries. Such action can be undertaken effectively, if it is remembered that a surfeit of restriction will lead only to more clandestine production. Prices should also be controlled. Alcohol is not one of life's necessities, yet in no Western country in recent years has the cost of this poison kept up with inflation. It is both immoral and dangerous that liquor today is relatively cheap; once again, however, the room for manoeuvre is limited: if prices were to increase too far, illicit production would gain the upper hand. One final measure – the institution of a comprehensive education programme – should be undertaken. Populations remain ignorant about how ethanol is metabolized, and while alcoholism is a social curse and a cause for collective concern, it remains a problem for the individual, one which, with awareness of risk and acknowledgement of personal capacity, he or she alone can tackle. As with the rest of life's dangers, alcohol consumption is a matter for personal discretion and education, beginning in the classroom, should provide us all with the means to act responsibly.

Such objectives are neither original nor radical, but they are at least realizable. They give grounds for hope that alcohol will cease to be the source of misery that it is today and that it will become simply a source of relaxation and pleasure.

NOTES

CHAPTER 1 DRINKERS IN ANTIQUITY

1 De Felice, *Poisons Sacrés, Ivresses Divines: Essai sur quelques formes inférieures de la mystique* (Michel Albin, Paris, 1936).
2 P. Cruveilhier, *Commentaire du Code d'Hammourabi* (Ernest Leroux, Paris, 1938). English translation, Chilperic Edwards, *The World's Earliest Laws* (Watts, London, 1934).
3 Genesis, 9: 20–5.
4 Psalms, 104: 15.
5 Proverbs, 31: 6–7.
6 Samuel, 1: 12–15.
7 Proverbs, 23: 29–35.
8 Genesis, 19: 30–8.
9 Jeremiah, 35: 5–10.
10 Homer, *Odyssey*, X, 550–60.
11 Cited by M. Keller, in *Alcoholism, Past, Present and Future* (International Congress on Alcoholism, Jerusalem, 1984).
12 P. Villard, 'L'alcoolisation dans l'antiquité classique: aux origines de l'alcoolisme', in *Alcoolisme et Psychiatrie, Rapport au Haut Comité d'étude et d'information sur l'alcoolisme*, ed. Postel and C. Quétel (1983), pp. 15–36.
13 See J. de Romilly, 'L'Ivresse', *Corps écrit*, 13, 1985.
14 Galen reproduced certain of Plato's thoughts on the physiological and anatomical constitution of the human body. See E. Rist, 'Le vin et la morale sociale selon Platon et Galien', *Presse Médicale*, 62 (1954), p. 1119.
15 J. Soustelle, *La Vie Quotidienne des Aztèques à la Veille de la Conquête Espagnole* (Hachette, Paris, 1955), pp. 185–7.
16 J. O. Leibowitz, 'Studies in the history of alcoholism: II Acute alcoholism in Ancient Greek and Roman medicine', in *British J. Addict*, 62 (1967), pp. 83–6.
17 R. Joris, 'Le vin comme médicament dans l'Antiquité', in *Proceedings of the Twenty-Ninth International Conference in the History of Medicine* (Cairo, December 1984).
18 In an article in *La Revue des Deux Mondes*, 15 November 1853.
19 See, for example, J. Coulomb, 'La mort d'Alexandre le Grand', *Histoire des Sciences Médicales*, 18 (1984), pp. 137–45.
20 J. M. O'Brien, 'Alexander the Great', *British Journal on Alcohol and Alcoholism*, 16 (1981), pp. 39–40.
21 This theme appears in De Felice, *Poisons Sacrés, Ivresses Divines*; H. Jeanmaire, *Dionysos, Histoire du Culte de Bacchus* (Payot, Paris, 1951); M. Detienne, *Dionysos Mis à Mort* (Gallimard, Paris, 1977); M. Maffesoli, *L'Ombre de Dionysos, Contribution à une sociologie de l'orgie* (Méridiens-Anthropos, Paris, 1982); Y. Durand and J. Morenon, *L'Imaginaire de l'Alcoolisme* (Éd.

Universitaires, Paris, 1972); J. Laffitte (ed.), *L'Imaginaire du Vin* (Centre de recherches sur l'image et le symbole, Marseilles, 1983).

22 A. Tchernia, 'Le vin de l'Italie romaine' (thesis, Paris, 1984); see also, M. Rambaud, 'Guerre des Gaules, Guerre du vin?', in Laffitte (ed.), *L'Imaginaire du Vin*, pp. 25–35.

23 E. M. Jellinek, 'Drinkers and alcoholics in Ancient Rome', *Journal of Studies on Alcoholism*, 37 (1976), pp. 1718–41.

24 J.-C. Sournia, *Histoire et Médecine* (Fayard, Paris, 1982), pp. 100–5.

25 E. Jeanselme, 'L'Alcoolisme à Byzance', *Bulletin de la Société Française d'Histoire et Médecine*, 18 (1924), pp. 289–95.

26 J.-C. and M. Sournia, *L'Orient des Premiers Chrétiens: Histoire et Archéologie de la Syrie Byzantine* (Fayard, Paris, 1966), pp. 41–4, 104–7.

27 Personal communication from L. Mavrommatis, historian at the University of Athens, December 1984.

28 R. Dion, *Histoire de la Vigne et du Vin en France, des origines au XIXe siècle* (Flammarion, Paris, 1977); this work is very well documented. See also, H. Enjalbert, *Histoire de la Vigne et du Vin* (Bordas, Paris, 1976).

29 P. Ménétrier, 'L'Alcoolisme, cause de la dégénérescence de la race chez les rois mérovingiens', *Bulletin de la Société Française d'Histoire et Médecine*, 14 (1920), pp. 301–9.

CHAPTER 2   WINE AND EAUX-DE-VIE

1 D. Seward, *Les Moines et le Vin, Histoire des Vins Monastiques* (Éd. Pygmalion, Paris, 1982).

2 Cited by Legrand d'Aussy, *Histoire de la Vie Privée des Français* (Paris, 1815), p. 46.

3 See the portrait of Pianormo Arlotto, ch. VII of Laurent de Médicis's book.

4 J. Cuba, *Hortus sanitatis* (Augsbourg, 1485).

5 B. de Laffumas, *Source de Plusieurs Abus et Monopoles qui sont glissés et coulés sur le peuple de France depuis trente ans ou environ* (Paris, 1596), cited by Dion, *Histoire de la Vigne et du Vin en France*, p. 488.

6 Agapios, *Goponicon* (Venice, 1647), cited by E. Jeanselme, 'L'Alcoolisme à Byzance'.

7 C. Berger, 'An vinum vitae et staturae detrahit?' (medical thesis, Paris, 3 March 1667).

8 Cited by M. Keller, *Alcoholism, Past, Present and Future*.

9 Ibid.

10 From the exhibition, 'Morbid Cravings, the Emergence of Addiction', held at the Wellcome Institute for the History of Medicine in London (October 1984).

11 R. Philippe, 'Une opération pilote: l'étude du ravitaillement de Paris au temps de Lavoisier', *Cahier des Annales: Pour une Histoire de l'Alimentation*, 28 (1970).

12 The word *frelater* first appeared in French usage in the sixteenth century and was derived from the Dutch *verlauten*, to decant. During production, wine requires decanting at several stages and it is common, and indeed accepted practice, at such points in the process to blend or mix it. The addition of sugar, spices,

alcohol, etc., however, is not viewed favourably, and it is for this reason that the word has developed its pejorative meaning.

13 Dion, *Histoire de la Vigne et du Vin en France*, pp. 427ff.

14 J. Guyot, *Étude des Vignobles de France* (3 vols, Paris, 1868).

15 Dion, *Histoire de la Vigne et du Vin en France*, p. 489.

16 de Laffumas, *Source de Plusieurs Abus*.

CHAPTER 3   FROM THE ENLIGHTENMENT TO MAGNUS HUSS,
1700–1850

1 There is a chapter dedicated to this motif in Nashe's *Pierce Pennilesse, his Supplication to the Devill*, in *The Works of Thomas Nashe*, ed. R. McKerrow (Basil Blackwell, Oxford, 1958).

2 William Pitt, a heavy port drinker, died of cirrhosis of the liver in 1806 at the age of 47.

3 T. G. Coffey, 'Beer Street, Gin Lane: some views of 18th century drinking', *Quart. J. Stud. Alc.*, 27 (1966), pp. 669–92.

4 Henry Fielding (1707–54) is best known for his novel *Tom Jones*, but in addition to being a writer, he served as a Justice of the Peace for Westminster.

5 D. George, *London Life in the 18th Century* (London, 1930).

6 The tea-drinking habit spread fast and even in colonial ports the government attempted to increase customs on this commodity, a measure which provoked the Boston tea party and the subsequent revolt in the American colonies.

7 T. T. Trotter, *An Essay Medical, Philosophical and Chemical on Drunkenness and its Effects on the Human Body* (London, 1804).

8 W. F. Bynum, 'Chronic alcoholism in the first half of the 19th century', *Bull. Hist. Med.*, 42 (1968), pp. 160–85.

9 Cited by J. O. Leibowitz, 'Studies in the history of alcoholism, I: Description of liver cirrhosis by S. Black, 1817', *British J. Add.*, 61 (1965), pp. 129–34. To Black's name can be added that of J. C. Lettsom, who described drink-related changes in the liver to the London Medical Society in 1792. Also of importance is Thompson's work, *A Practical Treatise on the Diseases of the Liver* (Edinburgh, 1841).

10 G. Fellion, 'Aperçu historique sur le traitement de l'alcoolisme' (thesis, Paris, 1951).

11 R. Macnish, *Anatomy of Drunkenness* (Glasgow, 1836).

12 The meaning of words changes over time. Today, in French the word '*abstinence*' has the sense of a complete end to alcohol consumption, as distinct from the relative connotation it has in English. Conversely, '*tempérance*' has the sense of moderation, whereas in English 'temperance', when applied to alcohol, usually refers to total avoidance.

13 S. Ledermann, *Alcool, Alcoolisme, Alcoolisation: Données scientifiques, de caractère physiologique, économique et social* (2 vols, Travaux et documents de l'INED, PUF, Paris, 1956 and 1964), vol. II, p. 117.

14 T. G. Coffey, 'Beer Street, Gin Lane'.

15 W. F. Bynum, 'Chronic alcoholism'.

16 C. W. Hufeland, *Über die Vergiftung durch Bränntwein* (Berlin, 1802).

17 C. von Brühl-Cramer, *Über die Trunksucht und eine Rationelle Heilmethode Derselben* (Berlin, 1819).

18 F. W. Lippich, *Gründzuge zur Dipsobiostatik* (Leipzig, 1834).

19 Much of the information in this section is taken from M. E. Lender and J. F. Martin, *Drinking in America, a History* (Free Press, New York; Macmillan, London, 1982).

20 Cited by M. Keller, *Alcoholism, Past, Present and Future*.

21 B. Rush, *An Inquiry into the Effects of Ardent Spirits on the Human Mind and Body* (1784).

22 W. J. Rorabaugh, *The Alcoholic Republic, an American Tradition* (Oxford University Press, Oxford, 1979).

23 H. G. Levine, 'The discovery of addiction: changing conceptions of habitual drunkenness in America', *Journal of Studies on Alcohol*, 39 (1978), pp. 143–74.

24 M. Habert, *Les Ligues Antialcooliques en France et à l'Étranger* (Jules Rousset, Paris, 1904). This study was incomplete even at the time of its publication. See also, H. G. Levine, 'The alcohol problem in America: from temperance to alcoholism', *British Journal of Addiction* 79 (1984), pp. 109–19.

25 J. Eberle, *Treatise on the Diseases and Physical Education in Children* (Corey and Fairbank, Cincinnati, Ohio, 1833).

26 J. P. Gaussens, *Histoire Institutionnelle de la Maison de Charenton.* (Mémoire, École nationale de santé publique, Rennes, 1969). H. Rauch, 'Contribution à la histoire de l'hôpital Saint-Méen de Rennes' (thesis, Rennes, 1969).

27 L. Trenard, 'Cabarets et estaminets lillois: 1715–1815', in *Actes du 106ᵉ Congrès National des Sociétés Savantes*, held at Perpignan, 1981 (Archives CTHS, Paris, 1984), pp. 53–72.

28 R. T. H. Laennec, *De l'Auscultation Médiate ou Traité du Diagnostic des Maladies des Poumons et du Coeur* (Paris, 1919), vol. I, p. 368.

29 Thus Dupuytren saw the situation less clearly than Macnish (see n. 11 above).

30 von Brühl-Cramer, *Über die Trunksucht und eine Rationelle Heilmethode Derselben*.

31 Léveillé, *Histoire de la Folie des Ivrognes* (Dantu, Paris, 1830). Cited by G. Fellion, 'Aperçu historique sur le traitement de l'alcoolisme'.

32 F. C. Steward has published a detailed list of expenditure in the major Parisian hospitals for the year 1840. This appeared in his *1843 Guide for Medical Men*, and has been analysed by K. B. Roberts, *History of Medicine* (Memorial University of Newfoundland, 1984).

33 The statement of a doctor from Coulommiers, made in 1843 and cited by J. Léonard, *La Vie Quotidienne du Médecin de Province au XIXᵉ Siècle* (Hachette, Paris, 1977).

34 J. Clément, *La Santé, ou la Médecine Populaire* (Paris, 1840).

35 E. Zola, *Le Docteur Pascal* (NRF, la Pléiade, Paris), vol. V, pp. 1096, 1655–6nn.

36 L. R. Villermé, *Tableau de l'État Physique et Moral des Ouvriers Employés dans les Manufactures de Coton, de Laine et de Soie* (EDHIS, Paris, 1983, originally published 1840).

37 See, for example, 'De la santé des ouvriers employés dans les fabriques de soie, de coton, et de laine', *Annales d'Hygiène Publique et de Médecine Légale*, vol. XXI. Also, 'Sur les cités ouvrières', *Annales d'Hygiène Publique et de Médecine Légale*, vol. XLII (1849).

CHAPTER 4   MAGNUS HUSS AND ALCOHOLISM

1 Petrus Bergius, 'Dissertation diaetetica in qua spiritus frumenti proponitur' (Uppsala, 1764).
2 Information kindly furnished by the Vin och Sprithistoriska Museum, Stockholm.
3 There is a resurgence of interest in the life and work of Huss. The most complete biography to date is, A. Huss, *Magnus Huss, An Eminent Public Benefactor* (Nordisk medicinarsbok, 1962, in Swedish). On Huss's work, see H. Bernard, 'Alcoolisme et antialcoolisme en France au XIXe siècle; autour de Magnus Huss', in his book, *Histoire, Economie et Société* (1984), pp. 609–28. Also, N. Saleur, 'Magnus Huss, "alkoholismus chronicus", 1849–1852' (thesis, Strasburg, 1985).
4 M. Huss, *Alcoholismus chronicus, eller chronisk alkoholsjukdom; ett bidrag till dyskrasiernas Kännedom, enligt egen och andras erfarenhet* (Stockholm, 1849).
5 M. Huss, *Chronische alkoholskrankheit, oder alcoholismus chronicus: ein beiträg zur kenntniss dern Vergiftungs-Krankheiten*, tr. Gerhard Van dem Busch (Stockholm and Leipzig, 1852).
6 Dr Broussais (1772–1838) based his system on his understanding of the process of inflammation and on the practice of blood-letting. Brownism was based on the medical theories of Dr John Brown (1735–88), an Edinburgh doctor, who held that all disease is the result of too much or too little excitement.
7 Renaudin, 'Analyse de: "De l'alcoolisme chronique", par le docteur Magnus Huss', in *Annales Médico-psychologiques*, 5 (1853), pp. 60–88.
8 *Mémoires de l'Académie des Sciences* (1853), p. 208.

CHAPTER 5   DRINKING HABITS

1 For Great Britain, see E. J. Higgs, 'Research into the history of alcohol use and control in England and Wales: the available sources in the public records office', in *British Journal of Addiction*, 79 (1984), pp. 41–8.
2 See, for example, J. Rainaut and G. Miletto, 'Un mode culturel d'alcoolisation en Provence au XIXe siècle, les chambrettes', *Bulletin de la Société Française d'Alcoologie* (1983), pp. 10–14.
3 The standard work here is S. Ledermann, *Alcool, Alcoolisme, Alcoolisation: Données scientifiques, de caractère physiologique, économique et social* (2 vols, Travaux et documents de l'INED, PUF, Paris, 1956 and 1964).
4 Figures cited by T. Zeldin, *Histoire des Passions Françaises, 1848–1915* (Seuil, Paris, 1979), vol. III, p. 429.
5 L. Pasteur, *Études sur le Vin, ses Maladies, Causes qui les Provoquent, Procédés Nouveaux pour le Conserver et Vieillir* (Paris, 1866).

6 E. Zola, *L'Assommoir* (NRF, la Pléiade, vol. II).

7 Carcassonne developed into a major market centre for wine producers during this period, see *Histoire de Carcassonne* (Privat, 1984).

8 Figures taken from *Le Grand Almanach des Familles*, 1884–5.

9 L. Mayet, *Études sur les Statistiques de l'Alcoolisme* (Plaquette, Paris, 1901).

10 C. Lian, 'L'alcoolisme, cause d'hypertension artérielle', *Bulletin de l'Académie de Médecine*, 74 (1915), pp. 525–8.

11 F. Barbier, 'La consommation des boissons à Valenciennes au XIXᵉ siècle: le vin et la bière, 1826–1895', in *Actes du 106ᵉ Congrès National des Sociétés Savantes*, held at Perpignan, 1981 (Archives CTHS, Paris, 1984), pp. 53–9.

12 *Le Grand Almanach des Familles*, 25 May 1884.

13 B. Hell, 'Manières de vivre, manières de boire: le homme et la bière en Alsace', in *Actes de la Rencontre 'Cultures, Manières de Boire, Alcoolisme'* (Éd. Bretagne, 1884), pp. 53–9.

14 T. Fillaut, 'L'Alcoolisme dans l'ouest de la France dans la seconde moitié du XIXᵉ siècle' (thesis, Rennes, 1981).

15 S. Ledermann, *Alcool, Alcoolisme, Alcoolisation*, vol. II, ch. XIV.

16 F. Lentz, *Étude statistique sur la consommation alcoolique en Belgique depuis 1831: considérations psychologiques sur l'alcoolisme, et sur les différents remèdes destinés à le combattre* (Brussels, 1920).

17 G. P. Williams and G. T. Brake, *Drink in Great Britain, 1900 to 1979* (Edsell, London, 1980).

18 S. Ledermann, *Alcool, Alcoolisme, Alcoolisation*, vol. I, chs I and IV.

19 D. Nourrisson, 'La loi, la politique et la morale, ou la question des bouilleurs de cru en Seine-Inférieure avant la Grande Guerre', in *Les Boissons, Production et Consommation aux XIXᵉ et XXᵉ Siècles*, op. cit., pp. 139–156.

20 C. Péguy, *Cahiers de la Quinzaine* (February 1903). Cited by D. Nourrisson, 'La loi, la politique et la morale'.

21 A. Dubac, 'Bouilleurs de cru en Normandie', in *Les Boissons, Production et Consommation aux XIXᵉ et XXᵉ Siècles*, pp. 121–37.

22 Evidently drink shops reflect their clientele and there is a history behind the names they are given. In France during the period 1850–1950, the following terms were employed: *marchand de vin, cabaret, taverne, caboulot, bistrot, mastroquet, troquet, buvette, café* and *rade*. If food was also served, the terms used were: *restaurant, buffet, brasserie* and *bouchon*. Indeed, there were many regional terms such as *estaminet* in Lille, *pied humide* in Lyons and *aubette* in Strasburg. In certain cases, the distribution of these names can tell us important facts about cultural history and regional migration within France.

23 L. Mayet, *Etudes sur les Statistiques de l'Alcoolisme*. These figures do not include Paris.

24 P. Manneville, 'Un entraînement forcé à l'ivrognerie: le paiement des ouvriers du port du Havre au XIXᵉ siècle', in *Les Boissons, Production et Consommation aux XIXᵉ et XXᵉ Siècles*, pp. 167–80.

25 'Les Cabarets', in *Le Grand Almanach des Familles*, 11 March 1885.

26 J. Rochard, 'L'Alcool, son rôle dans les sociétés modernes', *Revue des Deux Mondes*, 15 April 1886, pp. 871–900.

27 T. Fillaut, 'L'Alcoolisme dans l'ouest de la France'.
28 J. Lalouette, 'Le discours bourgeois sur les débits de boissons aux alentours de 1900', *Recherches*, 29: XII (1977).
29 An unpublished remark made by Charles Richet (probably in the 1920s). Kindly passed on by G. Richet.
30 S. Ledermann, *Alcool, Alcoolisme, Alcoolisation*,vol. I, p. 69.
31 J. London, *Le Cabaret de la Dernière Chance* (Éd. 10–18, Paris, 1974), p. 26. Originally published in English under the title, *John Barleycorn*.

CHAPTER 6 ALCOHOLISM AND MEDICINE

1 A. Terrise, 'L'Apparition de l'alcoolisme psychiatrique dans les thèses de médecine au XIXe et au début du XXe siècle', in *Alcoolisme et Psychiatrie, Rapport au Haut Comité d'étude et d'information sur l'alcoolisme*, ed. Postel and Quétel (1983), pp. 233–71.
2 *Dictionnaire Encyclopédique de Sciences Médicales*, dit Dictionnaire Dechambre (1865 edn), p. 624.
3 C. Pepin, *L'Alcoolisme* (Paris, 1897).
4 J. Rochard, *Traité d'hygiène sociale* (Paris, 1888).
5 An exhaustive bibliography on the subject would serve no purpose. J. Léonard indicates those authors whose names reappear frequently. See *La Médecine entre les pouvoirs et les savoirs* (Hachette, Paris, 1982), ch. XVIII and nn. 27–9.
6 It is difficult to distinguish the long-term harm done by different drinks because it is rare to find sample groups that consume only one type of alcoholic drink.
7 Cited by S. Ledermann, *Alcool, Alcoolisme, Alcoolisation: Données scientifiques, de caractère physiologique, économique et social* (2 vols, Travaux et documents de l'INED, PUF, Paris, 1956 and 1964), vol. II, p. 215.
8 Bell, 'On the effects of the use of alcoholic drinks on tuberculous diseases', *American Journal of the Medical Sciences*, 38 (1859), p. 407.
9 The invention of such terms was quite common at this time.
10 Ledermann, *Alcool, Alcoolisme, Alcoolisation*, vol. II, p. 141.
11 Ibid., vol. II, p. 117.
12 M. C. Delahaye, *L'Absinthe, histoire de la fée verte* (Berger-Levrault, Paris, 1983). Also, see T. Fillaut, 'Fée verte et poison social: l'absinthe en France au XIXe siècle', in *Actes, Cultures, Manières de Boire et Alcoolisme* (Rennes, 1984), pp. 47–52.
13 Motet, 'Considérations générales sur l'alcoolisme et plus particulièrement des effets toxiques produits sur l'homme par la liqueur d'absinthe' (thesis, Paris, 1859).
14 P. Jolly, *Le Tabac et l'Absinthe, leur Influence sur la Santé Publique, sur l'Ordre Moral et Social* (Baillière, Paris, 1875).
15 An expression taken from Lancereaux's comments on a report by J. Desbouverie, 'Répression de l'alcoolisme', *Bulletin de l'Académie de Médecine*, 19 (1888), p. 885.
16 See, for example, the 1889 work of Cadeac and Meunier, cited by H. Triboulet and F. Mathieu, *L'Alcool et l'Alcoolisme: Notions Générales, Toxicologie et*

Physiologie, Pathologie, Thérapeutique, Prophylaxie (Carré and Naud, Paris, 1889).

17 As a curiosity the table produced by Delobel can be consulted, 'Le Péril Alcoolique, l'Alcoolisme: Tableau des Maladies Dues à l'Alcoolisme', in *Paris Médical*, 8 February 1936.

18 C. Lian, 'L'alcoolisme, cause d'hypertension artérielle', *Bulletin de l'Académie de Médecine*, 74 (1915).

19 Roger, Widal and Teissier (eds), *Nouveau Traité de Médecine*, vol. VII, 'Les Intoxicants', p. 303. This chapter was the work of the specialists Triboulet and Mignot.

20 Triboulet and Mathieu, *L'Alcool et l'Alcoolisme*, p. 234.

21 L. Roché, report read to the Académie de Médecine, 1 February 1898.

22 Eonnet, in *Bulletin de l'Académie de Médecine*, 21 (1898), p. 326; 24 (1890), p. 669.

23 J. Reboul, *Alcoolisme Latent ou Inconscient: ses Conséquences Physiques, Intellectuelles et Morales* (Imprimerie Générale, Nîmes, 1898).

24 G. Variot, *Le Climat Marin et les Scrofules dans les Îles Bretonnes*, Rapport Présenté au Ministre de l'Intérieur (Davy, Paris, 1891); Vallin, 'L'Alcoolisme par l'allaitement', *Bulletin de l'Académie de Médecine*, 36 (1896), pp. 442–6.

25 Reports on 'L'Alcoolisme dans la Vallée d'Auge' and 'Les Enfants alcooliques: causes et effets de l'alcoolisme pendant la première jeunesse', *Bulletin de l'Académie de Médecine*, 50 (1903), pp. 88–9.

26 Armand-Delille, 'La santé des enfants de la population rurale nés pendant la période de restrictions d'alcools', *Bulletin de l'Académie de Médecine*, 131 (1947), pp. 692–3.

27 Dromard, 'Les Alcoolisés non alcooliques' (thesis, Paris, 1902).

28 Lecœur, 'Note sur les alcooliques en chirurgie', *Bulletin de l'Académie de Médecine* (1858–9), pp. 1256–71; Verneuil, 'Le Pronostic des lésions traumatiques et des opérations chirurgicales chez les alcooliques', *Bulletin de l'Académie de Médecine* (1870), pp. 961–86.

29 Charcot, for example, considered himself both a neurologist and a psychiatrist and would never have imagined that the two disciplines could exist independently.

30 V. Magnan, *De l'Alcoolisme: des Diverses Formes de Délire Alcoolique et de leur Traitement* (Delahaye, Paris, 1874). Magnan also conducted his own experiments, see: *Étude Expérimentale et Clinique sur l'Alcoolisme: Alcool et Absinthe, Épilepsie Absinthique*.

31 A. Papadaki, 'Statistique clinique des alcooliques traités à l'asile de Bel Air (Suisse) en 1901–1902', *Revue Médicale de la Suisse Romande*, 12 (1903). Also see, 'Analyse', *Archives de Neurologie*, II (1904), pp. 435–6.

32 Wright, 'Observations sur l'origine, le caractère et le traitement de l'œnomanie', in *The Alienist and Neurologist*, October 1880. H. Bernard, 'Pour une épidémiologie de l'alcoolisme en psychiatrie', in *Alcoolisme et Psychiatrie*, ed. Postel and Quétel, pp. 799–817.

33 Leclère, 'Les Internements pour alcoolisme à l'asile d'aliénés du Bon Saveur de Caen de 1838 à 1925', in *Alcoolisme et Psychiatrie*, ed. Postel and Quétel, pp. 321–66. Also, see D. Nourrisson, 'Aliénation et alcoolisme: l'exemple de la

Seine-Inférieure sous la IIIe République', in *Alcoolisme et Psychiatrie*, ed. Postel and Quétel, pp. 207–31.

34 C. Quétel, 'La marche croissante de l'aliénation alcoolique', in *Alcoolisme et Psychiatrie*, ed. Postel and Quetel, pp. 119–204. Quétel's interesting list is, however, incomplete.

35 Bouchereau and V. Magnan, 'Statistique des malades entrés entre 1870 et 1871 au bureau d'admission des aliénés de la Seine', *Ann. Med. psycol.*, VIII (November 1872).

36 Legrain, *Un Fléau Social: L'Alcoolisme* (Paris, 1896).

37 *Bulletin de l'Académie de Médecine*, 126 (1942), pp. 244–5.

38 Ibid., 128 (1944), pp. 659–60, 692–5.

39 Ledermann, *Alcool, Alcoolisme, Alcoolisation*, vol. II, p. 127.

40 C. Enachescu, 'Alcoolisme et création littéraire: essai d'analyse psychopathologique d'écrivains alcooliques', *Revue de l'Alcoolisme*, 16 (1970), pp. 141–50.

41 W. R. Bett, 'Vincent Van Gogh (1853–1890), artist and addict', *British Journal of Add.*, 5 (1954), pp. 7–14.

42 T. C. Lee, 'La Vue de Van Gogh', *J.A.M.A.*, 245 (1981), pp. 727–9. Digitalis poisoning is responsible for 'xanthopsy' or yellow vision. Other hypotheses have been suggested: for example, glaucoma or cataracts.

43 A. Manson, *Les Maudits* (Denoël, Paris).

44 J. Miermont, 'Ludwig van Beethoven et l'alcoolisme', *Psychologie Médicale*, 11 (1979), pp. 2083–92.

45 J. Boulay, 'Les Maladies et la mort de Moussorgski', *Sonances* (Quebec), 1 (1981), pp. 8–15.

46 We are restricting our exploration solely to the relationship between alcoholism and literature.

47 M. Costantini, 'Pour un alcooltest de l'art grec', in *L'Imaginaire du Vin*, ed. J. Laffitte (Centre de recherches sur l'image et le symbole, Marseilles, 1983), pp. 3–14.

48 Antheaume and Dromard, *Poésie et Folie, Essai de Psychologie et de Critique* (Doin, Paris, 1908).

49 A. Rauzy, 'Alcool, création et destruction chez Edgar Poe', *Psychologie Médicale*, 15 (1983), pp. 915–21.

50 W. Faulkner, *Œuvres Romanesques*, vol. I (Gallimard, Paris, 1977).

51 W. Styron, *La Proie des Flammes* (Flammarion, Paris, 1962); originally published in English as *Set This House on Fire*.

52 R. Yates, *Fauteur de Troubles* (Flammarion, Paris, 1984); *Revolutionary Road*.

53 See, for example, P. Sans, 'Introduction à la compréhension psychopathologique de l'œuvre de Malcolm Lowry', *Études Psychopathologique, Expression et Signe* (December 1977); F. Jesu, 'Effets de l'alcool, fonctions de l'écrit', in *Psychologie Médicale*, 13 (1981), pp. 495–502; J. Mambrino, 'L'œuvre de Malcolm Lowry', *Études* (November 1984).

54 M. Lowry, *Au-dessous du Volcan* (Buchet-Chastel, Paris, 1960); translation of *Under the Volcano*.

55 M. Lowry, *Pour l'amour de mourir* (Éd. de la Différence, Paris, 1976).

(See M. Lowry, *Selected Poems of Malcolm Lowry* (City Lights Books, San Francisco, 1962).)

56 M. Lowry, *Au-dessous du Volcan*, pp. 36, 87.
57 *Bulletin de l'Académie de Médecine*, 19 (1888), p. 885.
58 Roger, Widal and Teissier, *Nouveau Traité de Médecine*, pp. 262–3. The authors provide an extensive list of researchers who have worked on the role of alcohol in the diet.
59 J. H. Warner, 'Physiological theory and therapeutic explanation in the 1860s: The British debate on the medical use of alcohol', *Bulletin of History Med.*, 54 (1980), pp. 235–257.
60 L. J. Béhier, 'Note sur l'emploi interne de l'alcool à hautes doses dans les phegmasies et dans les maladies fébriles', *Bull. Gen. de Thérapeutique*, 150 (1865), p. 154.
61 While some doctors were prescribing rest cures in sanatoria, there were others who recommended milk products. In Eastern Europe, great success was claimed for treatment with *koumiss*, a fermented milk-based product. See A. Roubel, 'Sur le traitement de la tuberculose pulmonaire par le koumiss', *Rousski Vratch*, 11 (1912), p. 31; 12 (1913), p. 401; 13 (1914), p. 436.
62 Magnan, *De l'Alcoolisme*, pp. 55–6.
63 The debate among American doctors between 1919 and 1933 is discussed by B. C. Jones, 'A prohibition problem, liquor as medicine, 1920–1933', *Journal of the History of Medicine and Allied Sciences*, XVIII (1963), pp. 353–69.
64 Broca, 'Intoxication alcoolique latente (alcoolomanie): recherches expérimentales sur le sérum d'animal alcoolisé (anti-éthyline), essais chimiques', *Bulletin de l'Académie de Médecine*, 42 (1899), pp. 668–85; Dromard, 'Les Alcoolisés non alcooliques'; Sapelier and Dromard, *Le Sérum Anti-éthylique* (Paris, 1903).
65 P. Savy, *Traité de Thérapeutique Clinique* (3 vols, Paris, 1936).
66 P. Perrin, 'L'Alcoolisme, problèmes médico-sociaux, problèmes économiques', in *Expansion Scientifique*, (Paris, 1950).
67 Triboulet and Mathieu, *L'Alcool et L'Alcoolisme*, pp. 176ff.
68 P. J. Navarre, *L'Alcoolisme, le Mal, les Remèdes* (Mougin-Rusaud, Lyons, 1898), pp. 27–38.
69 A. Baratier, 'Les frontières de l'alcoolisme', *La Tribune Médicale* (1898), pp. 6–48.

CHAPTER 7   SOCIETY AND RACE UNDER THREAT

1 B. A. Morel, *Traité des dégénérescences physiques, intellectuelles et morales de l'espèce humaine et des causes qui produisent ces variétés maladives* (Baillière, Paris, 1857).
2 Ibid., preface, p. VI.
3 Ibid., pp. 4–5.
4 Darwin's *The Origin of Species* was published in 1859, two years after Morel's book.
5 H. Barella, 'Contribution à l'étude de l'alcoolisme', *Bull. Acad. Royale* (Belgium), 1898. A comprehensive list of the stigmata attributed to degeneration during the period 1850–1950 would be lengthy indeed.

6　See C. Herzlich and J. Pierret, *Malades d'hier, malades d'aujourd'hui* (Payot, Paris, 1984), esp. ch. IX.

7　Some of these writers are discussed by Y. Y. Simon, op. cit., and the list could be extended.

8　Morel, *Traité des dégénérescences*, p. 83.

9　This notion of human behaviour being influenced by climate is Hippocratic in origin.

10　Again, the working classes are equated with the criminal elements in society.

11　V. Magnan, *De l'alcoolisme: des diverses formes de délire alcoolique et de leur traitement* (Delahaye, Paris, 1874).

12　Moreau, *La Psychologie morbide dans ses rapports avec la philosophie de l'histoire* (1859).

13　Magnan, *De l'alcoolisme*: p. 69.

14　V. Magnan and Legrain, *Les Dégénérés, état mental et syndromes épisodiques* (RUEFF, Paris, 1895).

15　Dromard, 'Les Alcoolisés non alcooliques' (thesis, Paris, 1902).

16　Magnan and Legrain, *Les Dégénérés*, p. 16.

17　For example, Morambat's contribution to the debate, 'L'Alcoolisme et la criminalité', *Bulletin de l'Académie de Médecine*, 18 (1887), p. 843.

18　L. Jacquet, *L'Alcool, étude économique générale. Ses rapports avec l'agriculture, l'industrie, le commerce, la législation, l'impôt, l'hygiène industrielle et sociale* (Masson, Paris, 1912), preface written by George Clémenceau.

19　Morel, *Traité des dégénérescences*, p. 489.

20　M. Bée, 'L'image du buveur en Normandie, ou le syndrome de décadence dans "l'État moral" de 1902', in H. de Buttet, *Les Boissons, production et consommation aux XIXe et XXe siècles*, op. cit., pp. 181–96.

21　A. de Liedekerke, *La Belle Epoque de l'opium* (Éd. Différence, Paris, 1984).

22　J.-B. V. Laborde, *Les Hommes et les actes de l'insurrection de Paris devant la psychologie morbide* (Paris, 1872).

23　F. Dumoulin, *Le Débat sur l'alcoolisme après la Commune: 1871–1887* (Travail UER-Histoire, Nanterre, 1979).

24　E. Zola, *La Débâcle* (NRF, Pléiade, Paris), p. 877.

25　Of limited interest here is, J. F. Mouraux, 'Évolution de 1872 à 1949 des principales notions liées à l'alcool, à partir d'une analyse de textes du Trésor de la langue français' (thesis, Nancy, 1984).

26　C. Richet, *L'Homme et l'intelligence: fragments de physiologie et de psychologie* (Alcan, Paris, 1884), p. 104.

27　F. Dostoevsky, *Les Frères Karamazov* (Éd. Stock, Paris, 1949).

28　For a non-fictional account of the situation in the French navy, see, T. Fillault, 'Une action de promotion de santé en France à l'orée du XXe siècle: la prévention de l'alcoolisme chez les marins', in *101e Congrès des sociétés savantes* (Montpellier, 1985), vol. II, pp. 201–10.

29　S. Lagerlöf, *La Saga de Gösta Berling* (Stock, Paris, 1976).

30　See, for example, H. Triboulet and F. Mathieu, *L'Alcool et l'Alcoolisme: notions générales, toxicologie et physiologie, pathologie, thérapeutique, prophylaxie* (Carré et Naud, Paris) p. 183.

31 Erasmus Darwin, *Botanic Garden* (1794). Cited by C. Pepin, *L'Alcoolisme* (Paris, 1897).
32 Triboulet and Mathieu, *L'Alcool et l'Alcoolisme*, p. 170.
33 P. J. Navarre, *L'Alcoolisme, le mal, les remèdes* (imp. Mougin-Rusaud, Lyon, 1898), pp. 9–10.
34 E. Le Roy-Ladurie, *Le Territoire de l'historien* (NRF, Paris, 1973), vol. I, pp. 111, 139ff.
35 The article appeared in *Le Nouvelliste de Rouen* and is cited by Y. Pelicier, 'Des mots sur l'alcoolisme', *Confrontations psychiatriques*, 8 (1972), pp. 9–19.
36 For example, H. Martin, *Archives générales de médecine* (1877); Grenier, 'Contribution à l'étude de la descendance des alcooliques' (thesis, Paris, 1887); Sollier, 'Du rôle de l'hérédité dans l'alcoolisme' (thesis, Paris, 1889).
37 E. Pierret, *Le Péril de la race* (Perrin, Paris, 1907).
38 Lannelongue, *Bulletin de l'Académie de Médecine*, XXXII (1894), p. 191.
39 L. Mayet, *Études sur les statistiques de l'alcoolisme* (Plaquette, 1901, Paris).
40 P. Reynier, 'L'Alcoolisme et les tuberculoses externes chez l'adulte et chez l'enfant', *Bulletin de l'Académie de Médecine*, 58 (1907), pp. 407–14.
41 C. Richet, *L'Homme et l'intelligence: fragments de physiologie et de psychologie* (Alcan, Paris, 1884), p. 106.
42 Demme, *Uber den Einfluss des Alkohols auf den Organismen des Kindes* (Stuttgart, 1896).
43 G. Bilson, 'Muscles and health: "Health and the Canadian immigrant, 1867–1906"', in *Health, Disease and Medicine, Essays in Canadian History* (Hannah Institute, Toronto, 1984), pp. 398–411.
44 Barella, 'Contribution à l'étude de l'alcoolisme', p. 69.
45 J. Bergeron, 'Rapport sur la répression de l'alcoolisme', *Bulletin de l'Académie de Médecine*, 36 (1871), p. 993.
46 C. Pépin, *L'Alcoolisme* (1897), p. 103.
47 See, for example, J. Arnold, *De l'alcool considéré comme une source de force, et du parti que l'on peut en tirer dans la pratique de la guerre* (Paris, 1873).
48 Marshall, 'Observations on the abuse of spiritous liquors by the European troops in India', *Edinburgh Medical and Surgical Journal*, 41 (1834), p. 19.
49 *Bulletin de l'Académie de Médecine*, 18 (1887), p. 451.
50 Debove, 'L'Alcoolisme et ses conséquences pour l'individu, l'état et la société', *Press Médicale*, 95 (19 November 1898).
51 R. Dion, *Histoire de la vigne et du vin de France, des origines au XIXe siècle* (Flammarion, Paris, 1977).
52 M. Lipsky, 'Une famille de dégénérés hérédo-alcooliques dans l'œuvre de Dostoïevski: *Les frères Karamazov*' (thesis, Lyon, 1927).
53 D'Heucqueville, *Bulletin de l'Académie de Médecine*, 127 (1943), pp. 479–81.
54 A. Lamache, Davost, Chuberre and Delalande, 'La sénilité précoce des alcooliques chroniques', *Bulletin de l'Académie de Médecine*, 136 (1952), pp. 31–3, and 'L'activité génésique des alcooliques chroniques', ibid., pp. 530–2.
55 Herzlich and Pierret, *Malades d'hier* pp. 157–8.
56 J. Eberle, *Treatise on the Diseases and Physical Education in Children* (Corey and Fairbank, Cincinnati, 1833).

57 P. Lemoine, H. Harousseau, J.-P. Borteyru and J.-C. Mennet, 'Les enfants de parents alcooliques: anomalies observées à propos de 127 cas', *Quest-médical*, 21 (1968), pp. 476–82.

58 K. L. Jones et al, 'Pattern of malformations in offspring of chronic alcoholic mothers', *Lancet*, 1 (1973), pp. 1267–1271. See also, 'The fetal alcohol syndrome', *Tératology*, 12 (1975), pp. 1–12.

59 An extensive bibliography is contained in C. Samaille-Villette and P. P. Samaille, 'Le syndrome d'alcoolisme foetal, à propos de 47 observations' (thesis, Lille, 1976). See also H. Tuchmann-Dupleissis, 'Retentissement de l'alcoolisme maternel sur la descendance', *Bulletin de l'Académie de Médecine*, 164 (1980). The most recent comprehensive work on the children of alcoholic mothers is E. Klein, 'Kinder von alkoholikerinnen; Meinungen, Urteile, Vorurteile und Nachforschungen seit der 19. Jahrhundert', *Institute for the History of Medicine* (Cologne), 35 (1985).

CHAPTER 8   VIRTUE IN ACTION

1 As previously noted, in French the words *'abstinence'* and *'tempérance'* have the inverse meaning of their English cognates. Similarly, the English 'league' is more neutral than the French *'ligue'*, which harks back to the aggressive *Ligue des catholiques* of the time of Henri III. The actual behaviour of the English leagues, however, was often as violent as their French counterparts.

2 Bergeron, 'Rapport sur la proposition de loi de MM. Vilfen, Desjardins et autres', *Bulletin de l'Académie de Médecine*, 37 (1872), p. 133.

3 Taine was shortly to publish his book, *De l'intelligence*, and concerned himself with everything that affected this faculty.

4 Guerin, op. cit., pp. 226, 246.

5 For example, a letter from Decroix, President of the *Société de lutte contre l'abus du tabac* (Society Against the Abuse of Tobacco), which requested that the *Académie de Médecine* support the introduction of a law forbidding minors to smoke. 'Smoking leads to alcoholism', he wrote. There was no reply to his letter.

6 This has been well covered by F. Dumoulin, *Le Débat sur l'alcoolisme après la Commune, 1871–1887* (Travail UER-Histoire, Nanterre, 1979). Also see J. Léonard, *La Médecine entre les pouvoirs et les savoirs* (Hachette, Paris, 1982), ch. XVIII.

7 J. Baudrillart, *Livret d'enseignement antialcoolique à l'usage des lycées, collèges et écoles primaires, conforme au programme officiel* (Delagrave, Paris).

8 D. Langlois and H. Blondel, *Manuel d'antialcoolisme à l'usage des lycées, collèges, écoles primaires* (Nathan, Paris, 1905).

9 Cited by Milner and Chatelain, op. cit., p. 12.

10 J. Renault, *Bulletin de L'Académie de Médecine*, 121 (1939), p. 481.

11 Some of the information for this chapter is taken from M. E. Lender and J. K. Kirby, *Drinking in America, a history* (Free Press/Macmillan, New York/London, 1982).

12 M. Fishbein, 'Strokes: two American presidents who had strokes', *Postgraduate Medicine*, 37 (1965), pp. 200–8.

13 For France, see in particular M. J., 'Ce que j'ai vu aux États-Unis', *Revue Internationale de Droit Pénal*, 2 (1929). Vervaeck, 'Prohibition alcoolique et criminalité', *Revue Belge de Droit Pénal et de Criminologie* (1927), p. 1130. M. Legrain, 'La Prohibition de l'alcool en Amérique' (thesis, Paris, 1932).

14 Pruvost, op. cit., cites in his thesis the work of F. Riendau, 'Accidents consécutifs à l'emploi de l'alcool méthylique ou des succédanés de l'alcool entraînés par la loi de prohibition aux États-Unis' (thesis, Paris, 1932).

15 'Pluralism' as a policy was neither logical nor coherent. In 1950, William Faulkner published a humorous tract ridiculing developments in Lafayette (Mississippi), where proposals had been put forward to ban beer, but not whisky. None the less, they were adopted.

16 For a brief history of developments in Canada, see especially C. L. Krasnick, 'Because there is pain: alcoholism, temperance, and the Victorian physician', *Bull. Canad. hist. med.*, 2 (1985), pp. 1–22. The reader may also consult the article, 'Alcohol, society and the State: the social history of control policy in seven countries', *Addiction Research Foundation and WHO* (Toronto, 1981), vol. II, pp. 140–53. Also see, H. MacDougall, 'Enlightening the public, the views and values of the association of executive health officers of Ontario, 1886–1903', in *Health, Disease and Medicine: Essays in Canadian History* (Hannah Institute, Toronto, 1982), pp. 444–64.

17 Figures cited by P. J. Navarre, *L'Alcoolisme, le mal, les remèdes* (Mougin-Rusaud, Lyon, 1898), pp. 27–38.

18 Jones, 'The psychology of Jane Cakebread', *Journal of Mental Sciences* (April 1904). Cited by G. Fellion, 'Aperçu historique sur le traitement de l'alcoolisme' (thesis, Paris, 1951).

19 A. E. Dingle, *The Campaign for Prohibition in Victorian England, the United Kingdom Alliance, 1872–1895* (Croom Helm, London, 1980). For the same period, see R. M. MacLeod, 'The edge of hope: social policy and chronic alcoholism, 1870–1900', *Journal of the History of Medicine*, 22 (1967), pp. 215–45. This article looks at the campaigns of D. Dalrymple and N. Kerr in the period prior to the passing of the 1898 law.

20 For Sweden until the 1960s, see S. Ledermann, *Alcool, alcoolisme, alcoolisation: données scientifiques, de caractère physiologique, économique et social* (Travaux et documents INED, PUF, Paris, 1956), pp. 492–8.

21 M. Habert provides a comprehensive list for the early part of the twentieth century: see Habert, *Les Ligues antialcooliques en France et à l'étranger* (Jules Rousset, Paris, 1904).

22 J. F. Hutchinson, 'Science, politics and the alcohol problem in post-1905 Russia', *Slavonic and East European Review*, 58 (1980), pp. 232–54.

23 *Bulletin de l'Académie de Médecine*, 72 (1914), p. 275.

24 S. Soubramanien, 'Alcool et hindouisme, l'action de Gandhi', in *Alcool et religions* (Éds. CNDCA, Paris, 1985), pp. 109–15.

25 See Y. Durand and J. Morenon, *L'Imaginaire du vin* (J. Lafitte, Marseille, 1983).

26 See the report of the symposium 'Alcool et religions' organized by the *Comité national de défense contre l'alcoolisme* (National Committee for Defence Against Alcoholism) in 1985.

27 J. Hassine, 'Le vin dans la civilisation d'Israël', in *L'Imaginaire du vin*, pp. 71–8.

28 Lardier, *De l'intoxication alcoolique, sa prophylaxie*, a work introduced to the *Académie de Médecine* by Dujardin-Beaumetz in 1893.

29 Édouard Drumont (1844–1917) was a polemical journalist and violently anti-Semitic.

30 C. R. Snyder, 'Alcohol and the Jews', in *Arcturus Paperbacks* (Southern Illinois University Press, 1978).

31 R. H. Landman, 'Studies in drinking in Jewish culture. III: Drinking patterns of children and adolescents attending religious schools', *Quarterly J. Stud. Alc.*, 13 (1952), pp. 87–94.

32 'L'Alcoolisme en Israël', unpublished document of the Israel Institute for Applied Research, Jerusalem, 1982. Analysed in the *Bulletin Haut Comité Alcoolisme*, 4 (1984), p. 331.

33 See the wealth of examples contained in the catalogue for the exhibition 'Dutch Genre Painting' (Royal Academy of Arts, London, 1984).

34 Wine-growing is on the increase in Britain. In 1984 some three million bottles were produced. This expansion, however, is threatened by a renewed appearance of phylloxera.

35 Nashe has been studied by D. L. Hodges, *Renaissance Fictions of Anatomy* (University of Massachusetts Press, 1985), pp. 36–49.

36 R. P. Coton (the King's confessor), *Formulaire de confession pour ceux qui fréquentent les sacrements, avec la manière d'examiner la conscience, pour ceux qui se confessent rarement, ou qui veulent faire confession générale* (Paris, 1615).

37 Anonymous manuscript dated 1667, 'Quelques Petits Avertissements tirés des écritures saintes et des Saints Pères, qu'on peut donner aux pénitents dans le tribunal de la Confession'.

38 Cited by H. de Buttet, *Les Boissons, production et consommation*, op. cit., pp. 40–51.

39 Cited by V. Nahoum-Grappe, *L'Imaginaire du vin*, pp. 297–308.

40 The catechism enumerates the seven deadly sins: pride, covetousness, lust, anger, gluttony, envy and sloth.

41 Mgr Turinaz, *Trois Fléaux de la classe ouvrière: la violation de la loi du dimanche, l'alcoolisme et la mauvaise tenue des ménages ouvriers* (Paris, 1900).

42 Mgr Gibier, *Nos plaies sociales: la profanation du dimanche, l'alcoolisme, la désertion des campagnes* (Lethielleaux, Paris, 1903).

43 See, for example, K. McCarthy, 'Early alcoholism treatment: the Emmanuel movement and Richard Peabody', *Journal of Studies on Alcohol*, 45 (1984). Peabody was an Episcopalian cleric.

44 Scattered throughout the United States there are groups that have remained faithful to their religious roots and the culture of their original homelands. Some of these, the Amish in Pennsylvania, for example, are strictly abstinent.

45 C. W. Black, 'The temperance problem and the Free Churches', speech to the Temperance Conference, May meetings of the Congregational Union of England and Wales, 1953.

46 D. Brahimi, 'Le vin dans la poésie persane, d'Omar Khayyam à Hafiz', in *L'Imaginaire du vin*, pp. 97–107.

47 The poem is analysed by F. Rosenthal, 'Cannabis and alcohol, the green and the red', in G. G. Nahas and W. D. M. Patton (eds), *Marihuana, Biological Effects: Analysis, metabolism, cellular responses, reproduction and the brain* (Pergamon Press, Oxford, 1979).

48 J. Hure, 'Le thème bacchique en Islam au Ve siècle de l'Hégire, à Ishbiliya (Andalus) et Nishabur (Khorasan)', in *L'Imaginaire du vin*, pp. 87–96.

49 C. Geslin, 'Alcoolisme et syndicalisme ouvrier en Bretagne avant 1914', in *Culture, manières de boire, alcoolisme*, op. cit., pp. 221–6; D. Nourrisson, 'La classe ouvrière devant l'alcool: vice rédhibitoire ou instinct de survie?', pp. 226–34.

50 Vandervelde, *Le Socialisme et l'alcool* (Paris, 1906), p. 100.

51 P. E. Prestwich, 'French workers and the temperance movement', *International Review of Social History*, 25:1 (1980), pp. 35–52.

52 J. S. Roberts, 'Drink and industrial work discipline in nineteenth century Germany', *Journal of Social History*, 15:1 (1981), pp. 25–38.

53 J. S. Roberts, *Drink, Temperance and the Working Class in Nineteenth Century Germany* (George Allen and Unwin, London, 1984).

54 Although politically on opposite sides of the fence, both Nicolas II and Bela Kun were ardent Prohibitionists. They also met the same fate: one was shot on Lenin's order, the other on Stalin's.

55 A. Carpentier, *La Danse sacrale* (Gallimard, Paris, 1980), p. 25.

CONCLUSION TO PART II

1 P. Perrin, 'L'Alcoolisme, problèmes médico-sociaux, problèmes économiques', in *Expansion scientifique* (Paris, 1950).

2 Ibid., pp. 28, 26.

PART III MODERN ALCOHOLOGY

1 See the entry 'Alcoologie', in the *Glossaire d'alcoologie* (Haut Comité de l'alcoolisme, Documentation française, 1950).

CHAPTER 9 CLINICAL AND BIOLOGICAL CONSIDERATIONS

1 See, for example, the readers' letters in a large circulation magazine such as *L'Economist* (esp. 24 August 1985).

2 E. M. Jellinek and M. Keller, 'Rates of alcoholism in the USA, 1940–1948', *Quarterly Journal of Studies on Alcoholism*, 13 (1952), pp. 49–59.

3 E. M. Jellinek, *The Disease Concept of Alcoholism* (Hillhouse Press, New Haven, CT, 1960).

4 Ibid., p. 7.

5 Ibid., pp. 36–9.

6 P. Perrin, 'E. M. Jellinek et son oeuvre', *Revue de l'Alcoolisme*, 8 (1962), pp. 257–63.

7 P. Fouquet has written a great deal. See, in particular, 'Le syndrome alcoolique', *Études Antialcooliques*, 4 (1950), pp. 49–53; 'Le concept d'alcoologie', *Vie médicale*, 13 (1983), pp. 579–84; P. Fouquet and J. Godard, 'Le mouvement alcoologique français depuis 25 ans', *Alcool ou Santé*, 128 (1975), pp. 4–13; R. Malka, P. Fouquet and G. Vachonfrance, *Alcoologie* (Masson, Paris, 1983).

8 *Glossaire d'alcoologie.*

9 E. N. Heather, I. Robertson and P. Davies, *The Misuse of Alcohol: Crucial Issues in Dependence, Treatment and Prevention* (Croom Helm, London, 1985).

10 B. Hillemand, J. P. Joly and J. P. Lhuintre, 'L'Alcoolisme, problèmes sémantiques, classifications', *NPN Médecine*, 69 (1984), pp. 501–7.

11 *Commission sociale de l'épiscopat: dossier sur l'alcoolisme* (Le Centurion, Paris, 1978).

12 See the confessional account of an alcoholic doctor: G. Lloyd, 'I am an alcoholic', *British Medical Journal*, 285 (1982), pp. 785–6.

13 See M. Fontan, 'La personnalité éthylique', *Psychologie médicale*, 3 (1981), pp. 423–5; J. P. Delisle, 'La personnalité de l'alcoolique: problème de structure et question de traitement', pp. 439–41. The entire issue of the journal is given over to the treatment of alcoholics.

14 Such ambivalence is often present in the accounts alcoholics give of their condition.

15 Alcoholics' wives have been the subject of a great deal of study. See A. Rauzy, 'Remarques sur la personnalité des femmes d'alcooliques', *Psychologie médicale*, 3 (1981), pp. 471–7; L. Israël and N. Subra-Charpentier, 'La femme de l'alcoolique', *Confrontations psychiatriques*, 8 (1972), pp. 125–42.

16 Cited by M. Laxenaire, 'La personnalité du buveur', in D. Barrucand (ed.), *Alcoologie* (CERM, Paris, 1984).

17 *Glossaire d'Alcoologie.*

18 'La consommation d'alcool en France de 1950 à 1982', *Bulletin de Haut Comité de l'alcoolisme*, 2 (1984).

19 P. Denoix, 'Prévention et dépistage des cancers', *Rapport de la Commission du cancer, ministère de la Santé* (1974); O. Lasserre, R. Flamant, J. Lellouch and D. Schwartz, 'Alcool et cancer, étude de pathologie géographique portant sur les départements français', *Bulletin d'INSERM*, 22 (1967), pp. 53–60.

20 A. Romelsjö and G. Agren, 'Has mortality related to alcohol decreased in Sweden?' *British Medical Journal*, 291 (1985), pp. 167–70. The French figures only take into account patients in public psychiatric hospitals; those treated in private institutions or outside the hospital environment are not included. The real figure is therefore greater.

21 A. Féline and J. Adès, 'Aspects actuels de l'alcoolisation du sujet jeune', *Ann. Med. Psy.*, 138 (1980), pp. 80–6; M. Fontan, 'Les jeunes et l'alcool ou la drogue', in *Mieux connaître l'alcoolisme* (Documentation française, 1979), pp. 92–8.

22 M. F. Delorme and D. Barrucand, 'Aspects génétiques de l'alcoolisme', in Barrucand, *Alcoologie*, pp. 131–40.

23 An abundant bibliography on these subjects is contained in *Quotidien du médecine – Médecine cardio-vasculaire* (20 December 1984).

24 Bonnin, 'La parotidose des cirrhoses alcooliques', *Bulletin de l'Académie de Médecine*, 138 (1954), pp. 324–7.

25 Lereboullet and Pluvinage, 'L'atrophie cérébrale des alcooliques, ses conséquences médico-sociales', *Bulletin de l'Académie de Médecine*, 140 (1956), pp. 398–401; D. A. Wilkinson, *Cerebral Deficits in Alcoholism* (Addiction Research Foundation, Toronto, 1979); C. G. Harper, J. J. Kril and R. L. Holloway, 'Brain shrinkage in chronic alcoholics, a pathological study', *British Medical Journal*, 290 (1985), pp. 501–3.

26 A clinical and epidemiological study accompanied by an extensive bibliography can be found in Postel and Quétel, *Alcoolisme et Psychiatrie* (Rapport au Haut Comité de l'Alcoolisme, 1983).

27 F. Peigné, F. Veber and B. Elis, 'Alcoolisme féminin, corrélations avec la dépression et le comportement suicidaire', *Psychologie médicale*, 13 (1981), pp. 1191–3; C. J. Belin, 'Écriture, alcoolisation, dépression', ibid., pp. 1809–11.

28 *Les relations dose–effet de l'alcool* (Haut Comité de l'alcoolisme, Documentation française, 1985).

29 A. Leclerc and J. Brugère, 'Alcohol consumption and carcinoma of the larynx, the pharynx and the mouth: importance of the beverage', in *Symposium on 'Diet and Human Carcinogenesis'* (Aarhus, Denmark, June 1985).

30 Rouvillois and Dérobert, 'Alcool et accidents de la route', *Bulletin de l'Académie de Médecine*, 135 (1951), pp. 596–9.

31 'Comparaison internationale de l'alcool dans les accidents de la circulation', *Haut Comité de l'Alcoolisme – Informations*, 2 (1985), pp. 53–9.

32 The work of C. Got is summarized in *L'Alcool et la route* (Haut Comité de l'alcoolisme, Documentation française, 1984).

33 *Alcool et accidents: étude de 4,796 cas d'accidents admis dans 21 hôpitaux français entre octobre 1982 et mars 1983* (Haut Comité de l'alcoolisme, Documentation française, 1985).

34 B. Garros and M. H. Bouvier, 'Alcoolisation d'une population, ses risques', in *L'Alcoolisme, Morbidité, Mortalité* (Haut Comité de l'alcoolisme, Documentation française, 1984), pp. 21–36.

CHAPTER 10   HELP FOR THE ALCOHOLIC

1 A. Guilliet, 'Scandaleux et alcoologie', *Psychologie médicale*, 15 (1983), pp. 869–872.

2 D. Champeau, 'Le sulfate de magnésie intra-veineux dans le traitement de l'alcoolisme en cure ambulatoire', *Revue de l'alcoolisme*, 2 (1965), p. 4.

3 R. Robert and L. Waintraub, 'Du bon usage d'une loi réputée obsolète: rôle et résultats de l'action des Commissions Médicales d'application de la loi du 15 avril 1954 du département de Paris, étude de suites sur 5 ans', *Psychologie médicale*, 15 (1983), pp. 843–8; R. Quero, C. Bury and J. Breton, 'Aspects relationnels du fonctionnement de la Commission Médicale de la loi du 15 avril 1954 dans le département du Val-de-Marne', ibid., pp. 851–4.

4 Practical details and addresses can be found in *Vademecum alcool–drogue* (Centre d'étude et d'information sur le volontariat, Paris, 1984). In the UK, contact Alcohol Concern.

5 The work of these groups is followed with interest in scientific circles. See, for example, J. Ades, *Réflexion sur l'idéologie et le fonctionnement dynamique d'un groupe d'anciens buveurs* (Mémoire de CES, Documentation française, Paris, 1979); C. Orsel, 'Contribution à l'étude de certains groupes thérapeutiques chez les alcooliques' (thesis, Paris, 1948); M. Lasselin and M. Fontan, 'Pour une étude analytique des mouvements d'alcooliques abstinents', *Revue de l'alcoolisme*, 25 (1979), pp. 82–91; P. Chassan, 'Maladie alcoolique, abstinence et groupes d'anciens buveurs', *Psychologie médicale*, 15 (1983), pp. 907–9.

6 For twenty years Haas has been working with alcoholics at the hospital of Saint-Cloud. See R. M. Haas, *Médecin du bateau ivre* (Grasset, Paris, 1977); H. Niox-Rivière and D. Audoin, 'Réflexions sur l'autobiographique sevré', *Psychologie médicale*, 15 (1983), pp. 911–14.

7 Jack London, *John Barleycorn; on alcoholic memoirs* (Mills and Boon, London, 1914).

8 Ibid., p. 2.

9 There are numerous examples of this genre: Lucien, *L'enfant qui jouait avec la lune* (Salvator, Paris, 1984); P. Coran, *La Mémoire blanche* (Duculot, Gembloux, 1981); Francesca, *Des espoirs par gorgées* (Bertout, Luneray, 1984); X. Grall, *L'Inconnu me dévore* (Calligrammes, Quimper, 1984); M. Gari, *Le Vinaigre et le Miel, vie d'une paysanne hongroise* (Plon, Paris, 1984); A. Buffet, *D'amour et d'eau fraîche* (S. Messinger, 1986).

CHAPTER 11   PREVENTION

1 The most complete work on the subject is *Approche des coûts sanitaires et sociaux de l'alcoolisme* (Haut Comité de l'alcoolisme, Documentation française, 1985).

2 'L'enseignement de l'alcoologie', *Bull. Sté. Fse. d'alcoologie* (1980), pp. 8–56.

3 J. Zourbas, *Attitudes et comportements des jeunes de 7 à 11 ans à l'égard des boissons alcoolisées: enquête épidémiologique auprès de 1,285 écoliers* (Faculty of Medicine, Rennes, 1983).

4 *Alcool-Paroles* (Haut Comité de l'Alcoolisme, 1985).

5 D. Bratanov, 'Le problème de l'alcoolisme dans la littérature mondiale', *Revue de l'alcoolisme*, 15:3 (1969), pp. 215–32.

6 S. Ammar, 'L'Alcoolisme, problème de santé publique', *Tunisie médicale*, 4 (1972), pp. 1–7.

7 J. C. Duffy and M. A. Plant, 'Scotland's liquor licensing changes: an assessment', *British Medical Journal*, 292 (1986), pp. 36–9.

8 The Soviet Union has a curious regulation on its internal flights. Although vodka is banned from the passenger cabin, no such restriction is placed upon the pilot.

9 R. E. Kendell, M. de Roumanie and E. B. Ritson, 'Influence of an increase in exise duty on alcohol consumption and its adverse effects', *British Medical Journal*, 287 (1983), pp. 809–11.

10 Although regional differences in consumption levels have been recognized for many years, their exact scale can only be assessed with the aid of detailed statistical studies. For France, see *Les Différences régionales des consommations*

d'éthanol et des risques d'alcoolisation pathologique (Haut Comité de l'Alcoolisme, Documentation française, 1984); *Le Phénomène de l'alcoolisation en France, à partir des résultats nationaux des centres d'examens de santé de la Caisse nationale d'assurance maladie* (Colloque des centres d'examens de santé, 1984), pp. 421–58; I. Got, 'Les Indicateurs nationaux et régionaux de l'alcoolisation en France' (thesis, Paris, 1986). For Great Britain, see E. J. Higgs, 'Research into the history of alcohol use and control in England and Wales: the available sources in the Public Records Office', *British J. Add.*, 79 (1984), pp. 41–7; R. W. Latchman, N. Kreitman, M. A. Plant and A. Crawford, 'Regional variations in British alcohol morbidity rates: a myth uncovered?', *British Medical Journal*, 289 (1984), pp. 1341–5; *Health Education in the Prevention of Alcohol-Related Problems* (Scottish Health Education Coordinating Committee, 1985).

11 For a comparison of the international standards, see *L'Alcool et la route* (Haut Comité de l'alcoolisme, Documentation française, 1984).

12 M. Derely and E. Lehembre, 'Pour une approche humaine de l'alcoolisme en milieu de travail' (thesis, Lille, 1979).

13 A. Sauvy, 'Un mal anachronique', *La Santé de l'homme*, 171 (1971), p. 48.

14 *Alcohol, Society and the State: A Comparative Study of Alcohol Control, 1950–1980* (2 vols, WHO and the Alcohol and Drug Addiction Research Foundation, Toronto, 1981).

15 'Medicine in Eastern Europe', *British Medical Journal*, 288 (1984), pp. 1288–92.

16 R. Room, 'The World Health Organization and alcohol control', *British J. Add.*, 79 (1984), pp. 85–92.

17 See, for example, F. de Closets, *Le Système, et puis M* (Livre de poche, 1980), pp. 224–5.

18 For France, see ch. 5.

19 A French example is G. Domenech, *Éloge de l'ivresse* (Albin Michel, Paris, 1981).

20 See, J. Bury, 'Alcoolisme et mythe de Dionysos', *Psychologie médicale*, 13 (1981), pp. 505–11; A. Jeanmaire, *Dionysos, histoire du culte de Bacchus*, (Payot, Paris, 1985).

CHAPTER 12   MODERN ALCOHOLISM

1 The Haut Comité de l'Alcoolisme study by Stoetzel and Colas de la Noue (21 June 1985).

2 J. Godard, 'L'alcoolisme n'est plus ce qu'il était, réflexions et propositions', *Alcool ou Santé*, 147:4 (1978).

3 B. Shahandeh, *Rehabilitation approaches to drug and alcohol dependence* (BIT, Geneva, 1985).

4 *Dagens Nyheter*, 20 November 1984.

5 In the Soviet Union, another phenomenon can be observed in the Muslim republics of Central Asia. A modern-minded Uzbek or Tadjik will drink wine or vodka to demonstrate his attachment to Soviet domination, while those who remain abstinent indicate their devotion to local culture and Islam sentiments, which often mask an anti-Soviet outlook.

6 Work of the Alcohol and Drugs Addiction Research Foundation, Toronto (1979–80). In Canada, the inhabitants of the Yukon and the North-West Territories drink twice the amount consumed by the people of Quebec (a difference comparable to that which existed a hundred years earlier in North America between New Englanders and the pioneers of the 'wild West').

7 Davidson, 1971–85 study (INSERM, 1985).

8 'Alcoolisation, phénomène sans frontières?', *Alcool ou Santé*, 152:4 (1983); ibid., 153:1 (1984); *Cultures, manières de boire et alcoolisme*, op. cit.

9 *Production et commerce de l'alcool: conséquences pour la santé publique* (Publications OMS, 1986).

10 A study conducted in Zambia showed that 275 road-accident victims had alcohol levels above 0.8 g/l, and that of these some two-thirds were over 2.0 g/l. See, *Gazette médicale de France*, 6 April 1979. A disquieting example is furnished by Trinidad and Tobago. The average quantity of rum destined for the internal market has increased from 3 million litres of pure alcohol for the period 1958–67 to 7.5 million litres for the period 1973–82. See, B. Walsh and M. Grant, 'Le marché des boissons alcoolisées et ses influences sur la santé publique', *Forum mondial de la Santé* (OMS), 6 (1985), pp. 221–41. The article is followed by a debate in which representatives of the advertising industry deny that they have any influence over consumption levels.

11 S. Douki, Z. Hachemi, S. Ammar and M. Helayem, 'L'Alcoolisme interdit', International Symposium on Alcoholism and Drug Addiction, Casablanca (11–12 October, 1984).

12 For Britain, see R. Smith, 'Booze on the telly', *British Medical Journal*, 290 (1985), pp. 445–6.

13 Cf. R. Room, *Shifting Perspectives on Drinking, Alcohol Portrayals in American Films*; D. Herd, *Ideology, melodrama, and the changing of alcohol problems in American films*; *Représentations de l'alcool et de l'alcoolisme dans le cinéma français* (Colloquium held in Paris, June 1983).

14 F. Steudler, 'Cinéma, manières de boire et alcoolisme', in *Actes de la rencontre 'Cultures, manières de boire et alcoolisme'*, pp. 379–87. The same author, in collaboration with J. Ades, has made a film, *Alcool-décor* (Laboratoires de Riom, CERM).

15 Le Circle Rouge (the Red Circle).

16 For the cartoon, see, Y. Pilard, 'L'Alcohol et l'alcoolisme dans la bande dessinée d'expression française' (thesis, Bordeaux, 1984).

17 According to C. Beraud, average alcohol consumption levels have dropped by a quarter, but this has had no effect on mortality levels from cirrhosis. See his article, 'L'Alcoolisation en France', *Médecine digestive et nutrition* (May 1984), pp. 11–17.

INDEX

Note: Page references in *italics* indicate tables and figures.

Index compiled by Meg Davies (Society of Indexers)